GW01454425

A History of
Norton Rose

Sir Philip Rose.

MEN OF THE DAY. No. 243.

SIR PHILIP ROSE, BART.

BORN five-and-sixty years ago, of a family that had been settled in Buckinghamshire for nearly three hundred years, Sir Philip Rose was bred to the law and became a solicitor. His firm was that of Baxter, Rose, and Norton, as a member of which he passed the Great Northern Railway Bill in 1845 and laid the foundation of a large Parliamentary practice. From 1854 to 1860 he acted as the recognised agent of the Conservative Party, and, gathering up the scattered forces that remained after the defeat of Lord Derby's first Administration, reorganised it to excellent good purpose. Meantime he had in 1841 founded and become the Honorary Secretary, which he still remains, of the Consumption Hospital. To this hospital he gave all his spare time, and made it one of the largest, most prosperous, and most useful of all the hospitals. In 1872, however, having differed with his partners in consequence of their having undertaken to act for the Tichborne Claimant, he retired from the firm, and devoted himself completely to Buckinghamshire, Consumption, and Mr. Disraeli.

From early in life he had been the ally and adviser of Mr. Disraeli, and to the last he remained Lord Beaconsfield's faithful and most trusted friend. In May. 1874. he was, without any solicitation, made a baronet, and a few weeks ago he received the latest breath of the statesman he had known for forty years, and found himself left as his working executor.

Sir Philip is a very shrewd practical man of the world, excellent at business, and endowed with a considerable contempt for the Parliamentary results of the manœuvres with which he has become so well acquainted. He is a kindly amiable person too, and has a large amount of varied information.

A History of Norton Rose

ANDREW ST GEORGE

GRANTA EDITIONS

© Norton Rose, 1995

Published by Granta Editions, 25–27 High Street, Chesterton, Cambridge CB4 1ND,
Great Britain.

Granta Editions is an imprint of Book Production Consultants PLC.

All rights reserved. No part of this publication may be reproduced, stored in any
retrieval system or transmitted in any form or by any means electronic, photocopying,
recording or otherwise, without the prior written permission of the copyright holder
for which application should be addressed in the first instance to the publishers. No
liability shall attach to the author, the copyright holder or the publishers for loss or
damage of any nature suffered as a result of reliance on the reproduction of any
of the contents of this publication or any errors or omission in its content.

A CIP catalogue record is available for this book from the British Library.

ISBN 1 85757 028 6

Picture Credits
Acknowledgement is gratefully made to those who have given permission for the
reproduction of illustrations/photographs on the pages indicated: pp.57, 71 *Vanity Fair*
(by kind permission of Stephanie Zarach); pp.48, 49 Brompton Hospital;
p.70 *Hughenden papers*, National Trust; pp.81, 113, 166 Illustrated London News
Picture Library; pp.104, 106, 168 Stock Exchange; p.153 Newcastle City Library;
p.157 British Library Newspaper Library; p.209 *Daily Mail*.
All other pictures are the copyright of Norton Rose.

Every effort has been made to obtain permission for the reproduction of the
illustrations and photographs in this book; apologies are offered to anyone whom it
has not been possible to contact.

Designed by Jim Reader and Peter Dolton.
Design and production in association with
Book Production Consultants PLC,
25–27 High Street, Chesterton, Cambridge CB4 1ND, Great Britain

Printed and bound by Butler and Tanner Ltd, Frome.

Contents

List of Illustrations

Acknowledgements

WRITING THE HISTORY of a great and long-lived law firm has been both a pleasant and difficult task. Records and archives are widespread and the work involves pioneering and fundamental research at all stages.

I have received generous help from many quarters in writing this book. I should like to thank the senior partner, Tony Kay, and the partners and staff of Norton Rose for their kind and efficient help. I have enjoyed regular conversations about the firm with many partners, and I thank them for their time, interest and hospitality.

In particular, I am most grateful to the partners, Michael Macfadyen and Colin Graves, who have given time, energy and expertise to the project, and to the Librarian, Miriam Davies, who has helped at every turn.

I should also like to thank those partners and staff who have taken time from their work or retirement to talk to me. Among the most helpful have been: David Alexander, Giles Botterell, Michael Brown and Michael Davies (who both read the manuscript and made apt suggestions), Brian Davenport, Chips Jewell, Jim Leaver (who read the manuscript meticulously and helped to interpret the early partnership deeds), David Lewis, John Norton, Peter Purton and Anthony Surtees; I am also most grateful to Dick Clifford, Gerry Driscoll, Geoff Lewsey and Brenda Pearson. I was pleased to have been able to talk at length with Con Surtees, former senior partner, who died in 1994.

The Botterell, Norton and Rose families have been a model of happy co-operation. Much of the material in this book has been drawn from their collections, and I am most grateful to Giles Botterell, Petica Waley (the great great grand-daughter of Sir Philip Rose), and Gillian Roxburgh (grand-daughter of Henry Turton Norton) for their invaluable help, their generosity with family papers and photographs, and for their hospitality. I gratefully acknowledge their permission to quote from family papers and reproduce photographs. I am most grateful, too, to Olive Norton for her help early on.

Outside the firm I have been lucky to have had advice and guidance from Lord Blake and Lord Denning on political and legal history; from John Morris, senior partner of Sinclair Roche & Temperley, and from John Flintoff and Kendall Strange (partners in the Newcastle firm of Ingledew Botterell) on shipping; from Frank Rehder and Frank Ledwith on shipping insurance; and from Stuart Conacher at the Chamber of Shipping on shipping history. Miles Green, the fine local historian of Penn, Buckinghamshire, proved indispensable on local history.

I am especially grateful to Stephanie Zarach, Alison Leach and their team, who oversaw the production of this book and provided a constant flow of ideas and good sense. Sohrab Sorooshian has been the best of research assistants: intelligent, inventive and unimpeachable. I thank them all.

I have used the library and manuscript collections of: the Bodleian Library, the British Museum, the Financial Times Library, the Guildhall, the Law Society Library and the London Library; the Public Records Offices at Chancery Lane and Kew; the Newspaper Library at Colindale; the archives of the British Shipping Federation; the archives of Ashurst Morris Crisp; the local historical archives and public records offices of Doncaster, Middlesex, Newcastle-upon-Tyne and Sunderland; and I thank the Librarians and staff at each library for their help and co-operation. In particular, I should like to thank John Orbell and the staff of Barings' Archives for their unfailing flow of information and documents.

My last and greatest thanks go to Douglas Hamilton, senior partner of the firm from 1982 to 1994. He has provided wisdom, wit and great encouragement during the writing. I hope the book shares his broad vision of the law.

LEFT: *Queen Victoria's appointment of Philip Rose to baronetcy.*

BELOW: *Letter to Rose from Disraeli.*

Introduction

THE HISTORY OF a law firm traces a complex organism in a changing environment. If law is the record of a nation's development, then the chronicle of a law firm is the application of legislation to cases, of expertise to specific causes and of ideas to business life. Norton Rose grew from foundations established two hundred years ago and has evolved with the times, responding to challenges and creating opportunities.

There are three kinds of history in this book: first, that of the individual partners who helped to create the firm; second, the development of the firm itself; and third, the place of the firm within the legal and social environment of the last two centuries.

The first type of history concerns the firm's individual partners. Norton Rose began in 1794 with Robert Charsley. He practised alone. The following chapters trace the biographies of the firm's greatest partners. Individual portraits show the energy and enterprise of the Victorians, Sir Philip Rose and Henry Elland Norton, and the public profile of Sir Charles Norton a hundred years later.

In 1841, when Philip Rose founded the Brompton Hospital, the records of the founders' meeting describe him as 'without rank or fortune, a member of a profession which necessarily occupied much time and thought ... supposed, however falsely, to check and chill the sympathies of the natural heart, engendering indifference to human suffering'.[1] He achieved rank and fortune. One of the two greatest statesmen of the day entrusted his reputation to this friend and lawyer: Benjamin Disraeli chose Sir Philip Rose to be his confidant and executor.

Each law firm is the sum of its partners, a merger of individual lives and talents. Rose's partners were Henry Elland Norton and Robert Baxter, lawyer, preacher, railway entrepreneur and newspaper proprietor.

The second kind of history is that of the firm itself. In fact, this is a tale of two firms: Norton, Rose & Co. and Botterell & Roche (founded in 1861), which amalgamated in 1960 to form the firm now known as Norton Rose. Beyond the biography of each individual – the political successes of Sir Philip Rose, the entrepreneurial daring of Robert Baxter, the commercial vision of Wilson Roche and Con Surtees, and the professional expertise of all the partners – lies the biography of the firm itself. A law firm represents a gathering of individuals talented in politics, investment, management, consultancy and, of course, in many branches of legal work. Norton Rose continued to evolve, from its vigorous presence in the City during the nineteenth century, through its more subdued operations in the early part of the twentieth century, to its strength and diversity as an international practice today. The existence and collaboration of so many lawyers is a gentle rebuttal of Thomas Jefferson's remark, 'That one hundred and fifty lawyers should do business together ought not to be expected.'

Norton Rose prospered greatly during the 1830s and 1840s from the development of the railways. Then in the 1850s and 1860s it became expert in investment and corporate law, establishing the first investment trust in England. In the 1870s and 1880s the firm expanded and diversified into foreign government loans and what is now known as project finance and capital funding. By the turn of the twentieth century, Norton Rose had been a powerful force in the City for sixty years. In parallel, the shipping specialist firm of Botterell & Roche, which had been established in 1861, was a major force, both in shipping circles and as part of a strong regional network of marine practice and knowledge.

Beyond the history and evolution of the firm is a third kind of history, that of the firm's place in social, legal and public life.

Everywhere there is an interplay between lawyer and client, lawyer and public, profession and society. As the legal profession grew during Victoria's reign, both branches were less structured than they became in the twentieth century. Both Disraeli and his chief adversary, Gladstone, were intimate with the law and chose wider public careers. The nineteenth century's greatest novelists, Dickens, Thackeray and George Eliot, were close to the law by training or inclination. Poets and thinkers such as Robert Browning and Matthew Arnold set some of their works in court and wrote essays on legal and moral matters.

The profession became socially and intellectually much more respectable and powerful throughout the nineteenth century. In 1863 Philip Rose's friend, Benjamin Disraeli, observed punningly, 'Of all powers in the nineteenth century, the power of attorney is the greatest.' Another parliamentarian – a barrister – Pleydell Bouverie simply said in 1884, 'The two great evils in this country are taxes and solicitors.'

One of the most interesting aspects of the growth in the firm's standing is the impact of solicitors' changing view of their profession. The flair of Sir Philip Rose in the 1840s and of Henry Turton Norton (son of the first Norton) lay in their realisation that a solicitor could influence all parts of political, legislative and commercial life. It was during the last century, when Norton Rose and Botterell & Roche were establishing themselves, that the foundations of the profession were set down. Lawyers in the nineteenth-century City created the rules and means by which they were valued. They built and lived in an environment of investment. Their public status had fluctuated. Dickens was uncomplimentary about lawyers in *Bleak House*, and he was equally sharp about the City in 1865 in *Our Mutual Friend*; the gospel of investment was unseating the gospel of work:

> All is well known to the wise in their generation, traffic in Shares
> is one thing to have to do with in this world. Have no antecedents, no
> established character, no cultivation, no ideas, no manners; have Shares.
> Have Shares enough to be on the Boards of direction in capital letters,

oscillate on mysterious business between London and Paris, and be great. Where does he come from? Shares. Where is he going to? Shares. What are his tastes? Shares. Has he any principles? Shares. What squeezes him into Parliament? Shares. Perhaps he never of himself achieved success in anything, never originated anything, never produced anything! Sufficient answer to all: Shares. O mighty Shares! To set those blaring images so high, and to cause us smaller vermin, as under the influence of henbane or opium, to cry out night and day, "Relieve us of our money, scatter it for us, buy us and sell us, ruin us, only we beseech ye take rank among the powers of the earth, and fatten on us!"[2]

The nineteenth century, from which both firms grew, was a nursery of expertise, where specialisms took root and particular skills were cultivated. Beneath all the frenzy and speculation, which produced regular financial crises in the 1840s, 1850s and 1860s,[3] ran the desire for order, protection and regulation. Limited liability legislation[4] and Companies Acts[5] made investment a more technical, defined enterprise. As a result, Gladstone felt able to pronounce proudly that the economy of the early 1870s had advanced 'by leaps and bounds'. Looking back on the same period, the social commentator, A.R. Wallace, raised questions about customs, laws and social behaviour as the roots of economic explanation:

> In every case in which we have traced out the efficient causes of the present depression, we have found it to originate in customs, laws, or modes of action which are ethically unsound, if not positively immoral.[6]

Lawyers expanded their activities as the commercial environment grew. Norton Rose developed as a firm because of railway technology and related investment activities. As the firm's founders responded to the present and planned for the future, they prospered and became well known. Philip Rose received public attention through a baronetcy bestowed by Disraeli and Henry Elland Norton's family moved in leisured intellectual circles. Both these men and their families benefited from a change in the status of the solicitor, by 1900 no longer the poor cousin of the barrister but a self-confident member of a confident profession.

The qualities which make a good solicitor may have changed in degree but not in kind: intelligence, energy, discretion. In business Sir Philip Rose was at the heart of commercial and financial enterprise, just as Wilson Roche of Botterell & Roche had a profound impact on the shipping industry by creating the Shipping Federation. Lawyers in the nineteenth century were less regulated and therefore more able to move between the roles of lawyer, confidant, investment analyst, company director and management consultant. In nineteenth-century England successive governments turned public opinion into law; and throughout the twentieth century the law continued to be an instrument of opportunity. Early in the twentieth century, solicitors continued as guardians of the wealth created in the previous century, and the firm prospered in the family and property practice which sustained it through periods of industrial and commercial decline.

After the Second World War, the legal profession again entered a period of expansion both at home and overseas. The firm's post-war growth reflected this. There were opportunities at home and abroad arising from banking, property, project finance and investment. The firm expanded and developed internationally, first by international work brought by clients, and second by establishing overseas offices: in Europe in Brussels, Moscow, Paris, Piraeus and Prague; in South-East Asia in Hong Kong and Singapore; and in the Gulf in Bahrain.

The profession has kept pace with developments in business, since law follows and regulates movements of money and property. What the railways were to Sir Philip Rose and Henry Elland Norton in the 1840s, so corporate and investment finance are to the modern firm: a concentration of technology, finance, politics and legislation. The wider implications of the history of a law firm, its partners and its place in the legal profession, are clear for social, political and economic historians. Law remains an inter-disciplinary activity combining intellectual, financial, social and – of course – legal expertise. A firm of longevity and continuous presence is a remarkable organism within the legal environment. The history of such a firm as Norton Rose gives an opportunity to see a path of energy and excellence transcribed across two centuries of lived experience. Alongside the published histories of other established legal firms such as Freshfields, Clifford Chance, Linklaters & Paines and Slaughter and May, the story of Norton Rose contributes to a wider understanding of industrial, corporate and financial history.

There are patterns in the history of the firm and of the legal profession. In the chapters which follow, individual lives comprise the organism which the law firm became, from a sole practitioner through various types of management to the 100-strong partnership in 1994. The partners who created and extended the firm were quick to change; they acted and reacted in the commercial and legal environments, and expanded with or readjusted to the business climate. Each made lasting contributions to the firm, the law or the wider business community. Latterly, the impact of individual lawyers has been tempered by the complexity of the legal environment; success has come through acting corporately as part of an inter-disciplinary team.

Individual enterprise can, however, express itself through the corporate structure and organisation of the firm. The structure of the larger law firms caused some lawyers to become managers. The many partners chose or elected a few colleagues to run the partnership and allow individual partners the maximum autonomy with clients. In essence and in spirit, the entrepreneurial partners of the 1840s set the style for the firm. In larger groupings, ambition became collective: lawyers in the last twenty-five years of the twentieth century evolved larger partnerships to meet the more sophisticated requirements of major businesses, nationally and internationally.

Patterns set in the past affect the present. The firm which established England's first investment trusts emerged as an international corporate finance practice. The railway technology of the nineteenth century evolved into the information technology of the twentieth: Tennyson's image of the railways as 'the ringing grooves of change' became the 'information superhighway' of the 1990s. Foreign loans in the 1890s grew into a broad international finance practice; property and conveyancing developed to include environment and planning law; and a 100-partner firm adopted a quasi-corporate management structure. The firm found within itself a way forward and the expertise to make that way; 'expertise with expedition' was a motto of the former senior partner, Con Surtees.

The firm's future will mirror its past and build from its present: in expanding global markets, in developing countries and in established business centres. As the province of law broadens, so will the activities of firms like Norton Rose. This history shows that commerce, finance, technology and commodity both create and are created by the laws which govern us. Disraeli thought justice to be truth in action; the history of a law firm is law in action.

Notes

1. Brompton Hospital Founders' Meeting, 25 May 1841.

2. Charles Dickens, *Our Mutual Friend*, Book I, chap. x.

3. See: Morier Evans, *The Commercial Crisis 1847–8* (London, 1848), *The History of the Commercial Crisis, 1857–8 and the Stock Exchange Panic 1859* (London, 1859), *Speculative Notes and Notes on Speculation* (London, 1864); and John Laing, *Theory of Business* (London, 1867).

4. 1855–62. See: H.A. Shannon, 'The Coming of General Limited Liability', *Economic History (Economic Journal Supplement)*, 2 (1930–3), pp.267–91.

5. 1862.

6. A.R. Wallace, *Bad Times*, p.117, London, 1885.

1794–1844

The Founders: Charsley, Baxter, Rose and Norton

'LAWYERS BELONG TO the people by birth and to the aristocracy by habit and taste,' the philosopher Alexis de Tocqueville wrote in 1835. 'They may be looked upon as the connecting link between the two great classes of society.'[1] Forty years later, Philip Rose stepped from one class to the other when he was created a baronet at the instigation of his old friend Benjamin Disraeli, who had himself joined the peerage as Lord Beaconsfield. The two men had moved quietly between classes. Rose had reservations, confiding to his son, Frederick:

> The offer concerns you even more than me, for I don't expect to make old bones. If I thought that at my death you would feel it *infra dig* to continue the practice of your profession I would certainly refuse the honour. I owe all my success in life to the practice of the law, and I should be disgusted if a son of mine felt that because he had succeeded to the title of Baronet he could no longer continue the practice of an honourable profession.[2]

The founding partners of Norton Rose in the first forty years of the firm's life could not have known the firm would be flourishing two hundred years later; but they did have a sense of where and how the profession was developing, and of their own professional and social standing as lawyers. In his own papers, Frederick Rose remarked that the history of the solicitor's professional life in a high class practice 'if it could ever be told, which of course it cannot except as regards public work, would necessarily be interesting'. He continued, 'No class of professional men know so much of human life, of human frailty, of grim family secrets, as those men who are the confidential advisers of, practically, all classes of Society.'[3]

Frederick Rose was writing at the turn of the twentieth century, when the status of a solicitor was assured and consolidated alongside the other professional classes. But the standing of an attorney was far from secure when in 1836 Philip Rose joined a practice which had begun forty-two years earlier in the London Road at Uxbridge.

The Founders

The firm was founded by Robert Charsley of Middlesex in 1794. Charsley came from a family who had been stewards to the Curzon family in Buckinghamshire. The Charsley family was well established in the Thames Valley. A minute book of land tax commissioners of 1690 lists the clerk for the area as F. Charsley.[4] The name first appeared in Buckinghamshire on the Manorial Roll of Penn in 1738, when one John Charsley was Steward to the Manor Court. The Manorial Roll for 1804 lists Robert Charsley as holding the same position. Robert was the first solicitor in the Charsley family. He had been admitted to the Court of King's Bench in 1794 and was a practising attorney in Uxbridge. The family practice grew to include an office in Beaconsfield and an agency in the City.

Charsley practised alone from 1794 to 1804, when he was joined by Albany Carrington Bond and moved to 23 Billiter Lane, Leadenhall Street, in 1805, and then to 18 Mark Lane in 1806. Bond was a Vestry Clerk to the church of St Mary, Stratford Bow, and a Master in Extraordinary. The brief partnership ceased on Bond's death in 1808, leaving Charsley to practise alone again. He moved to 66 Mark Lane in 1814 and to 25 Mark Lane six years later. Then in 1821 he took into partnership one William Barker, a solicitor of four years' standing, and moved to 21 Mark Lane. The practice at this time was mostly what was known as 'family business'[5] (trust, probate and conveyancing) with commercial work arising from the firm's City connection and position.

Commerce lay east of the Courts. Literature of the early 1800s, such as Fanny Burney's play *A Busy Day* (1801), often sets up City *arrivisme* against West End *savoir faire*. The social status of areas now homogenised into central London was distinct: Bond Street seemed far from St James's and Kensington little more than a rural village. The City was both a social extreme and the commercial centre. The growth of the legal profession in the nineteenth century is in part the story of how those two worlds met, liked each other, and profited from the encounter. But in the early 1800s it would still have been difficult to envisage that a partner of the firm, known as Baxter, Rose, Norton & Spofforth in 1860, would help to establish the Junior Carlton Club through his association with the Conservative Party.

One morning in September 1802, William Wordsworth stood on Westminster Bridge and looked east, finding an image of power and presence in the city he saw there:

> Earth has not anything to show more fair;
> Dull would he be of soul who could pass by
> A sight so touching in its majesty;
> This City now doth, like a garment, wear
> The beauty of the morning; silent, bare,
> Ships, towers, domes, theatres and temples lie
> Open unto the fields, and to the sky, –
> All bright and glittering in the smokeless air.[6]

The bustle which Lord Byron had found was closer to the world around Mark Lane; he loved the dirt and din of the capital:

> A mighty mass of brick, and smoke, and shipping,
> Dirty and dusky, but as wide the eye
> Could reach, with here and there a sail just skipping

In sight, then lost amidst the forestry
Of masts; a wilderness of steeples peeping
On tiptoe through their sea-coal canopy;
A huge, dun Cupola, like a foolscap crown
On a fool's head – and there is London town.[7]

The City was changing rapidly; new forms of commerce were arriving and developing, both mercantile and financial. There were new joint stock enterprises, bill-broking and insurance work, as well as regular trust and family work for the lawyers. In 1829 the firm Charsley & Barker moved to 50 Mark Lane, which was to be the firm's office until 1850. The firm took on Thomas Mann Bridge in 1831; he had been admitted to the Court of King's Bench that year. The firm then existed under the name Charsley, Barker & Bridge and their work, according to Philip Rose's recollection,[8] was a mixture of commercial, trust, probate and conveyancing work. Charsley retired in 1833, and the firm's name changed to Barker & Bridge.

Philip Rose and Henry Elland Norton
Philip Rose was born in Wycombe, Buckinghamshire in 1816. He was the son, grandson and great-grandson of prosperous citizens, all of whom had been Mayors of Wycombe. The Roses of Wycombe issued from an old and established bourgeois family line that had lived in the Thames Valley at Waddesdon, Winchendon, Haddenham and Dodbrooke, all in Buckinghamshire. In 1704 one Thomas Rose was baptised in Thame, Oxfordshire; he moved to Wycombe in the early part of the eighteenth century and began the Wycombe line of Roses. In the 1870s, Philip Rose tried to prove that the family had migrated from Nairnshire, where the name was Rouse, Ross or Rosse. It remains uncertain whether Rose successfully proved this. The family in England dates at least from Caroline times, when John Rose was born in 1649.

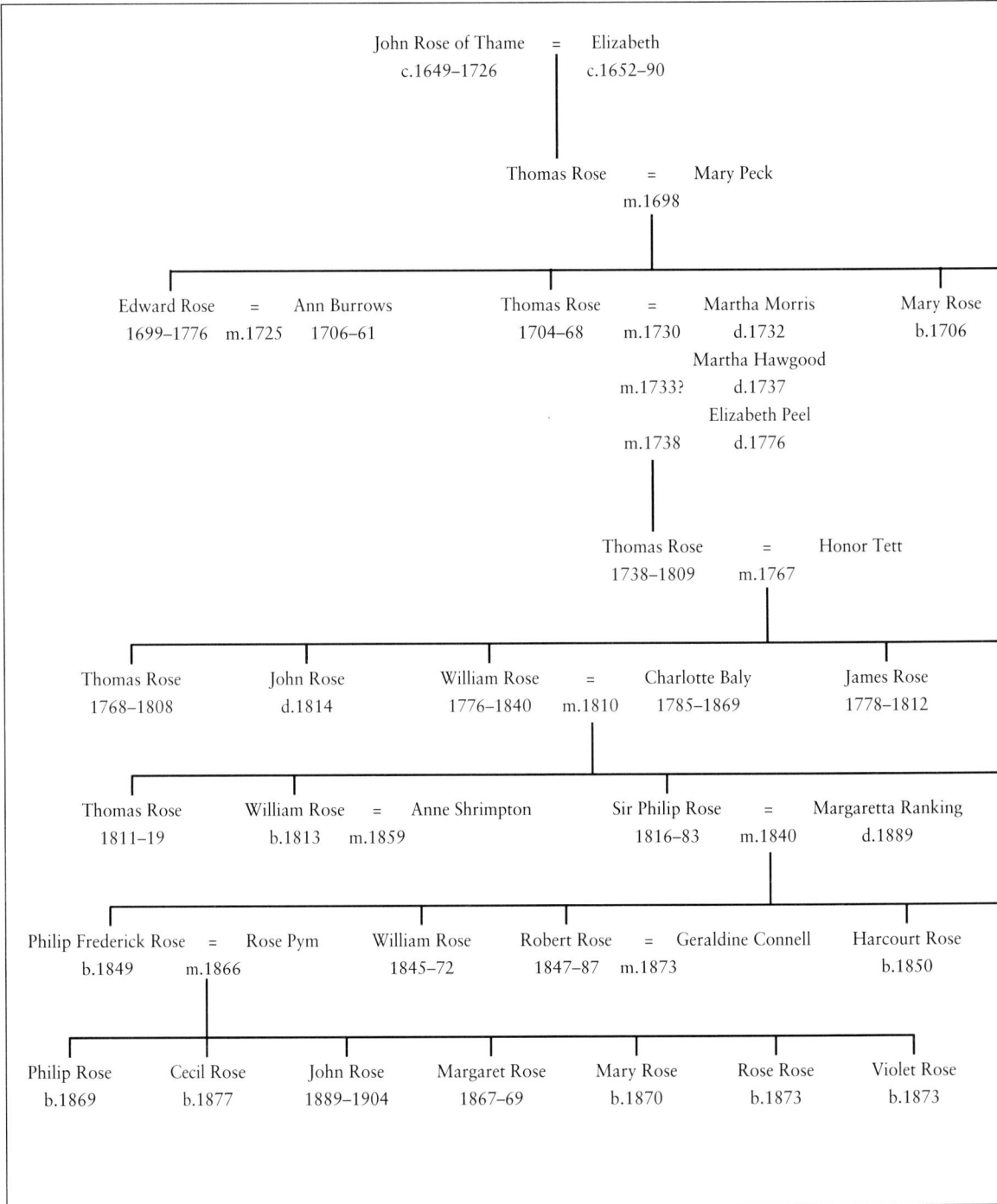

John Rose of Thame = Elizabeth
c.1649–1726   c.1652–90

Thomas Rose = Mary Peck
m.1698

Edward Rose = Ann Burrows
1699–1776 m.1725 1706–61

Thomas Rose = Martha Morris
1704–68 m.1730 d.1732

Martha Hawgood
m.1733? d.1737

Elizabeth Peel
m.1738 d.1776

Mary Rose
b.1706

Thomas Rose = Honor Tett
1738–1809 m.1767

Thomas Rose   John Rose   William Rose = Charlotte Baly   James Rose
1768–1808   d.1814   1776–1840 m.1810 1785–1869   1778–1812

Thomas Rose   William Rose = Anne Shrimpton   Sir Philip Rose = Margaretta Ranking
1811–19   b.1813 m.1859   1816–83 m.1840 d.1889

Philip Frederick Rose = Rose Pym   William Rose   Robert Rose = Geraldine Connell   Harcourt Rose
b.1849 m.1866   1845–72   1847–87 m.1873   b.1850

Philip Rose   Cecil Rose   John Rose   Margaret Rose   Mary Rose   Rose Rose   Violet Rose
b.1869   b.1877   1889–1904   1867–69   b.1870   b.1873   b.1873

Rose Family Tree – up to 1889

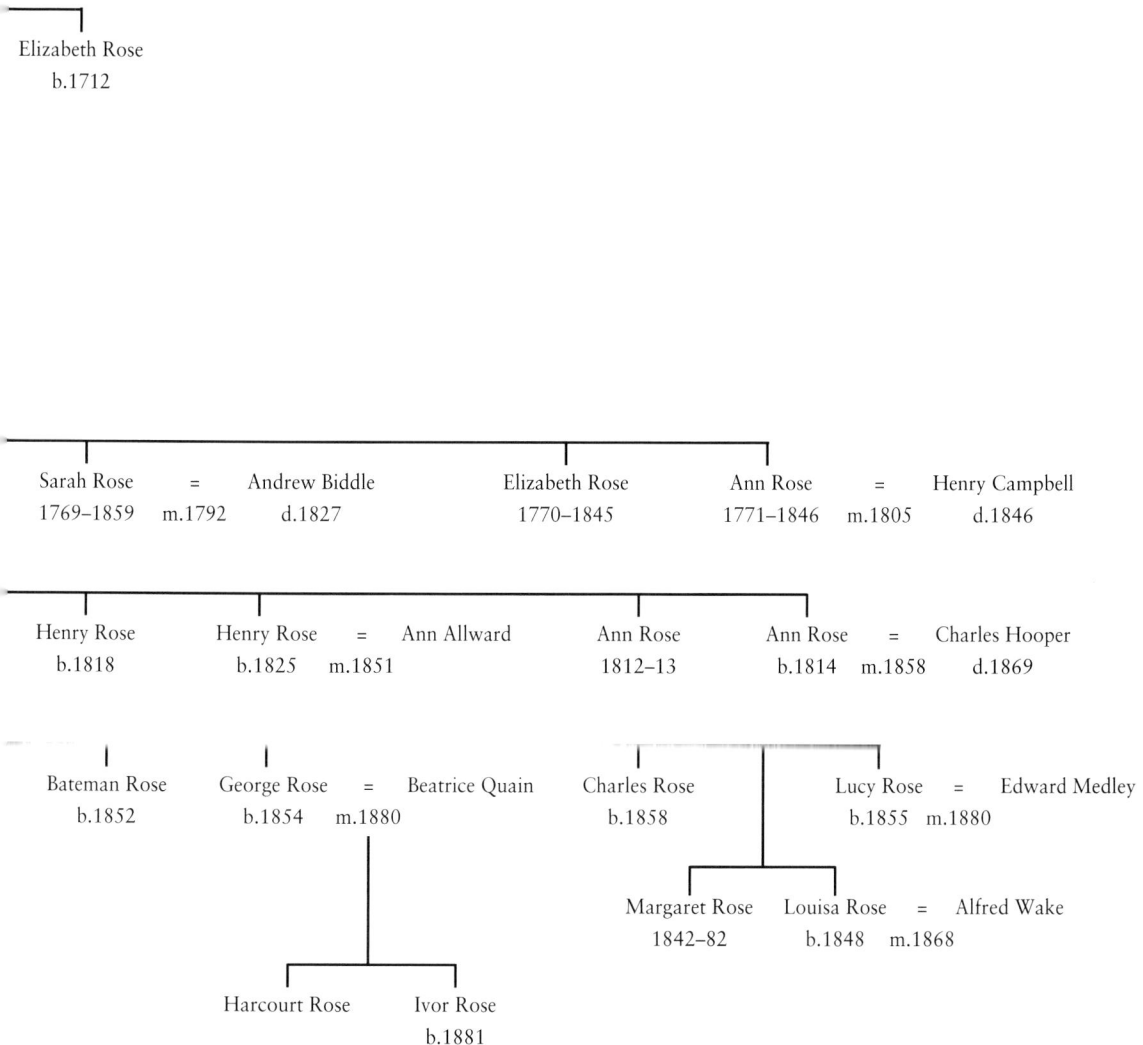

Elizabeth Rose
b.1712

Sarah Rose = Andrew Biddle
1769–1859 m.1792 d.1827

Elizabeth Rose
1770–1845

Ann Rose = Henry Campbell
1771–1846 m.1805 d.1846

Henry Rose
b.1818

Henry Rose = Ann Allward
b.1825 m.1851

Ann Rose
1812–13

Ann Rose = Charles Hooper
b.1814 m.1858 d.1869

Bateman Rose
b.1852

George Rose = Beatrice Quain
b.1854 m.1880

Charles Rose
b.1858

Lucy Rose = Edward Medley
b.1855 m.1880

Margaret Rose
1842–82

Louisa Rose = Alfred Wake
b.1848 m.1868

Harcourt Rose   Ivor Rose
b.1881

Philip Rose.

Dr William Rose was a hard, puritanical man, much interested in his children's success in life. Philip Rose later said that he would be frightened to approach his father if in difficulties and that he was the last person he would go to for advice or assistance.[9] Dr Rose died in the summer of 1846 and his wife in the spring of 1869. His eldest son, also called William, followed his father into medicine. Philip had to consider what he wanted to do, and on leaving school at Totteridge, Hertfordshire, he entered the law, becoming articled to John Charsley of Beaconsfield (1782–1855) in January 1833.

Philip Rose was not without training or education. Previously it had been neither customary nor necessary for solicitors to hold anything more than their articles.[10] The procedures for entering the Bar had been established for several hundred years. Since 1729, the aspiring solicitor had to meet entry requirements based on a five-year articled clerkship followed by a perfunctory examination. For some, there was a period as a salaried employee which could lead, after several years' practice, to a partnership.

As an articled clerk, Rose was assiduous and punctilious.[11] He was also ambitious and soon outgrew Beaconsfield, moving to London in 1836. He lived south west of the Inns of Court at 4 Arundel Street, Strand. He was articled at the firm of Williamson and Hills. Rose was

RIGHT: *Rose's practising certificates from the 1830s.*

14

In the Exchequer of Pleas.

66

Michaelmas Term in the Seventh Year of the Reign of King William the Fourth.

It appearing unto this Court that *Philip Rose of N°. 4, Arundel Street in the County of Middlesex late of N°. 1 new Basinghall Street in the City of London* Gentleman is duly qualified to Act as an Attorney of his Majesty's Court of Exchequer, at Westminster, and he having this Day taken in open Court the Oaths of Allegiance and Supremacy and also taken and subscribed the Oath appointed to be taken by Attornies, by an Act of Parliament made and passed in the Second Year of the Reign of his late Majesty King George the Second, intituled " **An Act for the better Regulation of Attornies and Solicitors ;**" This Court doth hereby admit him an Attorney of the said Court of Exchequer, and doth Order his Name to be Enrolled by the proper Officer of the said Court pursuant to the Directions of the said Act. DATED this *twenty seventh* Day of November in the Year of our Lord One Thousand Eight Hundred and Thirty-six.

Enrolled the same day

By the Court

CERTIFICATE for an Attorney, Solicitor, Proctor, or Notary Public, admitted or enrolled Three Years or upwards, and resident in London or Westminster, or within the Limits of the Two-penny Post.

£6.

No. 9787 9796

Stamp Office, Somerset Place.

I *Teesdale Cockell,* duly appointed by the Commissioners of Stamps Do hereby certify, That *Philip Rose ...*

... bath delivered into my Office a Note in Writing, containing his Name, and Place of Residence as herein set forth, pursuant to the Acts of Parliament relating to the Stamp Duties on Certificates to be taken out by Attornies, Solicitors, and others, and that he hath paid the Duty for this Certificate, by virtue whereof he is at liberty to practice as an Attorney, Solicitor, Proctor, or Notary Public, (if duly admitted or enrolled,) from the day of the Date hereof, until the Fifteenth day of November, One Thousand Eight Hundred and Thirty seven *both inclusive, and no longer.*

Given under my Hand, this *Eighteenth* day of *February* in the Year of our Lord One Thousand Eight Hundred and Thirty *seven*

Teesdale Cockell, Registrar.

Entered at my Office, this *20th* day of *February* 1837,

Note.—This Certificate must be entered at the proper Office of the Court in which you were admitted or enrolled.

Forasmuch as upon Examination and Inquiry touching the ability and capacity of *Philip Rose of Arundel Street Strand in the County of Middlesex Gentleman* ...

In the Kings Bench

Michaelmas Term in the seventh year of the reign of King William the fourth young at a time when the legal profession offered a broadening range of opportunity. The 1830s were an exciting time for the profession because it had begun to regulate its standards of entry. Since 1729, when an Act for the Better Regulation of Attorneys and Solicitors set out a five-year period of articled clerkship and drew up a roll of admissions to be administered by the judges, there had been little legislation to alter the shape or membership of the profession.

Articled clerks were taught by practical experience rather than from first principles, which meant that knowledge was as limited as the means of instruction. Articles themselves were not cheap. Stamp Duty on Articles was £100, set by William Pitt in 1794; this was increased to £110 in 1804 and £120 in 1815. It remained at £120 until 1853 when it was cut to £80; it was finally eliminated in 1947. The cost of a London legal education in the early nineteenth century was around £1,000, slightly less in the provinces where the Stamp Duty on Articles was half.[12] It included a premium payable to the firm by the articled clerk; this varied from around £100 in London in the eighteenth century (when the average annual income of a clerk was £75); by 1835 it varied between £200 and £500 according to the standing of the firm.[13] The last articled clerk in Norton Rose to be charged a premium entered the firm in 1951.

The 1729 Act had allowed attorneys the right of admission to the Court of Chancery, and in 1749 solicitors achieved similar rights of admission. The terms 'attorney' and 'solicitor' were practically inter-changeable, the latter formed by those hoping to seem more respectable. The distinction was formally abolished in 1875. Rose would have considered himself a solicitor (root *solliciteur*, to take charge of business) rather than an attorney (root *atorner*, to assign or appoint), since it was the title of choice for the upwardly mobile, which Rose certainly was. Since 1739 the London predecessor of the Law Society had existed as The Society of Gentlemen Practisers. But in the 1820s and 1830s things began to change rapidly. 1825 saw the foundation of a Law Institution (hall, library, club and offices) which was established by deed of settlement in 1827. In 1831 it received its Royal Charter and in 1832 changed its name to The Incorporated Law Society. In 1833 it instituted a series of lectures for Articled Clerks and employed three lecturers to give nine to twelve lectures annually at the Society's headquarters in Chancery Lane.[14]

By 1836 the Law Society was looking at worst to maintain and at best to improve the quality of its members, and so its Council set out an examination for membership. The common law judges appointed sixteen attorney members of the Council of the Law Society to examine candidates for admission as attorneys; and the Master of the Rolls appointed twelve solicitor members to examine candidates for admission as solicitors.[15] It was this examination that Philip Rose sat and passed in the summer of 1836. It took one day, and the standards were reportedly low. Several candidates handed in their papers within two hours (the rubric allowed five) and ten failed; however, the examiners subsequently passed six of these and, after reconsidering the remaining four, passed them as well.[16]

The pass rate in the second sitting of the examination in 1837 was also 100 per cent.[17] The rates of entry, however, fell from 500 in 1836 to around 400 per year between 1837 and 1852, while the numbers of barristers admitted showed no such decline. The yearly rate of growth in the number of practising solicitors in the first third of the nineteenth century had been 3 per cent, but this growth ended in 1835, perhaps because of the announcement of the first professional examination to be held the following year.

This meant that Rose was joining a profession which was, in all other respects, poised to expand, but for which the entry figures remained constant until the 1870s when the profession did begin to grow again and accelerate into the 1880s. In London, work tended to concentrate in foreign loans and numerous company flotations during the 1820s and in financial and commercial projects during the 1830s.

One result was a more significant role for the legal clerk, who was cheap to employ and who did not have to pass an examination to qualify him to do profitable work:

> Every hour is spent with pen in hand, either fumbling among drawers and boxes for antique precedents, or entering them in commonplace books, or modelling them into new forms for new circumstances as new clients may require them. A walk now and then to examine an abstract, or search for a cause, or with volumes of reports and a bag of briefs to Westminster Hall, is the only relief to weeks of endless writing.[18]

Henry Elland Norton came from a London family. Born on 12 November 1814, he was one of six children.[19] His middle name, Elland, was his mother's maiden name. He married Charlotte Anne Turton Newton of Southborough on 5 August 1846, and their first son took the Turton name. Henry Elland Norton was admitted in 1838. He had been articled to his uncle, Henry Norton of Gray's Inn at the firm of Egerton, Norton and Chaplin.

The new regulations governing the intake of the profession meant that both Norton and Rose entered at a time when incoming talent was dwindling but prospective business was increasing. Rose's first certificate refers to the rules drafted by the Council in 1836. It reads:

> Michaelmas Term 1836. IN PURSUANCE of the Rules made in Hilary and Easter Terms, 1836, of the Courts of King's Bench, Common Pleas, and Exchequer, WE, being the major part of the Examiners actually present at, and conducting the examination of Philip Rose of No. 4 Arundel Street, Strand, DO HEREBY CERTIFY, that we have examined the said Philip Rose as required by the said rules, AND we do testify, that the said Philip Rose is fit and capable to act as an Attorney of the said Courts. Dated the 16th day of November 1836. (Certificate No. 79.)

Rose swore his oaths of allegiance to the King's Bench on 21 November 1836, as the certificate reads, under 'an act [sic] of a [sic] Parliament made and passed in the second year of the reign of his late majesty King George the Second intitled *an act for the better regulation of Attornies and Solicitors*. This court doth hereby admit him … '. His admission to the Court of the Exchequer and the Court of Common Pleas followed the next day, and to the Court of Chancery on 26 November. Rose's first Practising Certificate (Stamp Duty, £6) is dated 18 February 1837; it was entered at the Court of King's Bench (the court where he was initially enrolled) and signed by the King's Bench Commissioner, Thomas Blanc.

Rose was at that time articled to Williamson and Hills of 4 Verulam Buildings, Gray's Inn. It must therefore have been a radical step in 1838 – the same year John Linklater went into partnership with Julius Dods – to go east to Mark Lane, between Eastcheap and Tower Hill, to join the partnership of Barker and Bridge. How did Philip Rose join this firm of Barker & Bridge? William Barker was the London agent for the Charsleys' legal business in Beaconsfield. In 1838, Dr William Rose, Philip's father, wrote to William Barker about his son's prospects and the possibility of a partnership in the firm. The letter is now lost, but the record of its existence and summary of its contents have survived.[20]

When Thomas Bridge retired in 1838, Rose joined William Barker by buying Bridge's interest for £1,500, which he had borrowed from one of his grandfathers. In addition, Robert Ranking, a surgeon from Hastings and Rose's future father-in-law, stood surety for Rose:

> Robert Ranking … hath agreed to enter into a Bond to the said William Barker in the penal sum of Two thousand five hundred pounds conditioned on the due performance of the said Philip Rose of the covenants and stipulations herein contained and which on the part of the said Philip Rose are or ought to be observed during and in respect of the said Copartnership[.][21]

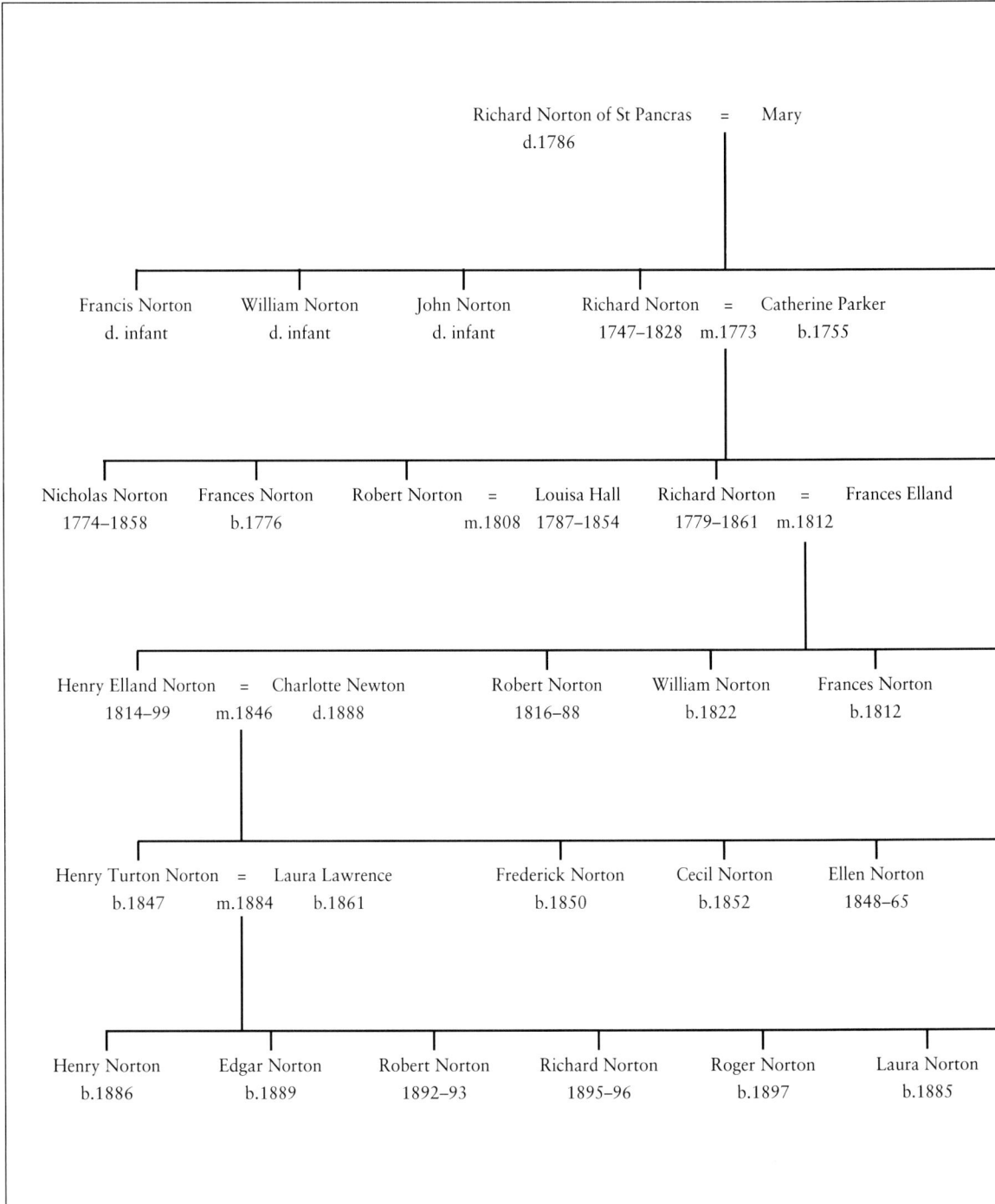

Richard Norton of St Pancras   =   Mary
d.1786

Francis Norton   William Norton   John Norton   Richard Norton = Catherine Parker
d. infant   d. infant   d. infant   1747–1828 m.1773 b.1755

Nicholas Norton   Frances Norton   Robert Norton = Louisa Hall   Richard Norton = Frances Elland
1774–1858   b.1776   m.1808 1787–1854   1779–1861 m.1812

Henry Elland Norton = Charlotte Newton   Robert Norton   William Norton   Frances Norton
1814–99   m.1846   d.1888   1816–88   b.1822   b.1812

Henry Turton Norton = Laura Lawrence   Frederick Norton   Cecil Norton   Ellen Norton
b.1847   m.1884   b.1861   b.1850   b.1852   1848–65

Henry Norton   Edgar Norton   Robert Norton   Richard Norton   Roger Norton   Laura Norton
b.1886   b.1889   1892–93   1895–96   b.1897   b.1885

Norton Family Tree – up to 1905

Mary Norton   Anne Norton = William Plaistowe
                              m.1782

Henry Norton   Elizabeth Norton   William Norton   =   Martha Miller   Alexander Norton   Edward Norton
1785–1837   1778–1865   1789–1856   m.1822   1796–1853   b.1792   1799–1866

Ann Norton   Louisa Norton
b.1818   b.1827

Elizabeth Norton   Louisa Norton   =   Richard Margerison   Henrietta Norton
b.1853   b.1854   m.1881   b.1856

Ellen Norton   Jane Norton   Ethel Norton
b.1888   b.1893   b.1902

The partnership 'in the Profession Business and practice of Attornies at Law and Solicitors in equity under the style or firm of Barker & Rose' began on 30 July 1838, and was to run from 1 January 1838 for seven years, with Barker and Rose as joint equals. Barker could terminate the partnership with six months' notice to Rose, who then had two months to buy out Barker's 'Goodwill' after appropriate arbitration. The last clause, titled 'Nineteenthly', refers to 'Umpirage … Arbitrators … Referees' and stipulates that disputes were to be settled by referees – 'two indifferent persons' – chosen by either party; if the differences persisted, the referees could choose an umpire.

The capital of the partnership was £1,000 (half each from Barker and Rose) deposited with the firm's bankers, Glyn, Halifax, Mills of Lombard Street. Barker and Rose were able to use Bridge's name for three years. Bridge himself agreed not to practise 'at or in London or any place or places within ten miles from the Royal Exchange', or to prejudice, infringe or invade the business of the firm. Indeed, Bridge pledged to 'at all times use his best endeavours to promote the interest and advantage of the said William Barker and Philip Rose'.

The partnership deed mentions the 'Salaries of all Clerks Writers and other persons which shall be needful', and this indicates a practice which was either used to having several clerks or ready to employ them. The other articles of the lengthy agreement (about 6,000 words), headed 'firstly' to 'nineteenthly', deal with the accounting year (January to January), share of profits and losses (equal), other partnerships, outside stewardships or clerkships, promissory notes from the firm, and standing bail (only with the consent of the partners). In essence, the agreement covers a number of points which occur in modern partnership deeds.[22]

A deed of 8 February 1844 endorsed on the back of the second page of the partnership agreement of 30 July 1838 terminates the partnership from 1 January 1844. Rose agreed to buy out Barker's 'Goodwill' for £1,400, half payable immediately and 'the other moiety

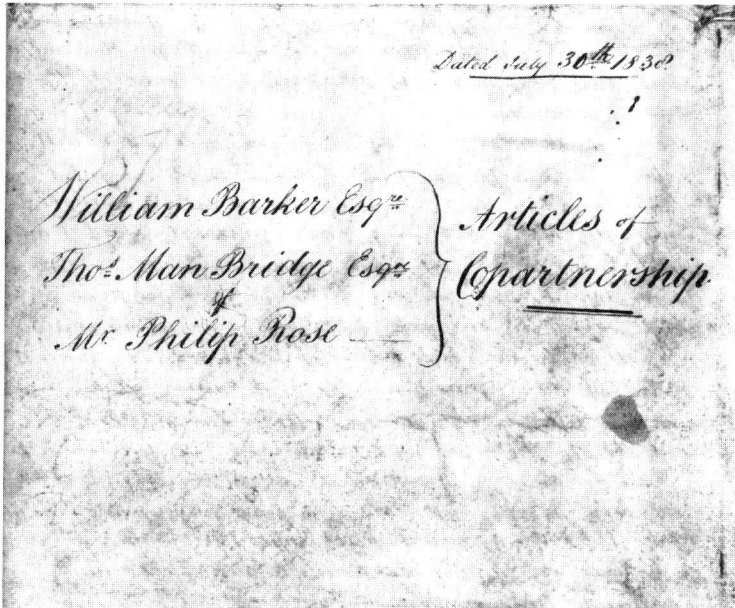

The 1838 Partnership Agreement.

thereof to be secured by the Bond of the said Philip Rose, payable on demand with Interest'. The deed was signed by Barker, and Rose, and witnessed by Henry Elland Norton. A further deed (9 February 1844) constitutes a new partnership between Rose and Norton from 1 January 1844 under the name Barker, Rose & Norton. This is Norton's first appearance in the firm's history. His uncle, Henry Norton, had died in 1837, and although no records exist for the firm Egerton, Norton and Chaplin, it seems that Norton must have stayed with them until joining Barker, Rose & Norton in 1843.

Under the 1844 agreement, Norton paid Rose £1,100 as a premium for admission and a further £145 as a third of the value of the office furniture, library, fixtures and effects at 50 Mark Lane. Of the total £1,245, Norton paid £700 immediately and agreed to pay the balance by instalments with interest secured by a bond and charge on

This Indenture made the *ninth*. day of *February*. in the year of our Lord One thousand eight hundred and forty four **Between** *Philip Rose* of Mark Lane in the City of London Gentleman of the first part and *Henry Elland Norton* of the same place Gentleman of the second part **Whereas** for several years previous and up to the first day of January last the said Philip Rose carried on the Business of an Attorney and Solicitor at No 50 Mark Lane aforesaid in partnership with William Barker of the same place Gentleman who had also for many years previous to his partnership with the said Philip Rose carried on the same business in partnership with Robert Charsley and Thomas Man Bridge and on the said first day of January last the said partnership between the said William Barker and Philip Rose was dissolved and the said William Barker assigned to the said Philip Rose the share of him the said William Barker in the Good will and effects of the said partnership (except the Capital and Credits thereof and all securities for the same and the Vouchers and Books of the said late Copartnership) and covenanted not to practise as an Attorney or Solicitor within the City of London or within ten Miles thereof

The 1844 Partnership Agreement.

his own share of the partnership's capital and credits. The
partners were entitled to the
partnership's goodwill, and were
required to advance the capital
(not less than £1,000) in the
proportions Rose two-thirds and
Norton one-third. Norton had
the option to buy from Rose,
before January 1854, a quarter
of Rose's two-thirds share of the
goodwill, which would bring
them to an equal partnership.
But in the meantime Norton was
the junior partner.

The shape and constitution
of the firm remained stable.
Bridge remained in contact with

Margaretta Rose.

the firm for some time, which suggests some amity between the
partners and retired partners. Rose's son, Frederick, recalls, 'Mr Bridge
… coming to our office at Victoria Street, Westminster, for several
years after I went there in 1860 in order to transact business with Mr
H.E. Norton, who always acted for him'.[23] Rose took over the
administration, and by the mid-1840s, he considered the firm a success.

He was so pleased with events that he had thought of taking
rooms in Albany, a West End status symbol, and of setting up a
Cabriolet, 'a type of vehicle affected in those days by smart young
men',[24] the equivalent of a Porsche Cabriolet in the 1980s. Rose was
then living at 41 Hans Place, Knightsbridge, which he had leased from
his father at £60 per year. The deed is dated 25 December 1839, a few
days before his marriage to Margaretta Ranking on 2 January 1840 in
Hastings. Dr Rose had probably intended to retire to London; at the

time was still in practice at Wycombe and had little need of a house in London, then a day's ride away.

Philip Rose and his wife moved from 41 Hans Place to 22 Hans Place, former home of the well-known and popular poet 'L.E.L.' – Miss Letitia Elizabeth Landon. The lease was for seventeen years, and Rose paid £110 per year as rack rent. Forty-four years after Rose left 22 Hans Place in 1856, his youngest son Charles Marston took the lease of a new house built on the site of his childhood home.[25] No. 22 and No. 23 – home of a Miss Marston, Charles' godmother – originally faced each other across the gateway to The Pavilion, home of Sir Francis Shuckburgh and now Pavilion Road. Pont Street, which connects Sloane Street to Walton Street, did not exist. The Pavilion grounds included Cadogan Gardens, Lennox Gardens and the adjoining streets; later, after The Pavilion was pulled down, they formed a cricket ground and skating rink. 'Many will remember,' wrote Frederick Rose in 1900, 'in the early days of the Roller Skate mania, the splendid elms standing in the grounds of the Princes Club, under which the ladies drank tea in the Summer.'

The period during which Philip Rose lived at 22 Hans Place was the most active of his life. The family grew, and the Roses added governesses[26] and tutors[27] to the household, always separate from the other staff who sat in the servants' pew at their local church, St Saviour's, Walton Street. The boys were sent to Harrow, Wellington and Eton; Rose was trying to give his sons a better start than he had had. Both Rose and his wife had been brought up as strict Evangelical Calvinists and they imposed a stern regime on the house. Margaretta came from a wealthy family, so she was no drain on Rose's financial resources; but her stamina was tested over the next sixteen years, when the Roses had ten children.[28] In 1856 they moved to No. 59 Rutland Gate and stayed there until 1868, when they moved to their last home, No. 1 (formerly No. 14) Cromwell Road where Rose died in April 1883.

In 1843, Rose, at 27, was keen, ambitious and ready to apply his religious ethic to his work; he rarely relaxed and seldom spent an evening at home, frowned on frivolity and practised charity on a manageable scale. He was a robust man, morally and physically, capable of long hours and dedicated work. His portrait from that time shows a level gaze, a full face with clear, even features and hair swept back from a high forehead. He is wearing a high-collared shirt – the Byronic collar – a black silk stock, light waistcoat and dark dress coat.

The partnership of the firm was changing from the older generation to the younger as Barker and Bridge made way for Rose and Norton. Apparently set to expand along the path of commercial, trust, probate and conveyancing law which it had already travelled profitably in the 1830s, the firm might have investigated the prospects opening up in finance, commerce and industry in the 1840s. But Joseph Gibbs, drainage engineer and a client of the firm, changed all that in 1843 by presenting Rose and Norton with the biggest opportunity they would ever get.

In 1835 Gibbs had evolved a project to run a railway from London to York. His application in the parliamentary session of 1836 was one of the few to fail. The Commons instead passed a bill for the northern route from Euston via Rugby, Leicester, Derby, Chesterfield and Castleford. A short extension of the North Midland Railway to York would link the two systems. Gibbs therefore contented himself with building a railway between London and Croydon. Then in 1843 he evolved another scheme, routing the line through Cambridge and Lincoln to York and using his expertise in drainage engineering to survey and plot the route north and south of Cambridge, especially over Hatfield Chase to the north.

On 17 April 1844 a notice appeared in *The Times* to the effect that a detailed prospectus 'with the names of the Provisional Committee' would be available within a few days from 'Messrs Barker, Rose & Norton of 50 Mark Lane'. This was the prospectus for 'The Great Northern Railway' (London – Cambridge – Sleaford – Lincoln – York).

But the Great Northern had a competitor, the projected Northern and Eastern Railway (London – Norwich – York).

One man controlled the destiny of the line to York and he had supported the link from York to the North Midland Railway, which made use of existing or projected lines. He was a linen draper called George Hudson, and he was to become the most powerful man in railways in the nineteenth century. Known as 'The Railway King', and hence George 'King' Hudson, he was as famous in his day as Brunel or Brassey after his investments during the railway mania of the 1840s made him notorious. He died in penury in 1871.

Hudson had advocated a route from York which ran through the West Riding of Yorkshire. But the late 1830s saw growing opposition from Lincoln – which wanted a rail link north and south – and from Doncaster, where two men had staged a fierce representation, urging that the railway should take a more southerly and direct route. They were Robert Baxter, a lawyer, and Edmund Denison, a Conservative MP. Meeting them was to change both the fortunes of Rose and Norton for the next fifty years and their ideas about what lawyers could achieve.

Robert Baxter

Robert Baxter (1802–89) was one of the most remarkable lawyers of the century. His obituary reads:

> So well did he succeed that his endorsement of a Bill in Parliament became at once a signal of ultimate triumph, and the great firm of Baxter, Rose, and Norton had more Railway Bills in Parliament at one time, almost, than all the other firms put together. This was a remarkable era in Mr. Baxter's lifetime, no less than it was in the national life of the country itself.[29]

Baxter had been articled to a solicitor practising in Lincoln's Inn in 1828. His family came from Stoke Golding, Leicestershire. He was the third son of Dudley Baxter, who was a magistrate, Deputy-Lieutenant of the county, and Colonel of the Leicestershire Militia, which he had equipped at his own expense during the Napoleonic War. Robert Baxter was clever, clear-headed, patient, deliberate and calculating. He was also prodigiously hard working, as his obituary reveals:

> We have known him come down from town late at night, call at once for a shorthand writer, and whilst munching a crust of toast, with a cup of tea, wade through a long report on the canvassing operations up to date – all the while dictating letter after letter bearing upon the details and requirements of the document before him. This would go on for hours, until the amanuensis had a fair day's work before him on the following morning, if, indeed it had not to be done that night before he went to bed.[30]

It continues:

> A truly great man, a man of mark, a man of his time, a man of high intellectual power, of warm, generous, overflowing sympathies, and of strong, religious convictions and aspirations, his 'footprints on the sands of time' are sharply marked and easily traceable by those who can take the lives of the great men as a prayerful incentive to make theirs sublime.[31]

Even though Baxter owned the *Doncaster Chronicle* where this obituary appeared, it is not over fulsome. It was thought a fair assessment of the man. Robert Baxter was in partnership with his brother Edmund and had offices in Hall Gate, High Street, Doncaster. This practice and Robert Baxter's ownership of the local paper gave him a prominent position in a small town. In the 1830s there were fewer than a dozen law firms in Doncaster, and had been since Baxter first went into practice in the 1820s, but the number increased dramatically in the 1840s and 1850s with the promise of railway business.

Baxter was active in local politics. He sat on a committee for The Suppression of Gambling Houses and Gaming Tables, formed in 1828. Its first general meeting was held in Baxter's office at noon on Monday 25 August, and Baxter became its provisional secretary.[32] Baxter worked as a party agent for Edmund Denison, and was a powerful speaker himself in times of rapid political change. Baxter's other public work was on the National Corporations Committee which lobbied against the Corporations legislation in the 1830s. A meeting of the Committee at Brown's Hotel, London on 13 August 1835 gave Baxter this commendation:

> Resolved unanimously. That the services which Mr Baxter has rendered to this Committee in promoting its objects and the advantages that have already resulted from them, are so important that his proposed departure from Town this evening cannot be looked forward to by this Committee otherwise than with the greatest concern.

> Resolved unanimously. That Mr Baxter be solicited to reconsider his intentions of withdrawing his attendance from the Committee and should the urgency of his private professional pursuits absolutely require his presence at home, that He be anxiously solicited to make the period of his absence as short as circumstances will permit – the Committee confidently hoping that he will return to Witness the successful termination of his valuable and unremitting Services.[33]

Baxter was gifted at presenting causes to the public, or to those who made decisions. In this he seems less like a lawyer and more like a combination of lobbyist, consultant and public relations agent. His greatest work still lay ahead, but Robert Baxter had a modified dual personality which was to affect his career. On the one hand, in public the man was undaunted by difficulties, 'and obstacles which would have overwhelmed weaker men were but as webs of gossamer in the ken of his keen, penetrating vision'.[34] But on the other, he was subject to bouts of depression and religious mania.

Baxter had two brothers: one was in practice with him, and the other was a clergyman in Doncaster. Baxter himself was a deeply religious man. Doctrinally, he was a member of the old High Church Party and was a Tory and State Churchman; but, theologically, he was a fervid evangelical, steeped in liturgical jargon. Around 1829 Baxter became closely involved with Edward Irving (1792–1834), the charismatic Scottish preacher, and founder of the Catholic Apostolic Church.

Irving had moved to London from Glasgow in 1822 to run the Caledonian Chapel in Hatton Garden. He was a great popular orator, and used his eloquence to attack prominent men like Jeremy Bentham, Lord Coleridge, George Canning and the Earl of Liverpool (Prime Minister, 1812–27). He wrote the anti-establishment *Argument for Judgement to Come* in 1823. William Hazlitt included Irving in his great *The Spirit of The Age*:

> Few circumstances show the prevailing and preposterous rage for novelty in a more striking point of view than the success of Mr Irving's oratory. People go to hear him in crowds, and come away with a mixture of delight and astonishment. They go again to see if the effect will continue, and send others to try to find out the mystery; and in the noisy conflict between extravagant encomiums and splenetic objections, the true secret escapes observation which is, that the whole thing is, nearly from beginning to end, a *transposition of ideas*.[35]

Irving and his followers differed from other sects in that they had the names of angels, apostles, and prophets, among their teachers, and they claimed the gift of prophecy and tongues. 'They also carry with them the promise of an early endowment of ministers in power, and foretell, as with authority, the speedy coming of Christ, and the out-pouring of the vials of wrath upon the world,' Baxter wrote in 1836.[36]

Baxter's involvement with the Irvingites grew throughout the 1820s until the early 1830s; it developed into a delusional and mystical relationship with one of the century's most powerful spiritual leaders.[37] In 1833 he wrote about his experiences in a turgid and weighty pamphlet. Baxter's *Narrative of facts characterising the supernatural manifestations in members of Mr Irving's congregation and other individuals in england* [sic] *and scotland* [sic] *and formerly in the writer himself* (London, 1833) is a technical account well versed in biblical scholarship, of the impact of Edward Irving's teachings in the 1820s and 1830s. It reads vividly and naively, like a medieval tract, where spiritual matters become palpable realities.

Baxter's *Narrative* tells how, 'called up to London ... by professional arrangements',[38] he fell in and then out with Irving. In January 1832, Baxter took the three-day journey from Doncaster to London and stayed for a month on business, probably connected with a countrywide action group opposing the current Corporations Bill. His tendencies at the time of Irvingism were to keep his religious life separate from his professional duties. However, during the visit he attended one of Irving's prayer meetings. He became more deeply involved with the cult and delivered a sermon to them in London. He was so close for a time to Irving that he sometimes deputised for him, taking family prayers. But he became disillusioned by the spring of 1832.[39] By the summer of 1832, Baxter had decided against Irvingism. He was still wrestling with it when he wrote *Irvingism in its rise, progress and present state* (London, 1836).[40]

Looking back in 1836, he recounts what happened:

> My own case may be an example: accustomed to try the powers and weaknesses of my own mind in public and in private; in business and in religious meetings; in speaking and in prayer; in reasoning, and in exposition; I found, on a sudden, in the midst of my accustomed course, a power coming upon me which was altogether new – an unnatural, and in many cases, a most appalling utterance given to me –

matters uttered by me in this power of which I had never thought, and many of which I did not understand until long after they were uttered … It was manifest to me the power was supernatural; it was therefore a spirit.[41]

Irving has made a lasting impact on English literary and ecclesiastical history, and has been written about by Coleridge, Mrs Oliphant, De Quincy and Carlyle. Baxter's involvement with him shows how close to the pulse of the 1830s he was, interested in both spiritual and temporal matters. What did this episode say about Baxter? That he was initially credulous, enthusiastic, energetic and, above all, a man of great personal and public probity. He can be excused because of the temper of the times, since the political turmoil surrounding the 1832 Reform Bill had occasioned all manner of searches, literary, religious and scientific, for certainties that did not depend on the whim of the majority.

Baxter's adulatory obituary in the *Doncaster Chronicle* attributes the Irving episode to his enthusiastic nature.[42] The brush with Irvingism and its excesses, however, showed Baxter had blind spots. These weaknesses surfaced in Baxter's behaviour during the famous Tichborne Case in the 1870s. It is certain that his vigorous non-conformist views had a bearing on the firm's espousal of an anti-Catholic client.

Having abandoned Irvingism, Baxter found another project in the late 1830s to which he could give himself wholeheartedly: the railway. The *Doncaster Chronicle* proceeded to give powerful advocacy to the London and York Direct System, as it was then called, in order to urge what the paper felt was 'intelligent, rational and practical public feeling on a question which … might have left Doncaster high and dry upon a loop line far away from the main system of the nearest railway … Mr. Baxter had many such irons in the fire, and how he grappled with their various interests and complex details at one and the same time, as he did, would be a mystery save for the hypothesis of marvellous ability and splendid capacity'.[43]

Around 1840, individual members of the legal profession like Philip Rose, Henry Elland Norton or Robert Baxter were on the verge of changing what lawyers customarily did and how lawyers habitually saw themselves. The railways provided a powerful combination of legal, financial, technological, political and social forces. Every sleeper laid had to be negotiated across land already owned; every bridge and every station built had to be planned, contracted, completed and seen through every stage of construction and function. Firms which specialised, as Barker, Rose & Norton had, in conveyancing, family, commercial and trust work could apply their traditional expertise to the new railway phenomenon. Lawyers everywhere were becoming railway-wise; the Huntingdon solicitor William Fowler, who was a friend of Rose, found himself acting for the railway district around his home town. The City too had realised that money could be made in railways: the Grand Junction Railway, London and Birmingham Railway, and York and Midland Railway paid 10 per cent dividends, while the Stockton and Darlington paid 15 per cent.

In 1839 the Government appointed a Commission of the Board of Trade to investigate a route to Scotland and as a caveat to their inquiry to report on the London–York route either in its west-coast form (Hudson's York and North Midland connection) or in the form proposed by Joseph Gibbs via Cambridge, Lincoln and Doncaster. The Commission reported in 1841, opting for Hudson's scheme which built on to existing lines, and remaining tepid about a Lincoln link. By the autumn of 1843, Hudson had forced his way on to the board of the North Midland Railway and staged the famous amalgamation between the Midland Counties, the Birmingham and Derby and the North Midland railways to establish 'The Midland Railway', with himself as Chairman, in the 1844 parliamentary session. At that time the journey from London to York took eleven hours but in an act of public showmanship Hudson took the train from Euston on 18 June and travelled the 303 miles to Tyneside in nine hours and thirty-two minutes.[44]

Hudson's combative and aggressive style was an outright challenge to the industry as a whole as it picked up speed in the 1840s. Indeed, four rival projects emerged in competition with Hudson's Midland Railway link to York: the Cambridge and Lincoln, the Direct Northern, the 'Great Northern' and the London and York. The 'Great Northern' was the railway scheme which Joseph Gibbs had brought to Philip Rose.[45] But on 3 May 1844 one of the rival schemes, the London and York, issued its prospectus under the aegis of the Earl of Winchelsea. Then on 11 June it produced an enlarged prospectus tabling a line which would cost £4.5m, and which at 327 miles would be longer than the original London and Birmingham and the Great Western railways combined.

Rose and Norton had to decide whether the firm should act for Gibbs and the 'Great Northern' in the face of such confident opposition.[46] Rose immediately staked £1,500 of his own money on the 'Great Northern' scheme; Norton was more circumspect – 'with his more cautious and timid temperament'[47] – and yielded to Rose's persuasion only as far as putting up £500. At this point, the firm was to act not for the Board of Directors of an established company but for a Proposed Committee drawn together to promote the appropriate Railway Bill. Rose offered the firm's time and expertise for nothing. It was a speculative venture, a piece of daring capitalism, and an immense risk in view of the other rival schemes. The greatest battle in railway history had begun.

The year 1844 and the next two sessions of Parliament were dominated by the battle for the Bill to build the direct London–York line. The Board of Trade Commissioners had before them the rival schemes of the London and York, the 'Great Northern', the Direct Northern and the Cambridge and Lincoln railways. The five

Commissioners – Lord Dalhousie, General Pasley, Captain O'Brien, G.R. Porter and Samuel Laing (a member of the founding family of Laing & Cruickshank and who later became a close associate of Rose) – complained: 'Five angels could not have performed satisfactorily if they had come down from heaven and sat four hours a day as a Board.'[48] The Board of Trade had not reached a decision when the Railway Bills went before Parliament, a fact which created problems for the lawyers. Eventually the Board of Trade reported in favour of a combination of the Direct Northern and the Eastern Counties Railway.

The Cambridge and Lincoln scheme consequently lost momentum. The field narrowed to the Direct Northern, the 'Great Northern' (represented by Barker, Rose & Norton) and the London and York scheme (represented by Baxter & Co. of Doncaster). In 1844, the 'Great Northern' and the London and York decided to amalgamate their railway schemes into what eventually became the Great Northern Railway. This brought about the union of the railway business of their two firms of solicitors. The lawyers were central to this extraordinary move, which effectively amalgamated two firms several hours apart and with only the mail as a means of communication.

Robert Baxter, Philip Rose and Henry Elland Norton agreed to form Baxter, Rose & Norton. Rose later said, 'The change of name was simple, and it was also phonetic, and the old name was changed so slightly that people hardly noticed it.'[49] Baxter was senior to Rose, by twelve years. Rose seemed content, but perhaps Baxter's extraordinary energy and charisma made taking a back seat easier. A memorandum of 21 November 1845 endorsed on the back of the partnership agreement (8 February 1844) shows that there were, in fact, three distinct partnerships. Rose and Norton had entered into business with Baxter but only in terms of railway business with which all three were connected and which was carried on at the firm's new London address – a kind of campaign office opened during the Railway Bills – at 3 Park Street, Westminster.

The memorandum reads: '[it is] … desirable to prevent misconception respecting the intentions' of Rose and Norton in the new partnership.[50] The memorandum holds Rose and Norton to the same terms as their original 1844 agreement. The most interesting part of the agreement was that it showed the three separate entities: the partnership between the brothers Robert and Edmund Baxter, the partnership between Rose and Norton, and the partnership – restricted exclusively to railway business – between Rose, Norton and Robert Baxter. The railways were the key. The firm devoted energy to the railway business because it promised to be so hugely profitable and held out the hope of future work.

Baxter moved from Doncaster to 3 Park Street for the parliamentary fight. By March 1845, positions were tougher and the rhetoric bolder. The Great Northern announced that it was going ahead, Board of Trade or no Board of Trade. The *Railway Times* commented:

> The monster bubble has burst; the mighty scheme which was to furnish the pockets of its supporters with the *spolia optima* of premiums to the tune of a million and a quarter has vanished into thin and unsubstantial air.[51]

A Board of Trade report, however, was one thing, a vote in the Commons another, and Royal Assent still another. This was a time of unprecedented activity; Baxter, Rose & Norton was at the centre. There were 224 Railway Bills in the 1845 session of Parliament. The parliamentary, litigious and public tumult was enormous. Parliamentary directives were ignored, declarations made, fortunes lost as investors switched between the four schemes.

Conditions in Parliament were scarcely ideal; the new Houses of Parliament were under construction, so the committees met in wooden sheds. The London and York, 'Great Northern' bill came up first. Such was the complexity for the firm and the Parliamentary lawyers that thirty-two barristers were retained. On the first day of the hearing, the appointed shed was filled to standing capacity with journalists, jobbers and hangers-on and had to be emptied to let the committee and barristers in. A larger shed was allocated for the next day's sitting.

By June 1845 there was one railway left in the race. The Cambridge and Lincoln and the Direct Northern had failed to comply with Standing Orders and were downgraded to 'projects' rather than Bills. The remaining scheme, the 'Great Northern', faced a barrage of what *Herapath's Railway Journal* called 'tedious, unimportant and insufferable nonsense' as the real opposition, 'King' Hudson, used a variety of delaying and spoiling tactics in committee and in the City.

These included a dubious circular to county and London postmasters to determine the addresses and means of the Great Northern's supporters; Hudson then claimed that the railway was funded by paupers and could not discharge its debts.[52] Hudson's action, in the midst of fraudulent Irish railway cases like the Dublin and Galway, so frightened Parliament that it staged a means test for the 'Great Northern' scrip holders. The inquiry – which continued all night on its first day – discovered that applications for £30,000 of shares had been signed by people who could not be traced and a further £45,000 of shares by people who had no means of paying.

Even if such difficulties could be overcome, victory in Parliament could only be worth something if the mechanisms were in place to move quickly and implement Parliament's decision. This meant that the 'Great Northern' scheme had to be ready to build its lines, stations and depots. The land had to be bought. During the period of the parliamentary fight, 1845–6, Baxter, Rose & Norton negotiated the purchase of the land required for the 327 miles of line from London to York.

The conveyancing task was immense, the clerks numerous, their schedules onerous and the activity constant. The firm took on nearly 300 clerks and housed them in a separate office in Great George Street, Westminster,[53] in addition to maintaining the general office in Park

Street and the all but abandoned office at 50 Mark Lane, which was kept open until 1850. In the 1840s, railway companies paid their solicitors on a transactional basis rather than by salaries or fixed fees, and most of the surviving paperwork relating to the business amounts to bills of costs and submissions of expenses.[54]

On 26 June 1846, Royal assent was given to the largest railway scheme ever sanctioned by Parliament. Baxter, Rose & Norton had helped to create what was to be known as the Great Northern Railway. The lobbying and public skills of Baxter had combined with the political and procedural talents of Rose and Norton, and the firm stood poised to expand along with the railway it had brought into being. Baxter became a Director of the Great Northern. The organisation of the firm fell to Rose and Norton (who was the financial controller), while Baxter's more public duties kept him busy in Parliament.

The railway business had a radical and lasting impact on the firm. It caused the practice to evolve an innovative system of government and organisation. Writing in 1900, Frederick Rose describes the firm:

> The business of the firm at that time was conducted, therefore, in a very different manner to that prevailing in most Solicitors' Offices. The usual custom was and is for each partner to deal with the particular branches of business in which his own particular Client happened to be interested under his own supervision. It was not so with Baxter, Rose & Norton. The whole business was divided into Departments and each Department was under the direct supervision of a particular Partner, though in some cases this rule was, to some extent departed from, notably in the Common Law and Chancery Departments each of which had its separate Chief and was entirely distinct from the other.[55]

The firm had found itself pushed into this particular shape by the railway, which itself represented a new technology requiring different sorts of legal and procedural expertise. The principle of internal cultural change matching the external demands placed on the firm was followed throughout the rest of the nineteenth century and then applied again during the firm's expansion after 1945.

Notes

1. Alexis de Tocqueville, *Democracy in America* (1835 [1961], p.325).
2. Rose Family Papers.
3. Ibid.
4. Inland Revenue Museum.
5. Frederick Rose, *Memoir*.
6. William Wordsworth, Sonnet Upon Westminster Bridge.
7. Byron, *Don Juan*, X, p.lxxxii.
8. Rose kept a diary of cases and case notes, now largely lost. Rose Family Papers.
9. Ibid.
10. By the 1870s only 5 per cent of solicitors admitted to the Roll were graduates. In 1939 fewer than a third of solicitors had university degrees; in 1969 the proportion had not reached a half. See: Richard L. Abel, 1988, pp.142ff and Tables 2.3ff.
11. Rose's first casebook is dated 'January 27th 1833'. Frederick Rose notes: 'It is an interesting family relic, as it shows how assiduously my Father applied himself when an articled clerk to the profession in which after he shone so greatly.' Rose Family Papers.
12. See: Abel, 1988, p.149.
13. See: Slinn, 1984, p.16; Lane, 1977, p.172; Kirk, 1976, p.51; Birks, 1960, pp.163–4.
14. Law Society, Annual Report, 1901, pp.12–13.
15. See: Abel, 1988, pp.156–7. The two boards combined in 1853 to administer a single examination.
16. See: Birks, 1960, p.179.
17. Its lowest rate was 48 per cent in 1952 and 1953.
18. Sir George Stephen, *The Guide To Service* (1842) in Slinn, 1987, p.11.
19. Norton Family Papers.
20. 'With this case book will be found some correspondence between my Grandfather

William Rose and Mr. Barker introductory to the partnership between my Father and Mr. Barker which was entered into in the year 1838.' Frederick Rose, Rose Family Papers.

21. Ibid.

22. Thanks to Jim Leaver who explained and transcribed the document.

23. Rose Family Papers.

24. Ibid.

25. 1899, £8,500 for a long lease; ground rent was £150.

26. Frederick Rose recalls: 'My father's idea was that we were to be educated at home until the time came for us to go to a public school, and very early in our childhood days he determined that male supervision and teaching were superior to female, so the Governesses were dispensed with, and a Tutor engaged.' Rose Family Papers.

27. One tutor, a Mr Genvy, used to ply Frederick and William with oranges and take them into 'Houses the character of which we Children knew nothing of ... a rather low class Public in the Paddington District, leaving us in the Tap Room quieted and consoled with oranges, whilst he drank at the Bar'. Ibid.

28. Margaret Amelia (born 1842, died 1882), Philip Frederick (born 1843), William Barker (born 1845), Robert Baxter (born 1847), Louisa Francis (born 1848), Harcourt Ranking (born 1850), Bateman Lancaster (born 1852), George Alfred Ste Croix (born 1854), Lucy (born 1855) and Charles Marston (born 1858 at 59 Rutland Gate where the family had moved).

    The children were named after their godparents, so it seems likely that William Barker Rose and Robert Baxter Rose took their names from Rose's partners, William Barker and Robert Baxter who may well have been godparents. This suggests a close and cordial working relationship in the 1840s, or perhaps a desire by Rose to please his seniors. Philip Frederick Rose took his name from the family doctor at William Street, Lowndes Square, Mr Frederick Brown.

29. *The Doncaster Chronicle*, 11 October 1889.

30. Ibid.

31. Ibid.

32. Baxter Papers, Doncaster Archive.

33. Ibid.

34. *The Doncaster Chronicle*, 11 October 1889.

35. Hazlitt comments: 'Mr Irving must have something superior in him, to look over the shining, close-packed heads of his congregation to have a hit at the *Great Jurisconsult* in his study … He has found the secret of attracting by repelling. Those whom he is likely to attack are curious to hear what he says of them: they go again, to show that they do not mind it … Mr Irving has in fact, without leave asked or a licence granted, converted the Caledonian Chapel into a Westminster Forum or Debating Society with the sanctity of religion added to it.' *The Spirit of the Age*, p.72.

36. Baxter opens his 1836 work on Irving with this: "It will be the remembrance of most of those who may peruse this Tract, that the Rev. Edward Irving was a minister of the established Church of Scotland. He came to London about the year 1820, and in a short time became popular beyond all example. The congregation who assembled to hear him comprised all the nobles and gentry of the land, and, in short, to use the language of town, Mr Irving was the "Lion" of the fashionable world, and the "Wonder" of the religious circles … It is enough to remark, that at this time, though his views were peculiar, and his manner of enforcing them striking, there were, apparently, none of the seeds of that system which in later years was evolved, and which distinguishes his present followers.' *Irvingism in its rise, progress and present state*, p.1.

37. Baxter wrote: 'Delusion is the only known term under which it [Irvingism] can be properly ranged; it has all the characteristics of this class, and will be found to vary only in the extent of power and depth of deceit displayed in it.' *Narrative of facts concerning supernatural manifestations*, p.xxv.

38. 'I scarcely knew how to shape my movements,' he confessed, 'my professional engagements no longer required my stay in town; and having no work set before me there, and great anxiety concerning my family, I determined to return to them, and there await the Lord's farther direction.' (Ibid., pp.52–3.)

39. Ibid, pp.3–4.

40. Ibid, p.22.

41. 'Without going again into detail, it may suffice to state, that instead of returning with apostolic power [as Baxter had been promised], I did return with a more

gracious gift, viz. with the eyes of my understanding enlightened, to see that what I and they had deemed to be the spirit of prophecy, was, in fact, the spirit of delusion. I left them about the last day of February 1832; and on the 26th April following, whilst they continued in their prayers and expectations, I returned to say I had been deluded, and to entreat them to open their eyes to the snare in which we were all taken.' *Irvingism in its rise, progress and present state*, p.24.

42. *The Doncaster Chronicle*, 11 October 1889.

43. Ibid.

44. See: O.S. Nock, *The Great Northern Railway*; Grinling, *The Great Northern Railway* and Simmons, *The Victorian Railway*.

45. See: *The Times*, 17 April 1844, advertisement for Gibbs's scheme.

46. On 23 May 1844 the London and York (now combined with the Great Northern) appointed Joseph Locke as its chief engineer, an international entrepreneur and one of the greatest influences in the business alongside Hudson and Brunel. A proposed route based on his survey was published by *The Times* in August 1844.

47. Frederick Rose, *Memoir*.

48. Nock, p.7.

49. Rose Family Papers.

50. Memorandum (21 November 1845) on p.2 of Articles of Partnership (8 February 1844).

51. Nock, p.6.

52. Petition sent to parliament, 4 August 1845.

53. Frederick Rose's recollection, Rose Family Papers.

54. Baxter Papers, Doncaster.

55. Frederick Rose, *Memoir*.

Lawyers and Politicians

ON THE EVENING of 2 May 1849, Benjamin Disraeli addressed the seventh anniversary meeting of the Brompton Hospital for Consumption and Diseases of the Chest, at the Albion Tavern, Aldersgate Street. In his speech, he praised the achievements of Philip Rose:

> Well, gentlemen, I say it is a very great encouragement that we should contrast the meeting in the Hanover Square Rooms with the results which have since occurred. I envy those who were present on that day. I envy the feeling of the gentleman who was Secretary at the Hanover Square Rooms, who read that day the number of letters from eminent individuals who could not attend. I envy him when I remember what he must feel at this moment when, in the eighth year, he reads the Report which he has communicated to us tonight. I confess to you that I share in his feelings in no ordinary degree. I recollect with pride that that gentleman is one of my constituents. I recollect with interest that I have known him from his boyhood; and that in his boyhood I observed that high principle and great energy which have made his subsequent career eminently prosperous. And I am pleased – I am more than pleased – I am deeply gratified that, in the chapter of circumstances that is called life, it is my lot to-day thus legitimately to bear my recognition to the private excellence and the public services, to the virtues and the talents of Philip Rose.[1]

Disraeli was not only paying tribute to Rose's work for the Brompton Hospital: the two men were friends as well. This association was the most prestigious of Philip Rose's public career, and brought great kudos to the firm, as well as much subsidiary business.

Philip Rose's public career had begun in the 1840s after his move to London and his marriage. The private excellence and public service which Disraeli praised in his old friend were qualities that sustained Philip Rose throughout a busy legal career and enabled him to pursue an active philanthropic role in Victorian London. He was the founder of the Brompton Hospital, instituted on 25 May 1841. The year before, a clerk in the firm had developed pulmonary tuberculosis; the disease was still at an early stage when treatment would have been successful, but he lacked the money to pay for it. Philip Rose attempted to have the clerk admitted to several London hospitals, but discovered to his dismay that cases of pulmonary tuberculosis were simply not accepted anywhere.[2] At that time Rose was not an influential man, although he had some contact with the medical world through his father and father-in-law. However, he decided to set up a hospital to fill this need. In his introduction to the Public Appeal in March 1841, he wrote:

> There is scarcely a disease of any severity which does not find ready admission into the wards of our general hospitals, and many complaints of comparatively rare occurrence and trifling importance have institutions especially devoted to their treatment. But consumption, the most frequent and fatal disease in existence, which, according to a high authority, destroys one third of our entire population, finds the doors of all our hospitals closed against it.

One of the hospital's founders, Mr S.C. Hall, remembers the first meeting of the founding committee at Philip Rose's house, 41 Hans Place, on 8 March 1841:

> ... there met at the house of Mr Philip Rose, five gentlemen, of whom it is my happiness to have been one. Mr Rose was a Solicitor, young in the profession and in life [Rose was twenty-five], he had little

power except that which was given him by a sagacious mind, large
intelligence, thorough integrity, and a nature purely philanthropic. He
had a Clerk who suffered under premonitory symptoms of
consumption … Mr Rose had resolved to procure the admission of his
Clerk into one of the Hospitals; but he was met at the threshold of
every one with a refusal of entrance … Scarcely a week passed before
Mr Rose had taken a house in Smith Street, Chelsea, appointed a
Matron, obtained the aid of willing Doctors, and ultimately the co-
operation of an influential committee, Mr Rose becoming the
Honorary Secretary and working day and night with an astonishing
amount of vigour which he exhibits today as he did long ago.[3]

Philip Rose knew that the hospitals would be reluctant to change their
policy regarding consumptive patients. He asked the committee
chairman, Nadir Baxter (who was no relation to Robert Baxter of the
firm), 'whether it would not be by far the more difficult task for a few
humble individuals to attempt to alter the very constitution of these
long-established institutions than to establish an independent one
having the benevolent and humane object of receiving for its inmates
those patients only who are expressly excluded from all others'.[4]

In the library at Philip Rose's house in Penn, there was a book,
now lost, containing the original letters, minutes of meetings and drafts
of resolutions relating to the establishment of the Brompton Hospital.
Frederick Rose recalls:

When I look through this book and see from it how discouraging
were the replies received from the persons whose aid and sympathy he
solicited in the first instance, I confess I am astounded at the pluck and
determination of my Father, who would not take "No" for an answer
but battled on until he had succeeded in his task.[5]

The Brompton Hospital project was a rehearsal for the skills and
processes that Philip Rose was to use in his professional life:

connections, information, publicity and the good opinion of those who had power to help him. It resembled piloting a Railway Bill through Parliament. In launching a public campaign, Philip Rose was doing for philanthropy what he would later do for his clients. He was one of the quickest among the legal profession to realise the power of public sympathy and shared information.

His charitable work with the hospital in the 1840s showed him stretching the image of the attorney into a public facilitator as well as a legal expert. The important point for the firm – and also for the history of the profession – was that Philip Rose's public career led him to move in wealthy and influential circles. When the Queen granted her royal patronage in 1842,[6] the future of the hospital was assured, and the social enterprise of a professional man rewarded.

Philip Rose's legal career showed that he was never frightened to change the institutions or bodies he encountered. Having founded the Brompton Hospital, he promptly expanded it by incorporating one of its rivals, the West London Dispensary for Diseases of the Chest;[7] the amalgamation brought support, enthusiasm and weight of numbers to the cause. Soon after the amalgamation, the first public meeting was convened, with a management committee of nineteen and a board of consultant physicians from University College and from King's College hospitals.[8]

In March 1842 an out-patient branch of the Brompton Hospital opened at 20 Great Marlborough Street; patients from the area bounded by Marylebone Road (north), Piccadilly (south), Dean Street (east) and Duke Street (west) could have home visits if they were too ill to travel. Over the next five years the hospital would treat 273 in-patients and 4,893 out-patients.[9]

In June 1842 the Committee of Management advertised for a house in Knightsbridge, Chelsea or Paddington; it found a suitable property in Brompton at the Manor House (near the Royal Hospital, Chelsea), took a ten-year lease and opened for the reception of twenty

The Manor House, Chelsea in 1841.

in-patients on 13 September 1842. A north wing was started on 11 June 1844, the foundation stone being laid by the Prince Consort; the west side was finished in 1846 and the east side in 1854, when the hospital acquired the freehold.

That year, when the Board Room had been completed, the Committee of Management raised a subscription for a portrait of Philip Rose, but he objected and insisted that the money should be used to benefit the patients directly.[10] The hospital's fund-raising events had included a concert by the coloratura soprano Jenny Lind (31 July 1848, Her Majesty's Theatre),[11] and a musical festival in the gardens of Chelsea College (17 and 18 June 1851).

Although philanthropic in origin and impulse, the foundation of the hospital turned out to be an astute commercial move by Philip Rose. The bankers handling the receipt of endowments read like a *Who's Who* of banking in the 1840s: Coutts & Co.; Drummond & Co.; Glyn, Halifax, Mills & Co.; and Williams, Deacon & Co. Rose's philanthropic efforts had positioned him in the City, in society and in

The Brompton Hospital in 1844.

professional life, giving him a high public profile. This in turn led to new business for the firm while it has continued to act for the Brompton Hospital since 1841.[12] Philip Rose had taken the image and function of the lawyer and applied them to create an institution which benefited both the patients and the firm itself.

But nothing increased the public standing of Philip Rose and the firm more than his association with Benjamin Disraeli.[13] It was a measure of Disraeli's regard for Philip Rose that he instigated his baronetcy, and made him one of his executors. Disraeli described this man who became his adviser as 'a dear friend'.[14] One biographer of Disraeli writes that Rose, who acted privately for him from the 1840s, 'was the most discreet of lawyers as well as Disraeli's confidant over decades of delicate service'.[15] Philip Rose drafted Disraeli's last will in 1878, and was one of two trusted executors, sifting and cataloguing private correspondence, attending to financial and literary beneficiaries, and shaping how Disraeli was to be seen by generations of admirers and historians.

Disraeli's relationship with the firm, through Philip Rose, is important for three reasons. First, in terms of the firm's history, it enhanced Philip Rose's profile and standing within the profession; second, in terms of the profession's history, it is an interesting example of the long association of lawyer and influential client – both private and political – in the nineteenth century; and third, it provides records which, coupled with the private records of the firm and the Rose family, create a unique picture of lawyer and client throughout four decades. They developed a trust and friendship beyond professional courtesy.

The two men had known each other since boyhood as Dr William Rose was the Disraeli family's physician. In 1846, Disraeli turned over his affairs to Rose, who was to remain his loyal and confidential man of business for life.[16] They became neighbours in 1847, when Philip Rose bought Rayners and its farms at Penn, Buckinghamshire, and when Disraeli bought Hughenden Manor, the house that was to be his home for the rest of his life. In 1847 Disraeli was overwhelmingly in debt, owing an amount approaching £20,000. Hughenden Manor, a mile north of High Wycombe in Buckingham-shire, had been on the market since the death of its former owner, John Norris, in 1845; the price was £35,000, including an estimate for timber on the estate.

Disraeli sought the advice of his London deputy and financial adviser, Richard Wright and Philip Rose. With their help, he signed a contract for Hughenden on 5 June 1847. He did not actually take title until April the following year, and was in danger of over-extending himself: even before he gained possession, he ordered trout from the river for his father, Isaac D'Israeli's limited diet. In his election address in Aylesbury in August 1847, Disraeli was careful to distance himself from Hughenden:

> Return me to parliament not because I am a relative of the Duke
> of Devonshire, not because my broad lands stretch from Buckingham
> to Aylesbury, but because my public character has shown you that I
> may be trusted, and what is more, that I am capable.[17]

After electoral success came the settlement. Disraeli's electoral expenses were £1,345 16s 4d, and outreached his capacity to pay. Philip Rose arranged a loan by mortgaging one of Disraeli's life insurance policies. Throughout the 1840s and 1850s, he managed the legal side of Disraeli's personal and financial affairs, and was sometimes even more closely involved than this. In 1847 Disraeli had asked Philip Rose to lend him £25,000 to complete the purchase of Hughenden, with Disraeli putting up the balance of £10,000 for the purchase price.

On 5 September 1848, according to a schedule of documents at the Buckinghamshire County Records Office, Rose and Disraeli signed a memorandum of agreement to complete a £25,000 mortgage and a bond to secure the repayment of £25,000 (probably based on Disraeli's expectation of £25,000 from the Bentinck family).[18] On 6 September, the date of closing, Disraeli was due to enter into two indentures: one with the vendors (probably the conveyance) and another with Rose (probably the mortgage). The mortgage was later transferred to Richard Durant and Enosh [sic] Durant Cumming, and then in 1858 to Montagu Warren Peacocke [sic].[19]

Looking after Disraeli's financial affairs was no mean feat, because the politician was forced to maintain a public image consistent with new responsibilities in Parliament. It was, writes one of Disraeli's biographers, 'a task to try even the ingenuity of Philip Rose.'[20] It is interesting to note that the relationship between client and solicitor also included investment advice and brokerage. In September 1849, Disraeli was still planning with Philip Rose, using the solicitor as a financial adviser:

My Dear Rose,

I see the "Economist" says, that tho' money is plentiful & cheap in the mercantile world, there is reason to believe, that mortgages will, for a long time, command 4½ pr Ct., & then it explains the apparent inconsistency of the two results.

I beg to remind you, of what I already mentioned to you, that under our marriage settlement, we have a large sum to lay out on real security, £30,000 of this still remains unappropriated, & if you know any client, who wants that amount at 4½ pr Ct. I shall be very glad to accommodate him.[21]

Earlier that year, when Disraeli became acknowledged as the leader of his party in the Commons, he received a letter from a long-term creditor, Robert Messer, to whom Disraeli had owed money for twenty-five years. In this and subsequent letters, Messer pointed out that Disraeli's position was now materially altered, and said simply that he wanted his debt paid, hinting darkly that he was anxious 'to avoid legal expenses'. Disraeli had begun speculating with Messer, the son of a rich stockbroker, in 1824; they had focused on investments in South America.[22] The speculation left Disraeli owing Messer money, although the surviving accounts are poor and show little of the amounts involved.[23]

Twenty-five years on, Messer's claim was for £1,100; Philip Rose negotiated it down to £500 to be repaid, with interest, over the next seven years. Robert Blake comments: 'Disraeli's finances continued long after this to be erratic, incoherent and uncertain, but this is the last we hear of the early imprudences which cost him so much difficulty for nearly a quarter of a century.'[24] This improvement was due in part to the roles played by Philip Rose, initially as his adviser who counselled, for instance, settlement with Messer; and finally as his executor, preparing Disraeli's life and papers for public scrutiny.

In 1851, Philip Rose's ingenuity was tested by a letter to Disraeli from a woman who lived in Devon. Her name was Mrs Sarah Brydges Willyams and her money was subsequently to provide Disraeli with much-needed security. She wrote from her home at Mount Braddon, Torquay, to ask Disraeli to meet her at the Great Exhibition by the Crystal Palace fountain.

Mrs Brydges Willyams was a childless widow, a Spanish Jew, already well over eighty. A contemporary, Charlotte de Rothschild recalled: 'the female Croesus ... has piercing black eyes, wears a jet black wig, with an enormous top knot, no crinoline, is quite a miser, starves herself into a skeleton, ... keeps neither horses nor carriages, nor men servants – only an enormous watch-dog to protect her and her gold.'[25] Mrs Brydges Willyams wanted Disraeli to be her executor. Disraeli sent her a copy of his novel, *Tancred* – 'a vindication, and I hope, a complete one, of the race from which we alike spring' – and called for Philip Rose.

Philip Rose recalled Mrs Brydges Willyams' approach in a memorandum[26] found among the Hughenden Papers. It shows the trust that existed between Disraeli and his lawyer:

> In the year 1851, Mr Disraeli brought me a letter he had just received, which required an immediate answer; – I remember his words – "I have received an important letter, and I come to you, as my best friend, to ask your advice." He then shewed me a letter written in a large bold hand, without the usual commencement or ending

This letter read:

> ... I have to ask, as a great favor [sic], that you will oblige me by being one of my Executors ... I think it right to add that whoever are my Executors, will also be my residuary legatees; and that the interest they will take under my will, altho' not a considerable one, will, at all events, be substantial.

Philip Rose continues:

> We consulted over this letter, and I gave my advice, which was in
> accord with Mr Disraeli's own instinct, that he ought not to be hasty,
> or eager, in accepting the proposal; and beyond a simple acknowledge-
> ment of the receipt of the letter, and stating that the subject required
> consideration, he allowed a month or six weeks to elapse before giving
> any definitive answer ...[27]

The history of Disraeli and Mrs Brydges Willyams was strange yet
uncomplicated. For some years previously, she had written regularly to
Disraeli after one of his political speeches, or upon the publication of a
new work, expressing her profound admiration for his writings, and
her sympathy with his noble vindication of the race of Israel. 'But,'
mused Philip Rose, 'like most public men, accustomed to receive this
sort of homage, especially from ladies, Mr Disraeli had taken no notice
of her letters; and had only ascertained by a casual enquiry of a
Devonshire friend, that a gentlewoman of that name resided at the
address from which the letters were dated.' The more Disraeli
discovered, the more intrigued he became with Mrs Brydges Willyams.
Philip Rose remarks:

> It subsequently transpired that Mrs Brydges Willyams was one
> Miss Mendez da Costa of the race of Israel, tho' a professor of the
> Christian Faith ... She was a lady of advanced age, of moderate
> fortune, inherited from her own family, but of great intelligence, and
> considerable intellectual powers, and had an enthusiastic pride in the
> race from which she sprung ...[28]

Disraeli visited Torquay frequently. He wrote over 250 letters to Mrs
Brydges Willyams. This correspondence, Philip Rose pointed out, 'so far
as it has been hitherto collected, is indeed worthy of being preserved, as
a brilliant specimen of social and political gossip written in the freedom
of private friendship – such as has been rarely equalled'.[29]

In November 1863, Mrs Brydges Willyams died at the age of 102 and was buried at Hughenden. As her executor and therefore residuary legatee, Disraeli inherited £40,000. Philip Rose's judgement in 1851 proved sound. Disraeli was back in the black, although he shared the news with as few people as possible. Philip Rose was a model of understatement, saying that the residue of the estate 'somewhat exceeded £30,000', but he was quick to suggest the use of public relations techniques:

> I wish you would consider whether some paragraph might not be advantageously put in the newspapers alluding to the bequest and the grounds for it. These things are catching and the great probability is that the example would be followed if properly made known.[30]

Until the Brydges Willyams' inheritance, Disraeli's finances had looked unhealthy; he complained to Lord Stanley on 4 November 1863, 'Of course, life is conspiracy and extortion.' But that year another piece of luck left Disraeli much better off than he had dared hope. This was the sudden and unexpected entry into the Tory cause of Andrew Montagu, a rich Yorkshire bachelor who offered to help the Conservative Party. Again Philip Rose was at the centre of the action. He acted as intermediary and put Montagu in touch with the Parisian banker, Baron Lionel de Rothschild (who was to lend Disraeli's government £4m at 13 per cent to buy Suez Canal shares in 1875).

The banker invited Montagu to discharge all of Disraeli's debts in return for a 3 per cent mortgage on Hughenden; Montagu agreed. Disraeli's debts, which had reached £60,000 in capital and accrued interest, and which were costing him £6,000 a year in interest, were rescheduled at £1,800 a year to Montagu. This sum Disraeli could pay from his annual pension of £2,000 after his second term at the Exchequer. The difference this made to Disraeli's troubled finances was enormous. With good personal judgement but poor political judgement, Philip Rose even prevailed upon Disraeli to recommend a peerage for Montagu, citing the example of William Pitt's banker; but Montagu declined.[31]

Disraeli always stressed the value of patronage, so prevalent in the Conservative Party. As his first private secretary, Ralph Earle, wrote in 1858: 'These questions of patronage are of the greatest importance and under present circumstances it seems to be only by attention to party claims that the Conservatives can be kept together.'[32] In 1875 Disraeli was called on by Robert Lytton, son of Bulwer Lytton the playwright, novelist, and old friend of Disraeli. Robert Lytton (also known as the poet 'Owen Meredith') was a career diplomat then stationed in Lisbon. He pointed out that India needed a new Viceroy and Disraeli obliged, at the same time putting forward Philip Rose's son, Harcourt, then serving on Lord Napier's staff in India, as a special aide to Lytton. Unfortunately, Lytton arrived in Calcutta to discover that Captain Rose had been 'invalided' home to England. The new Viceroy reported to the Prince of Wales:

> Invalided ... in consequence of an extraordinary accident: the bite of a donkey had reduced him to a condition that would be a very appropriate qualification for employment in any Oriental Court. ... The story is a strange one and I am quite unable to understand how the donkey could have perpetrated such an assault on the Captain.[33]

Philip Rose was careful to protect Disraeli's image from any opprobrium dating from his youthful friendship with a debauched Wykehamist called James Clay. Disraeli and William George Meredith,[34] who was then engaged to Disraeli's sister, Sarah, had set out on a tour of the Near East in May 1831.[35] They met Clay in Malta in August. He had chartered a fifty-ton yacht, *The Susan*, and had acquired a former servant of Lord Byron, a man called Tita Falcieri.[36] Clay was forthright and unembarrassed about his private life, to such a degree that his letters to Disraeli cataloguing his sexual exploits are still unprintable. Philip Rose later wrote on the matter in August 1882:

[James Clay] ... a thoroughly bad, unprincipled man. D.'s family had a horror of him, and dreaded his influence over D. – he was at Brasenose [College, Oxford] with Meredith and was, I think, a contemporary of Ralph D. at Winchester with whom he was intimate ... I fear there are many early letters of D. to Clay still extant in the possession of his son ... which it would be desirable to get hold of, if possible.[37]

Disraeli had remained in touch with Clay, who became a Liberal

Cartoon of Disraeli and Rowton.

MP; the two corresponded over the 1867 Reform Bill and Disraeli often visited Clay's house during the latter's last illness in 1873. Meredith had died from smallpox at Thebes on 19 July 1832.[38] Years later at the Carlton Club, in April 1881 soon after Disraeli's death, Philip Rose met the Reverend Edward Higgins, of Bosbury House, Ledbury, an acquaintance and friend from that time who wanted to write about 'Lord Beaconsfield's [Disraeli's] early life'. This was the first of many enquiries to be fended off by Philip Rose and Lord Rowton, the legal custodian of Disraeli's papers. Philip Rose recalls:

... As I was aware of the former intimacy between the Meredith and Disraeli families; and of the connexion that would have tied them still more closely together but for Mr Meredith's untimely death, I anticipated that any papers he might have left, so far as they referred to Lord Beaconsfield and his family, would require to be treated with great judgement and delicacy.[39]

The death of William George Meredith was still vivid for Philip Rose, nearly fifty years later:

It was with deep and painful interest, that I made a hurried examination of these papers, as I had a vivid recollection of the overwhelming grief, and consternation, in which the family at Bradenham were plunged when the news arrived that he, upon whom so many hopes depended, was lost to them.[40]

Philip Rose's private work for Disraeli brought Baxter, Rose & Norton into political life. Through Philip Rose's friendship with Disraeli, the firm became the agents of the Conservative Party. Baxter and Norton were less involved with the party political side of the firm's work. The former concentrated mostly on new railway business in parliament and the latter on the internal running of the firm. In effect, Philip Rose was the chief political adviser, and the man with the greatest expertise in that area in the firm.

The private work that he carried out for Disraeli was distinct from the work carried out by the firm for the party. The firm was engaged mostly in the handling of elections and the conduct of ballots across the country. It was lucrative business and the firm had one partner, Markham Spofforth, who worked full time on the account.

The relationship of a law firm to a political party differed from what might now be the case. Both institutions have changed radically since the 1850s; and the structure of political life was itself undergoing enormous change. While Peel and Disraeli dominated the Conservative Party during much of Victoria's reign, the party failed to dominate Parliament. Between 1830 and 1865 the Conservatives had a parliamentary majority for fewer than five years (under Peel, 1841–6), and for two and a half years were in office but without effective power (under Peel 1834–5; under Derby 1852 and 1858–9). Disraeli reorganised the party system, using the firm to help him. The result was that the Conservative party had an effective parliamentary majority for seventeen years between 1874 and 1900 (under Disraeli, 1874–80; under Salisbury, 1886–92 and 1895–1900).

Between the Reform Bills of 1832 and 1867, the Conservative Party organised itself through a kind of 'club government' from the Carlton Club, of which Philip Rose became a member in 1856:

> ... for a whole generation the club was the centre of such political organisation as the party possessed ... It is there that the county magnates meet and arrange candidatures with little regard to the embryonic and central organs of the party.[41]

But the party needed a more organised structure, one which would respond to the rigours and demands of a series of local campaigns fought by a national party. With the firm's advice, Disraeli began what the Carlton Club's historian, Barry Phelps, calls 'the first steps towards the creation of Conservative Central Office in 1867'.[42]

The elections of 1847 and 1852 had been bad for the Conservatives. But the later 1850s looked better for them. In part, this was because the party's Chief Whip, Sir William Jolliffe, was more able as a manager than his predecessor, William Beresford, and was more likely to listen to Disraeli. But Disraeli also revived the office of party agent, last occupied by Peel's appointee, Francis Robert Bonham. During the 1830s and 1840s, the party had in practice been run by Bonham, the key figure in extra parliamentary organisation and the Election Committee. While the whips were key figures and the Carlton Club was important, Disraeli saw room for a party agent who would act on a national level in the same way that local solicitors had acted in the provinces under Peel's leadership.

In 1853 Disraeli chose a new party agent, Philip Rose, who was already well acquainted with the party business. The two men agreed on the title of Principal Agent, to distinguish Rose from the general run of Conservative agents in the local constituencies. The party offices were with the firm's, first at 3 Park Street and then (after 1857) at 6 Victoria Street, Westminster. The necessity to have an office close to Westminster led the firm finally to close its premises at 50 Mark Lane in 1850.

This business was by no means new to Baxter, Rose & Norton, since the firm had maintained for some time a large practice in the legal expenses of parliamentary elections and the trial of election petitions in London, employing from time to time as many as 200 clerks. This was staple political legal work in the nineteenth century where there was much business in proving elegibility to vote, handling uncontested seats, and overseeing the ballot. 'This was a highly lucrative form of business,' Lord Blake writes in his history of the Conservative Party. 'It was worth while doing the purely agency work for the party in return for the fees to be gained from electoral litigation.'[43]

The railway business had taught the firm how to handle large volumes of work at high speed in consort with public bodies. The firm set up a central party organisation to advise constituencies on candidates, and it reinstituted the structure of local agents which had crumbled after the departure of Peel's agent, Bonham who filled the role of 'Principal Agent.'[44] It also advised on the drafting of some legislation: the firm was involved in a committee of the Cabinet convened in November 1858 by Disraeli to draft a Reform Bill for the next session.

However, while relations between Philip Rose and Disraeli were open and trusting, relations between the firm and the party soon became less cordial. Rose resigned as Principal Agent in 1859 over revelations about his part in compromising electoral petitions.[45] That year he was made instead County Court Treasurer for Buckinghamshire, a reward[46] for services to the party which still left him sufficient time to continue in practice. The party work had bored and irritated Philip Rose, as Frederick Rose recorded:

> Every Tom, Dick and Harry who had something to say about the organization of the party in any County or Borough came to the head Agent [the firm], and my father found that a great deal of his valuable time had to be devoted to seeing a lot of people, in whom he took no interest, but who never spared his time when they called to see him, and frequently hours of his time would be wasted in seeing people whose information was of no possible value ... My Father disliked being at the beck and call of all these local politicians.[47]

The job of Principal Agent fell to Markham Spofforth, who became a partner of Baxter, Rose & Norton in 1860 but who had been working independently on the Conservative account since 1853. He was paid £300 a year, and worked from the firm's office in Victoria Street. He joined the Carlton Club in 1865, bringing him closer to the informal side of the party.

Throughout the 1860s, Spofforth was responsible for the general electoral work and for the party agency work which the firm carried out for the Conservative Party. For these services the firm received £500 a year, small beer in comparison to the fees for railway work, but a useful entrée into the lucrative business of election petitions and a way to new business of a more general kind. Furthermore, party agency was the pathway to the profitable election work. But Spofforth produced fewer new clients to compensate for the meagre fees involved in party agency.

Spofforth attracted public criticism, and in fact was under investigation for gerrymandering when the 1868 election shook up the Conservative Party and it decided to structure itself without an external agent. He compromised himself first by selecting a candidate 'of the commercial spirit' for an election at Totnes, Devon, and then by advising the local agents at Beverley in 1868–9 to cover their tracks by destroying papers and 'bustling the chief briber out of the country'.[48]

The ensuing Parliamentary enquiries[49] cast some confusion over Spofforth's title: 'I do not consider myself the agent of the Conservative Party,' he said in 1866; when asked if he had been an agent in 1853, he replied that it was then when he was 'first consulted by the persons who came about seats and that sort of thing'. Although he suffered from these investigations and despite lacking Philip Rose's verve and tact, Spofforth made a good party agent, whatever his title. Disraeli wrote of him to the Lord Chancellor on 13 January 1875:

> Mr Spofforth served us for years, and years of adversity – if not always with perfect judgment, with great talent, honour and devotion. He was not well used by us but never murmured.[50]

When Spofforth resigned in 1869, he was rewarded for his long service with the post of Taxing Master in Chancery at a salary of £1,500 a year, the Victorian equivalent of being put on the boards of a few nationalised industries and quangos. Spofforth had been assisted by Robert Baxter's son, Dudley (1827–75). He graduated in 1849 from Trinity College, Cambridge, where he had read Classics and Mathematics. He had been in practice with Baxter & Sons in Doncaster. Although he was brought into the firm to help Spofforth's political clients, his most telling contributions to the firm's widening and deepening expertise were his works on taxation and government debt.[51] He also was to became a statistician, demographer, psephologist and electoral consultant, acting as a special adviser to Lord Derby and Disraeli over franchise reform and drafting the 1867 Reform Bill, which was redrafted by the Home Office draftsman.[52]

Dudley Baxter also brought an invaluable insight to the firm with his recognition of the power of the Press. Like his father and Philip Rose, he enjoyed a wide public life outside the firm which added to his activities as a lawyer. He had started writing to the local press in

Doncaster when he was 16. Between 1860 and 1874 he wrote thirteen works on statistics, railways, electoral reform and economics.[53]

Dudley Baxter also loosed a quiverful of letters to the editor of *The Times*. The correspondence columns from April 1866 to November 1873 testify to his unremitting activity on behalf of his technical views on electoral reform and also on behalf of the firm's political clients whose views he represented in an influential medium.

Intense public debate preceded the Derby government's 1867 Reform Bill to extend the franchise, and Dudley Baxter was at the heart of the fray, representing both himself and the Conservative view. He could be sharp, witty and forthright; he wrote on 18 June 1866 (*The Times*):

> Sir, – Facts are good. Admitted facts are better. But official facts are best of all, combining in the highest degree the elements of substantial truth and confessed accuracy with the *argumentum ad homines*, and slaying the government with their own sword. A Return has just been printed by the House of Commons, bearing the well-known signature of the Electoral Department of the Poor Law Board, showing the distance, in a direct line, of each town in the groups of the Redistribution Bill from each other town of the same group. If a Return had been invented for the purpose of demonstrating the folly of the Government groupings, it could not have been more effective.

He concludes, with a sarcastic note about the bribery engrained in the British electoral system:

> One signal merit of the Scotch and Welsh groups is still untouched. They are said to be free from bribery. The candidates for the Ayr burghs would not find it worth their while to bribe at Campbeltown, so far away from Ayr; or at Ayr, so far from Irvine; or at Irvine, so far from Inverary; or at Inverary, so far from Oban; because nobody can tell how the poll is going on at the other places. But the whole force of this argument depends on the greatness of the

distances and the impassability of the roads. It is an argument for grouping the most distant boroughs and the most inaccessible places – Lymington with Evesham, instead of Andover; Maldon with Totnes, instead of Harwich. Every railway diminishes its applicability. The telegraph is its perdition. Grouped boroughs are only fit for the civilization of Henry VIII or the Scotch Union; and the *beau idéal* of the Government must be a string of Highland fishing villages before the advent of General Wade.[54]

Your obedient servant

D.B.

Elsewhere Dudley Baxter's style is parliamentary in outlook but popular in impact. He writes in *The Times* of 30 June about the Prime Minister: 'I trust also that Mr Gladstone, whose generous feeling towards a political opponent I gratefully acknowledge, will himself welcome any well-founded corrections of information which has been furnished to him.' His readings at the Statistical Society, where he was a Fellow, also made the news, in particular his suggestion for using the railways as a sinking fund for the National Debt.[55]

It was part of the culture of the firm at that time to search for new financial instruments and seek out new ways of handling debt, profit and investment. The firm that was to create Foreign & Colonial, the first Investment Trust in England, and to form the Association of Foreign Bondholders, was clearly immediately in the forefront of financial enterprise and also *au fait* with the political and lobbying expertise needed to implement a bright idea. The firm's railway and political clients gave full scope to these imaginative and entrepreneurial instincts.

After the 1867 Reform Act, Dudley Baxter turned his attention to the subjects of poor relief, domestic economy and diets, writing frequently and at length on those topics. He posed a question in 1868 which provoked a leader in *The Times*. It was: 'What is the national income?' *The Times'* leader for 23 January 1868, reads as follows:

Mr Dudley Baxter has invited the Statistical Society to a calculation, the importance of which must be obvious, on many accounts, to those who think at all on the matter. What is the National Income? Everybody ought to know his own income, and the nation, which is the aggregate of us all, ought to be equally well-informed. Everything is becoming more and more a question of money …. In Mr Dudley Baxter's estimates we recognise only the well-intentioned outlines for a more careful handling of this question than has yet been attempted. We doubt whether the answer can ever be given with the simplicity here aimed at.

The following year, Dudley Baxter turned his thoughts to railway competition, referring in a letter of 12 January 1869 to the railway his own firm had created: 'The Great Eastern and Northern Junction was one of the greatest competition fights ever known. The Committee sat twenty-two days. The successful applicant, the Great Northern Railway, would laugh in the face of any one who suggested that competition was not their ground of opposition and the animating principle of the whole contest.' The successive months found him writing on taxation, the School Board, political economy, new forms of electoral reform, and on the 'State Purchase of Railways', which he stiffly opposed.

Dudley Baxter died in 1875, predeceasing his father, and was buried in Doncaster. Everywhere, he had brought his clients' concerns to a larger public. He felt able to write to *The Times* to put forward his clients' views even when his clients were not involved in specific litigation. He realised, with his father and Philip Rose, that a lawyer could legitimately pursue a client's interests even – or perhaps especially – when there was no litigation in progress. The firm had acquired a range of expertise in political and commercial consulting as well as in strictly legal matters. The confidence the firm gained allowed it to take on more ambitious projects in the City in the 1870s and 1880s.

The firm's connection with the Conservative Party had been severed in 1868 as Disraeli moved towards a new party structure. He had written to Lord Derby on 14 August 1863:

> The Carlton & Conservative Clubs are filled to overflowing and hundreds of candidates are waiting for their turn for a ballot, wh. will not in most cases come on for years.
>
> They are also necessarily so exclusive that the working corpus of our party can never be admitted. The Carlton will rarely admit a professional candidate and the Conservative a small percentage only.
>
> Our strength is great in country attorneys and agents who want a political and social focus in London. As Henry Drummond used to say, "of all powers in the 19th century the power of attorney is the greatest."
>
> They want to form a new political club to be called the Junior Conservative or something of the sort, but to effect the purpose aimed at, it must be started under powerful and unmistakeable auspices. Taylor [Col. T.E. Taylor, Junior Whip 1855–9, Chief Whip 1859–68] says it will organise, strengthen & encourage the party greatly & has written to me very strongly on the matter, with an unreasonable desire that I should communicate with you anent [sic]. What he wishes is that five trustees of the new Club should be yr Lordship, Ld Malmesbury, Ld Colville, Colonel Taylor and myself.
>
> I believe the affair has been long maturing, is needed & will be useful – but of course I await your wishes & opinion, on wh: all must depend.[56]

Disraeli had party reform in mind, and turned to a barrister called John Gorst in 1869 to reorganise the party structure. Spofforth was elbowed out by the election committee that was set up in June 1868, and at the end of 1869 he finally resigned because the new arrangements for the trial of election petitions had eroded the profitability as well as the power of the agency.[57] The firm was no longer charged with electoral work, and Philip Rose was consoled with a baronetcy as soon as Disraeli returned to office.[58]

In the 1860s and 1870s there was still private work to be done for Disraeli. In November 1871, Philip Rose wrote to *The Times* on behalf of his client, defending Disraeli from inaccuracies in articles from the *Newspaper Press* and the *Leisure Hour* about his early life:

> Sir – A narrative having been inserted into the recent publication of the *Newspaper Press* by Mr. James Grant, affecting to furnish a history of Mr. Disraeli's connexion with the periodical Press, the names of the journals he edited, describing even the furniture of the offices he inhabited, and speculating on the amount of salary he received, we are authorized to state that this narrative is entirely fictitious.
>
> Mr. Disraeli has never at any time edited any newspaper, review, magazine, or other periodical publication, and rarely contributed to any, nor has he at any time received or required any remuneration for anything he has ever written, except for those works which bear his name.

Philip Rose then inserts with his letter the stiff warning he had sent to the editor of the *Leisure Hour* in October, detailing the inaccuracies in a printed autobiography which touched on Disraeli:

> Sir – The attention of Mr. Disraeli has been called to an article headed "Mr. Disraeli at Twenty-five," which has been extensively copied into the London and country newspapers, and purports to be an extract from the Autobiography of Mr. John Timbs, which appeared in the October number of the *Leisure Hour* ... [Rose makes a series of four specific refutations of fact.]
>
> At the very period, 1830, when the autobiographer describes himself as often seeing Mr. Disraeli in Messrs. Marsh and Miller's shop [an Oxford Street publisher], Mr. Disraeli was in Greece, and did not return from his travels, as I personally well remember, until just previous to the General Election of 1832, when he returned to his

father's residence, in Buckinghamshire, to stand for the borough of High Wycombe.

I am to request that you will insert this authoritative contradiction in the earliest unprinted number of the *Leisure Hour*, and I am sure that you will regret that statements so utterly erroneous should have first appeared in a publication of such high character. I remain, Sir, your obedient servant,

Philip Rose

Philip Rose therefore had much to do to preserve Disraeli's reputation and guard him against gossip which could damage his political standing. But if Philip Rose was careful with Disraeli's past during his lifetime, he was to be even more jealous of it after his death.

One such example dated back to 1836 and was known as the Sykes affair. Philip Rose's handling of this in later years was loyal and exemplary. It was Disraeli's first public scandal. Philip Rose wrote in 1882: 'I can well remember the scandal in the country at this connection and especially at the visit of Lady Sykes to Bradenham accompanied by Lord L[yndhurst] and the indignation aroused in the neighbourhood at D. having introduced his reputed mistress and her paramour to his *Home* and made them the associates of his Sister as well as his father and mother.'[59]

The Memorandum, of June 1882, sees Philip Rose tidying up his friend's personal affairs, drawing a veil of decency over the past. It is headed, 'Very private and confidential. For Lord Rowton's eye alone – and then to be destroyed'.[60]

The Sykes and Bolton[61] Correspondence

The letters in this dossier relate to the intimacy that existed, from 1833 to 1836, between D. and the writer, Lady Sykes [formerly Clara Bolton], wife of Sir Francis Sykes Bart, which materially affected D.'s health, and nearly shipwrecked his career; – few other men could have had the necessary force of Will to escape from such an entanglement. –

There are a mass of letters undated, which it is not worth while to attempt to put in order, but sufft. are dated to shew the nature and progress of the connexion up to its final dénouement, and the disgraceful exposure of the Lady. …

It is unnecessary to enquire, but I think there is some internal evidence in the letters that the nature of the intimacy between D. and "the writer" was also known and acquiesced in by Sir F. Sykes.

When Sir Robert Peel formed his Govt. I have heard that it was currently reported that the notoriety of D.'s connection with Lady S. and of Lord Lyndhurst's alleged participation in it, operated to prevent the offer of office to D.[62]

The link between the two men developed and deepened in the 1870s. Disraeli had trusted Philip Rose with drawing up his will. It had been drafted on eleven sheets of paper, the last of which was signed 'Beaconsfield' and dated 16 December 1878, the day Philip Rose asked him to come to the firm's offices in Victoria Street to sign the document. Under the will, Disraeli's nephew, Coningsby Ralph Disraeli, had the use of Hughenden Manor during his lifetime; his secretary, Lord Rowton (formerly Montagu Lowry-Corry), received the letters, papers and manuscripts with authorisation to deploy as he wished.

Disraeli died on Easter Day, 17 April 1881. Philip Rose wrote to his son Frederick from 19 Curzon Street, Disraeli's London house:

It is all over, and the great man is gone – He passed away without suffering, calmly as if in sleep at 4.30 [a.m.] in the presence of Lord Rowton, Lord Barrington [,] myself and the physicians. We kissed his fine noble forehead and are now devoting ourselves to the necessary duties. I never saw anything more sad and impressive than his peaceful and tranquil expression and his appearance is one of the greatest dignity and repose.

I have written to Sir Nathaniel de Rothschild to be here between 9 and 10 and I think you had better come up to open the package in the

N/IV/C/5

19, Curzon Street. W.

Easter Tuesday my W81

Dearest Fred.

It is all over. and the great man is gone. — He passed away without suffering Calmly as if in sleep at 4. 30 in the presence of how Newton Lord Barrington myself and the Physicians We kissed his fine noble forehead and are now devoting ourselves to

the necessary duties I never saw anything more fixed and impressive than his peaceful and beautiful appearance and his appearance is one of the greatest dignity and repose.

I have written to Sir Nathaniel de Rothschild to be here between 9 & — 10 and I think you had better come up to open the housebags

in the Envelope. you gave her and which is in my Box here. Which you had better ask for when you arrive. before I introduce you to Sir J Nathaniel. — unless have Lord Newton present Who who not an Executor will be a useful adviser

This will make a great gap in my life

thoughts for many years have been Connected with him & his affairs & in his endeavours and to his comforts

Ever by loving Father

[signature]

[initials]

envelope you gave me and which is in my case here, which you had better ask for when you arrive, before I introduce you to Sir Nathaniel. – I shall have Lord Rowton present who tho' not an Executor will be a useful adviser.

This will make a great gap in my life – for a great portion of my thoughts for many years have been connected with him and his affairs and in the endeavour to add to his comforts.[63]

Benjamin Disraeli.

Disraeli died of bronchitis which had worsened into bronchial spasms and a coma punctuated by fits of restlessness. His secretary, Lord Rowton, had sent for Philip Rose and Lord Barrington; at about 4.15 a.m., Disraeli half lifted himself from the pillows and leaned forward 'with the same gesture which he had used on countless occasions in the past when he rose to reply in debate. His lips moved but no sound came to the intently listening group around his bed.'[64] He knew he was dying. He had confided to Philip Rose in March, 'Dear friend, I shall never survive this attack. I feel it is quite impossible.'[65] Then two days later, 'I feel I am dying. Whatever the doctors may tell you, I do not believe I shall ever get well.'[66]

After Disraeli's death, Philip Rose was concerned with the funeral arrangements. The service was to be simple, and Disraeli was to be buried in the vault of the churchyard at Hughenden with his late wife,

LEFT: *Rose's letter from Disraeli's deathbed.*

Mary Anne, whose funeral Philip Rose had attended in December 1868. Disraeli's funeral, on Tuesday 26 April 1881 at Hughenden was the simple occasion he had requested. The Queen sent a wreath of 'Osborne Primroses' which lay on the coffin as it was wheeled down the hill from the manor to the church; behind it walked Philip Rose, Lord Barrington, Lord Rowton and Sir Nathaniel de Rothschild.

The task of organising Disraeli's papers began immediately, and Philip Rose worked closely with Lord Rowton. The boxes of papers arrived at Rayners from Hughenden and Curzon Street throughout the remainder of 1881 and into the summer of 1882. Philip Rose lived long enough to see that his friend and mentor's reputation was preserved. He catalogued all of Disraeli's papers, writing memos to Rowton on the content and import of each, advising preservation or destruction of the material. He read each letter carefully with a view to propriety and posterity. 'It needs a perusal of the family letters to realise the full meaning and value of some of these miscellaneous letters,' he wrote, 'and it would therefore be better for Lord Rowton to read the family letters first in order.'[67] In December, Rose received Disraeli's mutilated private diary which ran from 1 September 1833 to 12 November 1837, accompanied by a collection of observations made by the statesman's father, Isaac D'Israeli, on men and things: Godwin, Wordsworth, Shelley, Byron, Babbage, translations and the French revolution.[68]

Rowton wrote to Philip Rose on Wednesday 7 June 1882, on the eve of a fishing trip to Norway. It is worth citing this letter in full because it encapsulates the relationship of two men who had worked together in confidence over a lifetime:

> ... Meanwhile, my dear Rose, you have made to me, with characteristic generosity, an offer wh: I can not decline, however reluctant I may feel to add one ounce to your burden in life. Of all living men, YOU, ALONE, can, with anything approaching to due intelligence put together the earlier materials which our dear old friend

has left behind him. And it is with real gratitude that I embrace your offer to look through the earlier letters, wh: he put together, last winter. I send, with this, a box containing, so far as I know, nearly all the intimate correspondence of Mr Disraeli when a young man. Tis not large, but it contains a mass, wh: it will be heavy labor [sic] to digest, tho', I believe, the work to you will prove as much one of interest, as of love.

I hope to be back in mid-July, when, I daresay, you will have found it in your power to look through a part.

I trust that you and I will then be able to take counsel as to the possibility and propriety of making something public, ere long.

I need not add that such an idea is, for the time, quite "entre nous".

Pray let Sir Nathaniel [Rothschild] know of this letter, if you see him soon – I am sure he will be glad to know how you and I are working to this end. And I, in these latter days, have been able to do a little to advance it.

It would give me much pleasure, some day soon, to hear that you are safely home – and that, in asking this favour of you, I am not presuming too much on the kindness of one on whose friendly aid I have often encroached, already, too largely ...

Is it not AMAZING to see how, in each and every point, our Chief's policy and principles are being vindicated!!

We shall yet live to hear men say that the crowning glory of his life was the acquisition of Cyprus!

Ever yours, my dear Rose

Rowton[69]

This was the first of a series of letters between Rowton and Philip Rose throughout the second half of 1882. But Rose's reply on 13 June from his home in Cromwell Road, South Kensington, best conveys his mood at the time:

... I received the box, No. 15, and will gladly undertake the duty you have confided to me; and, by the time of your return, I hope to have the contents arranged in such order, that you may see, at a glance, what has to be done, and what use ought to made of the materials.

... I can hardly conceive of anything more interesting than what may be hereafter worked out of these materials. Many letters might be advantageously published without a word of comment, but there will be a great deal to do when you return if you can give me access to the large wooden boxes of the elder Disraeli, and to one or two other boxes in which are letters of about the same period, and are of a kindred character.

... And now, dear Monty, let me wish you a very pleasant holiday and good sport, resulting in improved health. I am not WELL, and suppose I shall never again be what I once was. It is only when I get to serious business that I realize how frail I am, but this work interests and amuses me, that you must not suppose you are adding to my burdens – on the contrary, you are rather increasing my pleasures.[70]

Notes

1. Rose's copy of the transcript of this speech is marked: 'Honorary Secretary, afterwards Sir Philip Rose bart. and one of Lord Beaconsfield's Executors.' Hughenden Papers, Bodleian Library.

2. 'It will be found that under the fifth section of the standing orders of St George's Hospital, under the heading of Patients: No person shall be admitted as an in-patient who shall be labouring under any contagious disease or WHOSE CASE SHALL BE CONSUMPTIVE.' (M. Davidson and F.G. Rouvray, *The Brompton Hospital*, 1954, p.1.)

3. S.C. Hall, *Retrospect of a Long Life 1815–1883*.

4. M. Davidson and F.G. Rouvray, *The Brompton Hospital*, 1954, p.7; see also P.J. Bishop, B.D.B. Lucas and B.G.B Lucas: *The Seven Ages of The Brompton, A Saga of a Hospital*, 1991.

5. Rose Family Papers.

6. Sir Henry Wheatley wrote to Rose from St James' Palace on 31 May 1842: 'I beg to acknowledge the receipt of your letter of the 28th Inst., accompanied with the papers relating to "The Hospital for Consumption", which I have not failed to submit to The Queen, and Her Majesty, desirous of affording relief to the poorer Classes of Her Subjects afflicted with that destructive Complaint, will be graciously pleased to grant Her Patronage to The Institution; and The Queen will be further pleased to give an Annual Donation of £10 towards its support.'

7. 83 Wells Street, Oxford Street; the patron was the Duke of Argyll and the President, Lord Worsley, MP.

8. The visiting and consulting physicians were: John Forbes, Robert Liston, Hamilton Roe, Theophilius Thompson and C.J.B. Williams.

9. Fifth Annual Report, 29 May 1846.

10. The 1990 Annual Report to the Governors: 'On the occasion of the completion of the new Board room at the Hospital some of the Members of the Committee of Management thought that a fit opportunity presented itself of testifying their esteem towards their Honorary Secretary [Rose], and their appreciation of his zealous and successful exertions on behalf of the Institution by placing upon its walls a portrait of the Benefactor who had so large a share in its origin and progress, and who may justly be regarded as its Founder. A Subscription for this purpose was rapidly filled up, but its original design was abandoned at the earnest request of Sir Philip (then Mr) Rose. It was then determined to devote the subscriptions to the formation of a fund to be called the "Rose Fund", and to apply them, with such other contributions as might be obtained, in providing relief for the Patients, by gifts of clothes and small pecuniary assistance on their leaving the Hospital.

    The Fund thus raised now amounts to £2,413.6s. 2d. Consols (Report of 1900) the dividends of which sum, together with the annual subscriptions to this particular Charity, constitute the income applicable to the above benevolent objects.

    Its administration is entrusted to the Committee of management of the Hospital, and forms part of their ordinary business at their weekly meetings; when the amount of relief to be supplied, as well as the objects to be relieved during the succeeding week are determined.'

11. Rose wrote to Disraeli on 22 July asking him to use his influence with *The Times* to place an article about the event on 31 July. A short, factual article appeared in *The Times* on 31 July, but not, as Rose had hoped, written by Disraeli.

12. See: *Consumption Hospital Brompton*: *Register of Interests Under Wills &c* (2 Vols), Norton Rose Archives, for benefactions, donations and legacies to the hospital.

13. The Rose–Disraeli letters are in the Hughenden Papers, Bodleian Library, Oxford. The Toronto University Press edition of Disraeli's letters reached Volume V (1848–51, in the UK on 11 March 1994, ed. M.G. Wiebe, J.B. Conacher, John Matthews and Mary S. Millar, 591pp). This is the readiest access to the letters detailing the relationship between Rose and Disraeli.

14. Weintraub, p.654.

15. Ibid, p.431.

16. Letters IV 28 April 1846.

17. Ibid, p.273.

18. See: Blake, pp.251–4.

19. Disraeli's Letters (no. 1702 and nos. 1602, 1713, 1727, 1731, 1738, 1741 and 1742) in Toronto edition of Disraeli's letters.

20. Weintraub, p.290.

21. Hughenden Papers, Bodleian Library.

22. See: Blake pp.24–5, pp.268–9.

23. Hughenden Papers, Bodleian Library.

24. Blake, p.269.

25. Weintraub, p.307.

26. Hughenden Papers, Bodleian Library.

27. Hughenden Papers, Bodleian Library.

28. Ibid.

29. Ibid.

30. Hughenden Papers, 16 November 1863, Bodleian Library. And see: Blake, p.424.

31. There is evidence to suggest that Montagu wished to protect his illegitimate heir.

32. Hughenden Papers, 26 October 1858, Bodleian Library. And see: Blake, p.387.

33. Weintraub, p.550.

34. Hughenden papers. 'Rayners, October 1881 Memorandum [includes Rose's account of Disraeli's tour with Meredith and the letter announcing Meredith's death to Disraeli's father and sister]: These letters should be given to the world, if only to prove how false and groundless was the impression, in the minds of some, that D. was devoid of any depth of feeling.'

35. See: Disraeli's *Home Letters* (ed. R. Disraeli).

36. Hughenden Papers, June 1881 Memorandum, Bodleian Library. Tita Falcieri has an interesting after history. Rose writes an elegant and fascinating note.

37. Hughenden Papers, August 1882 Memorandum, Bodleian Library.

38. See: Blake, pp.63–70.

39. Hughenden Papers, Bodleian Library.

40. Ibid.

41. R. Blake, *The Conservative Party From Peel to Thatcher*, 1985, pp.137, 140.

42. Barry Phelps, *Power and the Party, A History of the Carlton Club 1832–1982*, London, 1983.

43. *The Conservative Party from Peel to Thatcher*, p.141.

44. See: H.J. Hanham, *Elections and Party Management, Politics in the Time of Disraeli and Gladstone*, p.357.

45. *Hansard*, CLV, pp.1276–96.

46. Disraeli had doubts: 'Any appointment which has the appearance even of preferring private interest and feelings to the efficiency of the public service must be avoided,' he wrote on 27 December 1858. Blake, p.390.

47. Rose Family Papers.

48. *House of Commons Report 1867* (XXIX, xii) and *House of Commons Report 1870* (XXIX, 9). And see: Hanham, p.277.

49. H.C. (1867). XXXIX, p.979.

50. Cairns Papers, in: Feuchtwanger: *Disraeli, Democracy and the Conservative Party*, pp.106–7. And see: Blake, p.142.

51. Dudley Baxter became a partner of Baxter, Rose & Norton in 1865, together with his brother, Francis Eldon Baxter; both men owed their partnership to their father.

52. See: Blake, pp.462–3.

53. The Volunteer Movement, its Progress and Wants, 1860; The Budget and the Income Tax, 1860; the Franchise Returns and the Boroughs, 1866; The Redistribution of Seats in the Counties (1866); Railway Extension and Results, 1866; The National Income, 1868; Results of The General Election of 1868, 1869; Taxation of The United Kingdom, 1869; History of the English Parties and Conservatism, 1870; National Debts of the Various States of the World, 1871; Political Progress of the Working Classes, 1871; Recent Progress of National Debts, (1874); Local Government and Taxation, 1874.

54. Wade's military roads effectively opened the Highlands in the eighteenth century.

55. The Times, 30 November 1866. Dudley Baxter's long letter looks at the effect of wars on national debt and at the merits of provisions made through Annual Surpluses, Terminable Annuities and a Sinking fund Invested in the National Debt itself à la Pitt.

56. Derby Papers (cited in Blake, pp.138–9).

57. See: Hanham, pp.358–68.

58. See: Blake, p.536.

59. Hughenden Papers, Bodleian Library.

60. Rowton was less bourgeois than Rose, and left the correspondence intact. See: Blake, p.449.

61. Clara Bolton, whom Disraeli met in 1832. According to Rose, 'By his family she was looked on as D.'s mistress.' It seems likely that the affair, if any, confined itself to London and was over by 1833.

62. Hughenden Papers, June 1882 Memorandum, Bodleian Library.

63. Hughenden Papers, Bodleian Library.

64. See: Blake: Disraeli, p.749.

65. See: Weintraub, p.655.

66. See: Blake, p.747.

67. Hughenden Papers, July 1882 Memorandum, Bodleian Library.

68. Ibid., Rayners, December 1882 Memorandum, Bodleian Library.

69. Hughenden Papers, Bodleian Library.

70. Ibid.

1844–94

The Firm, the City and the Railways

IF THE EIGHTEENTH century discovered law, then the nineteenth century discovered legislation. The lawyer was at the heart of commerce, finance, politics, industry, and even fiction. The novelist, George Eliot, was expressing a view commonly held in the nineteenth century when she remarked that the law and medicine were serious professions to undertake, since lives and fortunes depended on them.

Over the century, the population of England doubled. The number of people living in London trebled.[1] Working life in London allowed people to be geographically and socially mobile; London was no longer the city loved by Dr Johnson, but the metropolis of Dickens bustling with opportunity, with loss and gain, with a sense of life's upward and downward possibilities. Lawyers figured as legislators in Parliament, reformers in the courts, facilitators in commerce and deal-makers in finance.

The City continued to fascinate the Victorians throughout the period from the first great crash in 1825 to the financial slump of 1875. It represented a world of possibility evolving new techniques and new names such as financier, entrepreneur, dealer, jobber and insurer. What most engaged the Victorians was the behaviour of the market itself. One commentator, John Laing, recalled in 1867:

> For some years past trade has exhibited a gradual transition from
> stagnation to feverish excitement, embracing cycles of about ten years.
> These crises occurred in 1837, 1847, 1857, and in 1866, with pressures
> of varying intensity between. This sequence has continued long enough

for the presentiment that it represents what will be the order for some time to come.[2]

The 1847–8 crisis was caused by circumstances similar to those which had obtained in 1825–6: a mania for Joint Stock Companies. Speculation in the 1840s was directed at railway construction at home and abroad, but the 1847 crash was caused by a combination of the bad harvest and a fall in corn prices (because of French imports), the bankruptcy of the corn houses and the ensuing money panic. The 1857 crash began with merchants trading in America who had borrowed from British banks. On 27 October the Liverpool Borough Bank failed, followed on 17 November by the Wolverhampton and Staffordshire Bank, the Western Bank of Scotland, and the Northumberland and District Bank. Writing about the 1857 crisis, Morier Evans reflected in 1859:

> ... in an age, like the present, of great luxury and ostentation, mere moral warnings will prove weak in their effect, when the desires that necessitate wealth are many, and riches appear accessible without toil. A revision of the law that will cause the miseries of the panic to fall most heavily on the parties who have most deserved to suffer them, can alone prevent a recurrence of those terrible events that constitute, in the record of the last sixty years, such a chequered and unclean page in the history of the progress of modern commerce.[3]

The 1847–8 and 1857–8 market crises directed public thinking towards regulating the financial markets. But for its part, the firm had emerged unscathed from the rough and tumble of the mid-Victorian City. By the 1860s Baxter, Rose & Norton was experienced not only in trust work, but also in the corporate work involved in railway finance and in the processes involved in establishing and running a railway.[4] Philip Rose himself continued his work as Disraeli's solicitor and as a political agent.

Frederick Rose remembers the period:

During the 1850s my father mainly directed his energies to general business, and, having many clients of position whose business was then very considerable in amount, among whom I may mention Mr Disraeli and Lord Bateman [the same private work as for Disraeli], his time was very fully occupied.[5]

The firm had evolved a particular shape and structure because of the railway business which was to the nineteenth century what corporate law is to the twentieth. From 1848 to 1878 the firm maintained twenty-three railway company accounts, including the Great Northern Railway, the Metropolitan District Railway and the Great Eastern Railway.[6]

Instead of the more usual pattern of a practice comprising a coterie of all-rounders, Baxter, Rose & Norton had structured itself along specialised lines, anticipating one of the rules of professional organisation in the twentieth century. Each department was under the direct control of one partner: Philip Rose handled private clients, Baxter oversaw the parliamentary lobbying work, Norton ran the

Great Northern Railway at Peterborough.

Bills of costs, Great Northern Railway.

Bill Department (i.e. the costs department) and Spofforth the political agency. In 1861 Henry Rose, a relation of Sir Philip and a solicitor of ten years' standing, became a partner in the firm.

The number of partners in a firm bore little relation to the number of clerks, the standing of the firm or the amount of business. An estimate of partnership numbers relative to other firms can never be accurate, but in 1850 the firm had three partners, Freshfields three, Frere Cholmeley three, Linklaters & Paines two and Ashurst Morris Crisp two.[7] This shows the ratio of partners to juniors and clerks could be as high as 1:20. In the 1840s the ratio at Baxter, Rose & Norton had indeed been as high as 1:100 during the height of the railway boom. By the 1860s, the number of clerks returned to its more usual seventy. A marriage greeting given in 1866 to Frederick Rose, who had become a partner in 1866, is signed by the firm's partners and clerks, seventy-three in all.

The principle of specialisation continued to shape the firm after the railway mania had subsided. Baxter, Rose & Norton divided itself into the Bill Department (Chief Clerk, Edwin Scanes), the Parliamentary Department (Chief Clerks, William Livesey and W.J. Sleat), Chancery Department (Chief Clerk, Christian Corfield) and Common Law Department (Chief Clerk, Henry L. Buck). The clerks were attached to these departments, or to the partners.[8] One clerk, Samuel Keer, worked alone. Frederick Rose described him at work:

> One man will I refer to because his life was such a curious one, Samuel Keer. A large office like ours possessed of course a vast quantity of papers relating to Clients, and we had large strongrooms down in the basement of No. 6 Victoria Street, lit of course only by gas lights, and to which access was only attainable by a staircase leading from the Accountants' Office.
>
> Down in this dungeon, for it was little better, lived Mr Keer from year's end to year's end, and, if any particular deeds or papers were wanted, Keer was the man who could at once find them. He was nevertheless a most cheery, sociable being, but in Politics an outlandish Socialist. Many a chat have I had with him whilst serving my articles. Sometimes I had very little to do, and used to pay Keer a visit in order to pass the time, and then I got to know what his views on politics were. He died many years ago.[9]

Edmund Harvey was Chief Clerk of the Accounts Department with several clerks reporting to him. Philip Rose was to learn later, at the conclusion of the Tichborne Case, that Harvey had proved to be 'a terrible scoundrel' and prize embezzler.[10] He had been with the firm for some time as Ledger Clerk. He had been injured in childhood and used crutches to walk because of pain from a suppurating hip joint. His predecessor as Chief Clerk of Accounts was a man named Steinson. In the late 1850s, Steinson left the firm after Harvey had discovered irregularities in the books. While these were the result of inefficiency rather than dishonesty, it was clear that Steinson had covered his miscalculations by altering the cash books.

Harvey benefited from Steinson's departure. His annual salary was £400,[11] which he was able to augment to about £1,000 from the secretaryship of the Colne Valley and Halstead Railway (a position given him by Robert Baxter) and the bizarre guardianship of two lunatics (a duty given him by Philip Rose). The true extent of Harvey's frauds was to be revealed in 1872 (see Chapter 5).

At that time, fraud in the City was rife, and notorious fraudsters like Walter Watts (of the Globe Assurance Company), William Robson (of the Great Northern Railway and Crystal Palace Company) and Leopold Redpath (also of the Great Northern Railway and the Peninsula and Oriental Steam Navigation Company) were convicted in show trials in 1850, 1856 and 1857 respectively.[12] These men had perfected techniques of false accounting, writing fake cheques and issuing bogus shares. The will and the means for fraud were part of the City scene in the 1850s.

Philip Rose's private secretary was a man called Edward Pierce, who took notes in shorthand and made fair copies of Rose's correspondence; his work can be seen in the remaining copies of Rose's letters. When Pierce retired from the firm, Markham Spofforth's secretary, R.V. Tomlinson, was promoted to work for Rose, and was reputed to be an accurate and first-rate assistant. When Rose retired from the partnership, he used his influence to arrange for Tomlinson to become Secretary of the Alabama Great Southern Railway Company (a post which Tomlinson held for life).

The next step for the firm to take was not clear in 1860, nor could it have been for any law firm. The Joint Stock Companies Act (1844) and the Limited Liability Act (1855) introduced incorporation by registration and limited liability for shareholders. Limited liability was extended to banking in 1858 and to insurance in 1862. English law was the most permissive in Europe. This typically Victorian legislation sought to foster enterprise and investment in new projects. The 1855 Limited Liability Act and the 1856 Joint Stock Companies Act granted limited liability to groups of seven or more in almost any field, 'with a freedom amounting almost to licence'.[13] These developments were consolidated into the Company Act of 1862.

Banks and insurance companies came under the same umbrella in 1858 and 1862. The 1861 Insolvency Act replaced the 1849 Insolvency Act which had precisely defined bankruptcy and the bankrupt; in essence, it encouraged entrepreneurship by protecting debtors from creditors and made taking chances less risky. Changes in the law, particularly changes which affected commercial and financial enterprise, necessarily created work for the firm. But most important was the 1862 Companies Act, which created in the 1860s a mania for the formation of public companies since it limited the liability of a shareholder to the value of the shares held.

One of the earliest companies formed under the Act, and formed by the firm, was the General Credit and Finance Company Ltd (GCFC), based in Lothbury. The firm wrote the memorandum and articles of association for the company, and drew up the first prospectus. Philip Rose was a board member[14] and persuaded the GCFC to give him a room in which he could work with his other City clients, 'the number of which,' his son, Frederick, later wrote, 'increased in consequence of his renown as a city Lawyer versed in the company Law, and a Financier of admitted authority'.[15]

The GCFC was chaired by Rose's old railway associate, Samuel Laing. He was later to become a close colleague of Rose through the Foreign & Colonial Trust. Also on the board were: William Patrick Andrew of the Sind, Punjab and Delhi Railways; Samuel Beale, the attorney and chairman of the Midland Railway; Edward Blount of Blount & Co.,[16] bankers; Thomas Brassey, the railway construction engineer who had worked with Baxter and Rose on the Great Northern Railway; Charles P. Devaux of Devaux & Co.; Sir Stuart Alexander Donaldson, the former Colonial Secretary of New South Wales; Rose's friend, the entrepreneur, James Thompson Mackenzie (listed in the Prospectus as 'Deputy Chairman of the Eastern Bengal Railway'); John Moore, MP; Mr Alderman Salomons, MP; Samuel Leo Schuster; Charles Turner, MP; and George Worms. The bankers were the London and Westminster Bank and the Union Bank of London (who were also the bankers to the London, Brighton and South Coast Railway).

The Prospectus appeared in May 1863 as a direct result of the Companies Act limiting the liability of shareholders to the amount subscribed. The rationale for the company was, for its time, far-sighted and innovative:

> The foundation of institutions on the Continent, which combine large Capital and Credit for financial and industrial enterprise has now become an established fact, and in many cases their success has been remarkable. Such institutions may be abused, and become mere instruments of speculation; but when prudently conducted and directed towards legitimate business it cannot be denied that they meet one of the real wants of the age.
>
> England has hitherto not participated in this movement, and the consequence is, that Paris has, to a considerable extent, superseded London as the centre of financial enterprise.
>
> London, nevertheless affords by far the best sphere for a well-managed undertaking of this description. It is the greatest money-market of the world; the point to which all foreign nations resort to raise capital: the place where large contracts can be made and loans negotiated. There is clearly no other money market where concentrated Capital and Credit ought to command a more secure or larger profit.[17]

The GCFC London had a counterpart in Paris, 'La Société Générale pour favoriser le développement de l'Industrie et du Commerce de la

France'. The Paris company subscribed for 20,000 of the 125,000 shares on offer. The company's purpose and object were outlined in the Prospectus:

> The business will be to negotiate Loans and Concessions: assist industrial enterprises, Public works and Railway undertakings; negotiate Foreign, Indian and Colonial Bonds; conduct Mercantile transactions; and establish agencies for large commission business; in a word, to undertake all such operations as an intelligent and experienced Capitalist might effect on his own with a Capital of millions, with the exception of such purely speculative transactions as are prohibited by the memorandum of Association.[18]

The directors took no salary until shareholders' profits reached 5 per cent, after which the directors could take 10 per cent of the year's profits; the directors reserved the right to 20 per cent of any future share issues, while the other 80 per cent of shares (less a guaranteed 20,000-share purchase by the Paris company) was to be divided *pro rata* amongst the existing shareholders. In essence and practice, this was an early investment trust, although it was not conceived as such.

Philip Rose took on more corporate finance work and less private client work in the 1860s, transferring his private clients to Norton although, as his son, Frederick, wrote in 1900, 'He never wholly deserted them and used to deal with matters of principle, whilst leaving Mr Norton to handle the detail.'[19] Rose looked overseas for the first time in the 1860s. He became particularly adept at arranging foreign loans for Belgian, French and Australian companies;[20] 1864 found Rose in St Petersburg with Sir Henry Wolff on financial business; and he visited Paris in the following year to do business with Lewis 'Moses' Merton over the conversion of Turkish Government loans. The subsequent Turkish Bond issue in 1865 came to be known on the London Stock Exchange as the 'fly paper' bonds because of the brown paper they were printed on.

In connection with the Turkish loans, Rose visited Constantinople twice, once at the height of the cholera epidemic of 1866, during which his daily meetings with Fuad Pasha apprised him of the terrible extent of the epidemic – this must have influenced Rose in his insistence on clean water on his estate at Rayners, even though by the 1860s the worst of England's cholera epidemics was over. On the second of Rose's visits to Constantinople, in the 1870s, he was decorated with the Order of the Megidie by the Sultan for services rendered to the Turkish Empire.

The City environment was becoming more sophisticated and stable since the crisis of 1866–7 when the Bank of England suspended the production of banknotes and raised the base lending rate to 10 per cent after the bill-broking house of Overend Gurney & Co. Ltd had to close its doors on 11 May 1866. The lawyer, Sir Thomas Paine of Linklaters & Paines, remembered it in his journal as:

> the heaviest financial and commercial crisis, whether considering its immense extent, or the number of the sufferers, which has fallen in my time, though the South Sea Bubble in the preceding century was probably, having regard to the much smaller amount of the then available capital of the country, more widespread and lasting in its effects. For some time previous speculation had been rampant in almost all directions, but especially in those of a financial character. And the immediate effect was to bring down the greatest discounting house in the City and probably in the world.[21]

The mid-Victorian City was becoming more regulated as a result of the growing sophistication about the form and function of financial markets. On 11 November 1868, the firm founded the Association of Foreign Bondholders (so called in the first Prospectus, but later changed to the Corporation of Foreign Bondholders) to protect the interests of those who held foreign bonds in general, and the foreign bonds floated by the firm in particular. The Corporation remained clients of the firm until 1897 when it evolved into a city discount house.

The firm's work for the Corporation of Foreign Bondholders was assisted by the arrival of a new partner in 1872, Henry Turton Norton, the elder son of Henry Elland Norton.[22] There were now two generations of Roses, Baxters and Nortons in the practice. Henry Turton Norton was to exert a great influence over the shape and direction of the firm in the 1890s, especially in the development of its City reputation and in the balance of its business. He had been educated at Marlborough College and then at St John's College, Cambridge, where he excelled at mathematics. From Cambridge, after changing to law and gaining his MA, he came to London to join the firm. Henry Turton Norton represented a new type of solicitor: educated at public school and university, unlike the senior partners in the firm at the time. The emphasis of the firm's work was also beginning to change, as new City business grew from the firm's railway work.

By 1872, the Corporation of Foreign Bondholders had grown in size, scope and influence. It was run by a Council of members. The Council report for 1872 states:

> the Council, since its formation, has sedulously fulfilled the functions of protecting the rights and interests of the Holders of Foreign Bonds, by establishing rules and regulations calculated to effect that purpose; it has advocated the cause of its clients when the occasion required it with Governments and with the Stock Exchanges of Europe, in the public press and in the Legislatures, and it has co-operated with and appointed nine Special committees of Bond-holders.[23]

The Corporation was based at 115 Palmerston Buildings, EC, and provided offices, secretaries, clerks, accountants, bankers, legal advisers, councillors, agents and correspondents abroad. It was an extraordinary example of an institution born of need which itself incorporated many of the techniques of the firm's successful railway business: public pressure in the press, lobbying in parliament and the organisation of interest groups into new configurations. Lord Clarendon pronounced it a sound and wise institution, and Earl Granville urged the utility of the Corporation's Council in matters of foreign policy to the Foreign Office.[24]

The Council's members included George Bentinck, MP (with whose family Rose had handled Disraeli's finances for Hughenden in 1848), the stockbroker, Philip Cazenove and the MPs, George Goschen and R.W. Crawford. They had realised the scope for foreign investment and also accepted that investment information was neither a matter for government nor for the individual, but for an intermediate institution which provided offices and, above all, market information and analysis.

The Corporation expanded in 1872 to 1,000 members. They joined 'by taking one Bond of £100 each', after which they could 'derive the benefit and revenue that may be realised'. The members were also entitled to use the offices for meeting, discussion and common action and to have use of an archive of periodicals, parliamentary returns, financial and governmental documents, prospectuses, bonds and particulars of loans and records of the principal exchanges. Letters of introduction were provided for members, agents and correspondents of the Corporation abroad.

In the 1860s, Baxter, Rose & Norton developed a practice based on a scope and reach which followed investment round the world. The Corporation of Foreign Bondholders, created by the firm, was an international network of power, money, contacts and information which included a vast archive of 503 volumes of press cuttings and area reports gathered on an unprecedented scale. The Corporation was aware of its own power, describing itself as 'a union ... which constitutes a real force against their antagonists. ... The very association brings with it elements of independent influence, the full value of which is little appreciated.'[25]

The organisation also promulgated a form of information technology, with the Council's 'numerous announcements communicated to the newspapers and telegraphic agencies'[26] home and abroad, and to the Stock Exchange, the Bourses in continental Europe, and the Council's worldwide Agents, '… who are in a position to give official intelligence and advice to Foreign Governments and financial bodies'.[27] The Council also co-ordinated its activities with the new Trust Associations – like the General Credit and Finance Company or the Foreign & Colonial Trusts from the 1860s – on the grounds that 'the occasions which arise for co-operation with the Council and committees give the general body the advantage of the counsel and assistance of the men of standing and ability who are engaged as trustees or otherwise in the conduct of the affairs of these large institutions.'[28]

One of the earliest books on investment trusts, written by Arthur Scratchley (*On Average Investment Trusts*, 1875), stated that the Council of the Corporation of Foreign Bondholders 'numbers among its members financial notabilities of the highest rank',[29] and listed Philip Rose among them. The Corporation's reports covered a wide range of countries. Here is a selection showing the range of the Corporation's Annual Report, 1873:

> Holland: The relations of the Council with the Bourses of Amsterdam and Rotterdam are constant, because Holland for centuries has taken part in financial operation in various countries abroad, and still maintains her high position in this respect. This has created a spirit of enlightenment widely diffused among the community as to all Foreign investments, and which enables her representatives to take an early and leading action wherever intervention is required.
>
> Germany: The growth and prosperity in Germany has enabled its citizens to take a still greater share in American and Foreign Loan transactions, and thus common ties of interest with ourselves are being constantly formed.

Italy: The vexations practised on the Bondholders by the Italian Government have been pressed on the attention of the Council, and the Council have addressed serious remonstrations to the Minister of Finance.

Greece: The deplorable condition of Greek credit remains without remedy.

Egypt: A natural interest and anxiety are entertained with regard to the state of Egyptian finances, to which the Council have directed their attention.

Morocco: It is a matter of great gratification that the succession of the new Sultan, so commonly a danger in Morocco, has been accomplished with little disturbance.

Japan: Many communications have been made to the Council with regard to Japan, of which the financial operations are assuming importance.

Guatemala: The political troubles proved greater than had been expected, and the Government had to contend with a further outbreak of civil war.

Colombia: Considerable difference of opinion has prevailed in the bondholding interest as to the conversion of the old New Granada Debt into Colombian 4½ per cent. Bonds.

Ecuador: The Council are not able to report the removal of the shades of repudiation from the Republic of Ecuador.[30]

The information offered by the Council was shaped for the community of investors, individual and institutional, which grew during the 1860s and 1870s. Arthur Scratchley writes in 1875:

> Trusts offer ... a useful mode of arranging operation in the case
> of the wealthier classes, while to small capitalists they give the means

of making a safe beginning … As they are able to take a leading part in operations, they will be able to encourage the more deserving proposals for obtaining money by public subscription.[31]

The firm's expertise in investment trust work actually dates from its formation of the world's first purpose-designed investment trust on 19 March 1868: the Foreign & Colonial Government Trust. The project was born, like many of the firm's other business, from railways.

One of the prime movers in the foundation of The Foreign & Colonial Trusts was Samuel Laing, a key figure in the Victorian political and financial world. He was a barrister, railway commissioner and private secretary to Henry Labouchere, the President of the Board of Trade (and also a Governor of the Brompton Hospital) in the 1840s. In 1848 Laing had been made chairman of the London, Brighton and South Coast Railway; passenger traffic doubled in the next five years. In the 1850s he became MP for Wick, and in 1859 Secretary to the Treasury, a position he left in October 1860 to be the financial minister in India.

Laing said to Palmerston: 'You want me to go to India to doctor a sick budget with a deficit of six millions; that is a question of military reduction, and the possibility of military reduction depends on peace. Tell me candidly what you think of the prospects of peace, that I may regulate my financial policy accordingly.'

Palmerston replied: 'I do not trust the man at the Tuileries an inch farther than I can see him; but for the next two or three years, which is enough for your purpose, I think we are fairly safe of peace; therefore go in for reduction.'[32]

Laing went to India. On his return he devoted his energies to financial affairs and to the new limited liability companies spawned by the 1862 Companies Act.

Laing had come to the firm through his business partner James Mackenzie. He used to meet Rose in Mackenzie's offices, then in Old

Broad Street. Frederick Rose, who was Laing's successor at the London and Brighton, recalls:

> The personal friendship and business relations which were thus established early in the "sixties" between my Father on the one hand, and his two friends, Mr Mackenzie and Mr Laing on the other, continued until his death.[33]

The other force in the formation of the Foreign & Colonial, and its first chairman, was Lord Westbury, an influential figure in City finance and legislation. He was well known to Philip Rose as plain Mr Richard Bethell from his days at the Bar.[34]

RICHARD, BARON WESTBURY

Lord High Chancellor of England.

He was an eminent Christian,

An energetic and merciful statesman,

And a still more eminent and merciful Judge.

During his three years' tenure of office

He abolished the ancient method of conveying land,

The time-honoured institution of the Insolvents' Court,

And

The Eternity of Punishment.

Towards the close of his earthly career

In the Judicial Committee of the Privy Council

He dismissed Hell with costs,

And took away from orthodox members of the Church of England

Their last hope of everlasting damnation.[35]

Mackenzie may have floated the Trust in order to dispose of large batches of foreign stocks he was holding, and which would have fetched a lower price on the open market. This would be consistent with his behaviour over the London and Brighton railway, where he held large amounts of stock and safeguarded himself by restricting the issue or sale of shares by the directors. Frederick Rose complicates matters by trying for clarity:

> No doubt Mr Mackenzie held a great many of the Securities which were acquired by the Trust, and out of those Securities the Trust afterwards made enormous profits. But to say that Mr Mackenzie could not have sold those Securities without knocking the market down considerably, was an absurdity, in those days when foreign Stocks were greatly appreciated as investments; and although he doubtless made a handsome profit on the Securities he sold to the Trust, at the prices set forth in the Prospectus, he could by judiciously feeding the Markets, have realized quite as good prices if he had desired to part with his holdings in the ordinary manner through brokers.[36]

The idea behind the Trust evolved by Rose, Mackenzie and Laing was simple. In the 1860s, returns on foreign bonds were high – 5 per cent or 6 per cent – relative to their low risk. But defaults occasionally occurred. The private investor, unable to follow the Wall Street adage[37] ('put all your eggs in one basket and then watch that basket') and with little to invest, often lost all of the return and some of the capital when a foreign bond defaulted.

A common practice in the 1860s was to amortise loans by annual drawings; most foreign bonds could be bought at discount and redeemed at par; so the luckier investors who had invested in the bonds of solvent foreign governments were able to make a profit on capital. The Trust, Frederick Rose thought, was intended for small investors and not for those whose capital was sufficient to admit of their forming a Trust for themselves by spreading their capital over a range of investments. He continues:

> I am not able to say whether the original idea of the Trust originated with Mr Mackenzie, Mr Laing, or my Father. It was probably in its embryo stage the invention of a combination of all

three, but the idea seemed so sound and good that very early in the day my Father brought it under the notice of Lord Westbury, who took it up at once, and, in its final stage, as issued to the public, it had, as I am aware, received a good deal of consideration, and, if I may use the expression, "touching up" at the hands of that eminent Lawyer, who, indeed, consented to become Chairman of the Trustees, the other gentlemen selected being Mr George Woodhouse Currie [brother of the Glyn Mills banker, Bertram Currie] Lord Eustace Cecil [MP], Mr G.M.W. Sanford [MP], and my Father himself.[38]

The Trust Deed was drafted by Edward Fry, QC (later a judge and Lord Justice of Appeal) with alterations by Westbury. The seventy-six page Prospectus, promising a clear 7 per cent on investment, was formidably professional and thorough. *The Times* responded to it by stating, 'This scheme in its principle supplies a want that had long been felt,' offering 'to that large number of persons who are always disposed to encounter the risk of foreign investments the means of restricting that risk to its smallest amount.'[39] *The Economist* dissented from the generally warm reception, thinking the Trustees' promises 'far too sanguine to ever be performed':

> The prospectus promises a clear 7 per cent, and if people get as much as that while sitting still and doing nothing, they are very lucky; they need ask for no further benefits. We own to some doubts whether even so much will be *netted* by a miscellaneous dealing in foreign stocks in the present state of the world.[40]

The Trust's first public issue was a success. It was followed by four additional issues, and by a Trust under exactly the same conditions and structure for investment in American and Canadian Railway bonds and shares. The issue was sold through the firm's offices at 6 Victoria Street, where during 1867–8, the firm had accepted Francis Jeune[41] to give him experience of working in a solicitor's office. This again showed the changing status of the lawyer, for Jeune had been to Harrow (with Rose's sons, Frederick and William) and Balliol College, Oxford; his father, the Bishop of Peterborough, was a friend of Baxter, and thus the connection was made. Jeune was a vigorous and dextrous seller of Foreign & Colonial Certificates.

The Trust grew throughout the 1870s, until in the later years of the decade a problem became evident. The initial calculations in the 'Government Trust' were clouded by uncertainty in the foreign markets, with the danger that those certificate holders lucky enough to be paid off in the early years of the Trust stood to gain at the expense of those investors committed to stay in longer. Certificate holders eligible for payment by the annual 'drawings' were certain to receive their £100, but when the term of the Trust expired, the remaining securities would realise only enough to pay the remaining certificate holders at a discount.

The firm decided a Private Member's Bill to alter the deeds of the Trust was in order. Philip Rose was confronted by 'the obstinacy and pig-headedness of that autocratic individual',[42] Lord Redesdale, chairman of the Committees of the House of Lords. Redesdale met Rose and Currie, and killed the Bill. But the Trust faced the possibility of Lottery Law. Its position was resolved in 1879 by the Master of the Rolls, Sir George Jessel, in his dealings with another Trust, the Government and Guaranteed Securities Investment Trust. This, like the Foreign & Colonial Trusts, was not a Company registered as such under the Companies Acts, but a Trust governed by a Trust Deed drawn up by Fry and Westbury.

Jessel decided that the Government and Guaranteed Securities Investment Trust was a trading partnership of more than seven persons, and that it should therefore be registered under the Companies Acts; since it was not so registered, it was illegal and a winding-up order was made. The judgment was reversed in the Court of Appeal, which determined that Trusts were not trading companies, and were no more illegal than any private trust simply because there were seven or more persons entitled to interests under it. This was one of the rare occasions on which Jessel was overruled.

However, in February 1879, Sir George Jessel's judgment on the Government and Guaranteed Securities Trust was in force, and its announcement coincided with Rose's departure for Pau, South West France, to visit his daughter Amy, at that time seriously ill. It was a Wednesday. He attended a London & Brighton midweek board meeting in the morning, and left for Pau in the evening.

The next day a lawyer, Charles Edward Lewis of Lewis, Mums & Longdon, delivered a writ at the firm's Victoria Street office for the winding-up of each and every one of the Foreign & Colonial Trusts on the grounds that they were illegal, and asking for the immediate appointment of a receiver. With the writs, Lewis produced a letter offering a solution to the problem which entailed his appointment as a Trustee.

Lewis obtained a Notice of Motion and the case was due to be heard within a week, on the next Motion day. The Trustees called an emergency meeting, but Currie and Cecil were implacably opposed to Lewis as a fellow Trustee. If the Trustees did nothing, and ignored Lewis' proposal, then the Foreign & Colonial would cease to exist because the Master of the Rolls would have to treat it as a case analogous to the now defunct Government and Guaranteed Securities Trust. Frederick Rose cabled his father in Pau. Rose had technically withdrawn from the partnership in 1872, after the Tichborne case, but he remained active and influential at the firm throughout the 1870s. Reports of his retirement were greatly exaggerated.

Philip Rose returned to London immediately. Frederick met him at Victoria, where Rose said: 'Lewis has been too clever for us, but he really deserves success by his quickness in taking advantage of Jessel's judgment.' Rose had seen this as an opportunity rather than a threat. On his way back from Pau, he had drawn up a reconstruction scheme which consolidated the Trust's five issues into one company. Immediately on reaching the firm's offices he arranged for it to be typeset and sent to the certificate holders. Rose then persuaded Lewis to become a Trustee and drop the writs.

Lewis proved to be an agreeable colleague. Later, as Sir Charles Lewis, he seconded Frederick Rose's appointment as a Trustee on the death of Philip Rose.[43] Frederick Rose summarises:

> But for my Father's influence with his colleagues in the Trust, they would I feel certain, have declined to accept Mr Lewis as a colleague, and if they had not, he would certainly have pressed his actions in a hostile manner, and brought about a liquidation of the various issues of the Trust, to the great loss of the Certificate Holders, whose property would have been thrown upon the Market in such large quantities as to lead to great depreciation.[44]

Philip Rose's actions were typical: prompt, decisive, creative and profitable. He had been involved in a similar corporate crisis while acting for the London and Brighton railway in the 1860s. It started with Rose's friend, the financier, James Thompson Mackenzie, who was working in Old Broad Street and with whom Rose had founded the GCFC. In 1867 Mackenzie had bought a large quantity of 5 per cent Preference Stock in the railway on the understanding that the Directors did not issue more of the same stock for an agreed period. Mackenzie hoped to sell the stock, gradually, to investors. He found that the market price of the stock was falling; this surprised him, especially since the reputation of the London and Brighton was such that its stock in the 1860s was known as 'Brighton Consols'.

As the price continued to drop throughout 1867 and 1868, Mackenzie was left holding stock worth considerably less than he had paid for it. Other sellers of Brighton Preference Stock were feeding the market. At first Mackenzie blamed the Directors, but subsequently discovered the seller to be the Union Bank of London, the railway's own bankers, who were selling off stock pledged as security for an overdraft of £600,000. The bank had become wary of the railway's financial position, and was trying to reduce the overdraft. Mackenzie went to Rose.

The firm discovered that although the Directors of the Brighton company appeared to be in charge, they were opposed by a body of dissenting shareholders. Philip Rose immediately wrote to them,[45] and at the same time obtained a full list of the shareholders. On that list was the great barrister Richard Bethell, Lord Westbury, who had substantial holdings in the company.[46] In an aggressive and purposeful bid, Rose co-ordinated the dissent behind Westbury, and forced the Board of Directors to resign, using the report of a Committee of Investigation (chaired by Westbury) to show how, as Frederick Rose put it, 'the finance of the Company was utterly rotten and the dividends fictitious'.[47]

The rectified accounts show that interest on unproductive capital had been charged to capital and not revenue, and that no dividend had been earned on the ordinary stock. Rose was charged with finding a new Board of Directors. His son recalls:

> … Lord Westbury took little, if any, part in the business after the completion of the labours of the Committee of Investigation, and beyond intimating that he wished his Son-in-Law, Captain Cardew, to be one of the new Directors, his position as Chairman of the Committee of Investigation giving him the undoubted right to make this stipulation, he practically delegated to my Father the duty of choosing the other Members of the Board.[48]

Rose balanced the claims of the victorious dissidents as they vied for a seat on the reconstituted board, but he had also to handle the curious matter of the Surrey and Sussex Junction Railway, then under construction by Waring Brothers, the railway contractors. The Surrey and Sussex was an independent company financed by the London and

Brighton; money had been committed by the old Brighton Board of Directors to a project which was *ultra vires* and therefore outside their province.

This was what the Directors stood charged with; if they lost, they were personally responsible for refunding to the London and Brighton all the money spent on the Surrey and Sussex. Rose was satisfied that the ousted Directors[49] had acted in the best interests of the Brighton company, but was nonetheless obliged by the new Board to press a claim of *ultra vires* against them. A judge in Chancery, Rose felt, would find against the Directors, which would ruin them; so he advised the new Board to go to arbitration. The Duke of Richmond, the arbitrator, decided that the old Directors had behaved honestly and that the Brighton company should assume the liabilities of the Surrey and Sussex.[50] The completion of the Surrey and Sussex was delayed for ten years by the Brighton's parlous financial state, but it eventually emerged as the Croydon, Oxted and East Grinstead Line.

Railways were steady, lucrative business for the firm. The London and Brighton company retained the firm for an initial five years at £5,000 a year. The firm drew up an agreement with the London and Brighton company in July 1869 which consolidated and formalised the relationship they had had since July 1867. It reads:

> ... the said firm of Baxter Rose Norton and Company shall and will for the period of five years [from July 1869] undertake the conduct of the legal business of the Company of any nature whatsoever as and whenever required by them to do so and shall and will also for the same period advise the Directors in any matter in which they may require advice and assistance and shall devote as much of their time and attention as may be necessary efficiently to perform such duties and shall not during the continuance of this agreement undertake any cause or engage in any business of opposition to the Company.[51]

The agreement maps out the firm's responsibilities and commits the Brighton Company to provide an office for the firm at London Bridge. The new chairman of the company was Samuel Laing. The firm continued to represent the Brighton company throughout the 1880s, but the 1887 agreement mentions 'Two Thousand Two Hundred pounds being the same as has been received by the firm during the past five years under the within written Agreement', and from 1888 onwards the fee dropped to £2,000. The railway business remained with the Rose partners in the firm.[52]

The railway gradually grew in prosperity, not least because Laing identified a source of traffic based in what was to become 'the stockbroker belt'. In a sense, Laing invented the commuter. As the *Dictionary of National Biography* put it:

> … [Laing's] confidence was more than shared by a number of London stockbrokers who lived down the line, and knew, or thought they knew, a great deal about it. Hence the enormous amount of speculation that took place for a long period in Brighton Deferred Stock ("Brighton A's"). When speculative operations for the rise turned out well, their authors naturally regarded the management of the line with approval, but when they did not, Laing came in for more than a fair share of abuse.

The unique records which survive for the London, Brighton and South Coast Railway give a vivid picture of the day-to-day work undertaken by the firm since it first acted for the company in 1867. John Brewer, who became a partner of the firm in 1873, is mentioned as the 'Chief Assistant', whose salary 'shall be limited to the sum of Two Thousand Pounds that is to say One Thousand Five Hundred Pounds for the General and Ordinary Parliamentary Business of the company and Five Hundred Pounds to be expressly appropriated to the Conveyancing business and settlement of outstanding landowners' claims in connection with the Surrey and Sussex and other abandoned lines …'

The £5,000 'fixed remuneration' was paid quarterly to the firm, with special provision for inordinate parliamentary business.

The relationship between a law firm and an important railway client makes fascinating reading. Because the railway was a conduit for the flow of Victorian life, because it was both property and system, because it was landlord and tenant, and because it entailed a wide variety of contracts, a railway company and its solicitors saw all of human life pass before, along, through and around it.

The records of over twenty-five years testify to close co-operation between solicitor and client over the workings of a railway. They witness the firm's work in prosecutions, personal loss and injury cases, industrial accident claims, pensions disputes, share transfer and registration disputes, land acquisition and rating disputes, parliamentary business and petitioning, construction and commercial contracts. The appendix to this chapter (see Appendix B p.219) gives the range and scope of the work, from the political lobbying and consultancy involved in steering railway bills through Parliament to individual actions, prosecutions and settlements. The lawyers fulfilled a role akin to a management consultant

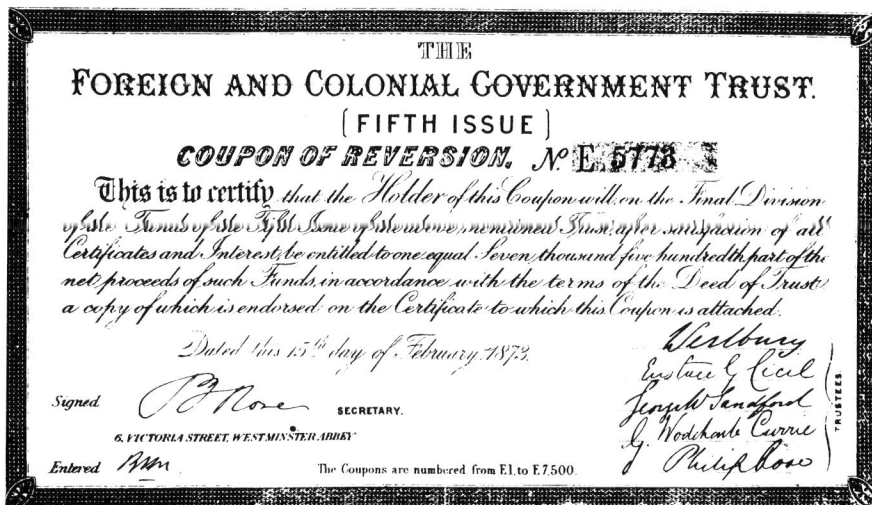

Foreign and Colonial Trust Company certificate.

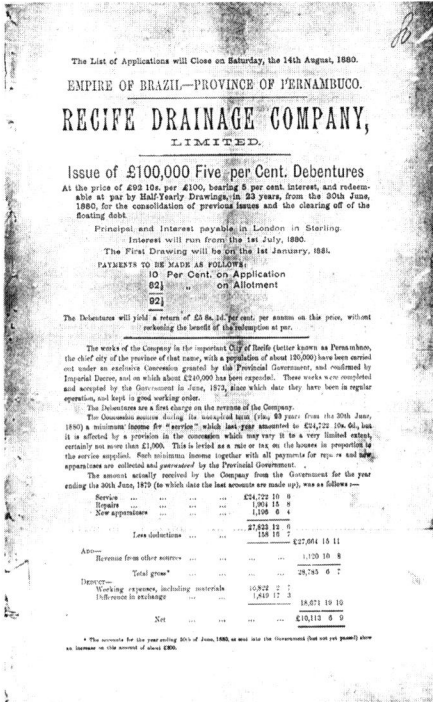

Recife Drainage Company
Debenture issue.

or strategic adviser in the twentieth century.

The variety of the partners' directorships and involvement with related business ventures testifies to the raised status of the lawyer to a figure whose presence was the *sine qua non* of respectable concerns. Philip Rose's directorships included the Alabama Southern Railway Company Ltd, the Anglo-French Fire Insurance Company Ltd, the Eagle Insurance Company, the Tramways Union Company Ltd, the London, Brighton and South Coast Railway Ltd, the Railway Debenture Trust Company Ltd, the Railway Share Trust Company Ltd, the American Investment Trust Company Ltd, and the Foreign & Colonial Government Trust Company Ltd. In 1881 the *Directory of Directors* lists Rose as director of the Recife Drainage Company Ltd, and in 1883 the Mortgage Company of England and the Submarine Continental Railway Company Ltd.[53]

Henry Elland Norton's interests were less expansive; between 1880 and 1894 he was a director of the Law Reversionary Interest Society (established in 1853 'for the purchase of reversionary property and life interests, and for the grant of life annuities, endowments and reversionary payments'. The company achieved limited liability status in April 1882). Then from 1891 to 1894 he was a director of the Weymouth and Portland Railway Company which transported stone from Portland's quarries for London's houses; and in 1892 he was a director of the East India House Estate Company Ltd.[54]

His son, Henry Turton Norton, was a director and vice-chairman of the British Fire Assurance Company Ltd from 1889 to 1894; director of the Glyncorrwyg Colliery Company Ltd from 1885 to 1894 (chairman from 1891), and a director of the Law Debenture Corporation in 1892.[55]

Frederick Rose was a director of the American Investment Trust, Foreign & Colonial Government Trust, the London board of the Life Association of Scotland, and the London,

Lord Westbury.

Brighton & South Coast Railway; he was also chairman of the Hayling Railways Company Ltd.[56]

Sources for solicitors and their clients are rarely comprehensive, and City records earlier than *Burdett's Official Intelligence* (first volume, 1882) or *The Directory of Directors* tend for the most part to omit solicitors in the details of company's directors and officials. However, the firm's expertise in railway business gave rise to a pattern of work in corporate investment finance. Sometimes there was a direct link with railway technology. In 1864, for example, Baxter, Rose, Norton, Spofforth & Rose, as the firm was known then, had acted as lawyers to the Telegraph Construction and Maintenance Company Ltd, which boasted the engineers Thomas Brassey and Daniel Gooch on the board, and Cazenove & Co. as its brokers. The company was formed to make telegraph lines:

The facility of intercourse which telegraphic communication now, in such extensive operation, has afforded to the public in its varied communities – Political, Commercial, and Social – has rendered that which was, but a few years ago, regarded merely as a scientific experiment, absolutely necessary for the purpose of our social system, and a highly remunerative investment.[57]

Railway Debenture Trust Share issue.

The company was particularly interested in the laying down and maintenance of submarine telegraphic cables. The legal structure of the company was complex, since it also involved leasing arrangements for submarine telegraph serving Alexandria, India and Suez. This was a technology derived from railway engineering, which explains the presence of Brassey and Gooch on the board.

The firm also developed business which had evolved from the financial and investment structure of the railways. One example of this was the Railway Debenture Trust Company Ltd (RDTC) which was a client of the firm between 1873 and 1898. Philip Rose was a director, and Samuel Laing, the chairman. The firm drew up the memorandum and articles of association under the Companies Acts of 1862 and 1867, limiting the liability of shareholders to the amount of their shares; this limitation of liability was to prove popular with investors.

The purpose of the RDTC was to take capital raised by issues and debentures and invest it in 'mortgages or obligations of railways and other debentures or bonds, but not more than one tenth of the capital so raised can be invested in any one security'.[58] No more than one fourth of the capital raised was to be invested in undertakings such as gas, docks, waterworks or telegraph – all of which were businesses similar to but distinct from railways.

The company was run from the offices of the GCFC at Lothbury; its bankers were Glyn, Mills, Currie & Co., and its auditors were Price, Holyland & Waterhouse of Gresham Street. The debentures of railways in France, Germany, Austria, Russia, the United States, Canada and 'other countries and colonies' promised a return of 6 per cent with a risk comparable to that on English railway investment. The prospectus reads:

> There are many investors … who would prefer the solid security
> of Railway Debentures to loans of foreign countries subject to political
> vicissitudes, – if such securities could be brought within their reach in
> a convenient form, whilst practically having a security equal to that of
> English Railway Debentures …
>
> The Railway Debenture Trust Company, Limited, will effectually
> meet these wants, *being founded on the principle of seeking safety
> rather than speculatively high interest on its investments.*[59]

Everywhere the safety of the investment was stressed: 'From the experience of the Board of Directors they feel justified in stating their belief that seldom has an institution been founded so free from risk, and yet possessing elements that hold out so good a prospect of a highly remunerative return to the shareholders.' After the railway mania of the 1840s, after the crashes of the late 1850s and late 1860s, and with continuing legislation to protect investors, the risk-free approach was deigned to appeal both to private and institutional investors.

The first of three share issues (150,000 shares, capital £3m with 200 £1 founders' shares) was 50,000 shares of £20 each, only £10 of which was to be called up: £1 payable on application, £3 on allotment and the balance throughout May and June of 1873. In essence, the Trust put within reach of individual investors the benefits and means of investing any amount of capital, small or large, on the security of railway debentures, and added a further security of a guarantee fund furnished by a large share capital of £3.2m.

The same team of lawyers, bankers, accountants and directors founded the related Railway Share Trust Company Ltd in May 1873; in essence, its aim was the same as the Railway Debenture Trust, but it sought to invest in shares or securities (with the same proportional limitation on investment in other gas, water or telegraph shares) instead of debentures. In the first seven months' trading, the Railway Share Trust Company returned net profits of 10¼ per cent on £500,000 of the 'paid-up A Capital' with a dividend of 8 per cent.

Once again, expertise in risk management, investment strategy and trust administration had developed from railway work. Abroad, the firm represented the Buenos Ayres [sic] and Rosario Railway Company Ltd (1890–6), the Argentine Great Western Railway Company (1891); and during the 1890s the Agency, Land and Finance Company of Australia, the Army and Navy Investment Trust and the Bankers' Investment Trust.

One case, however, was to alter the firm in the 1870s and change its structure thereafter. It was the most famous action of the century, and the longest trial heard in an English court. It split the firm, and caused one senior partner to resign and another to leave to set up practice on his own. It fired the imagination of public and Press. It was the Tichborne Case.

Notes

1. See: A. Briggs, *Victorian Cities*; A. St George, *The Descent of Manners*.

2. *Theory of Business*, 1867, p.236.

3. *The History of the Commercial Crisis 1857–58*, 1859, p.12.

4. See: Appendix B.

5. Frederick Rose, *Memoir*.

6. Railway clients of the firm, 1848–78: 1854 East Lincolnshire; 1854 Great Western and Uxbridge; 1854–70 South Wales Mineral; 1854–66 Wycombe; 1855–74 Llynvi Valley; 1855 South Yorkshire; 1856–62, 1869, 1871 Leominster and Kington; 1862–7 East Somerset; 1862–9 Forest of Dean Central; 1862–3 West Somerset; 1863–4 Barnsley Coal; 1863–74 Berks & Hants; 1860–74 Colne Valley and Halstead; 1864–7 Marlborough; 1863–73 Trent, Ancholme and Grimsby; 1863–7 West Riding and Grimsby; 1864–7 Weymouth and Portland; 1866–74 Metropolitan District; 1866–74 Wolverhampton and Walsall; 1867–73 Great Eastern; 1868 London, Brighton and South Coast. (Source: Bradshaw's 1848–78.)

7. Numbers of partners in comparable firms, 1850–1930.

	1850	1870	1890	1910	1930
Norton Rose	3	5	4	5	5
Freshfields	3	4	4	4	5
Frere Cholmeley	3	4	6	6	6
Linklaters & Paines	2	4	4	4	9
Ashurst Morris Crisp	2	4	4	5	5

Source: Law Society.

8. Rose Family Papers.

9. Frederick Rose, *Memoir*.

10. Rose Family Papers.

11. A nurse or cook in 1868 could earn £20–30, a governess £60 – *The Times*, 19 March 1868 (the paper itself cost 3d.). Dudley Baxter described £100 a year as 'the equatorial line in British incomes', the point above which income tax liability was incurred.

12. See: D.M. Evans, *Facts, Failures & Frauds*, 1859; and A. St George, *The Descent of Manners*, 1993.

13. See: P.L. Cottrell, *Industrial Finance 1830–1914* (1980), chapter 3; and L.C.B. Gower, *Gower's Principles of Modern Company Law* (1979), pp.39–49.

14. Share Prospectus, London, May 1863.

15. Rose Family Papers.

16. See: E.C. Blount, *Memoirs* (Ed. S.J. Reid, 1902), chapters III, VI.

17. Share prospectus, London, May 1863.

18. Ibid.

19. Frederick Rose, *Memoir*.

20. Ibid.

21. See: J. Slinn: *Linklaters & Paines*, pp.66–7.

22. Henry Turton Norton, born 21 June 1847. His siblings were Frederick Charles Norton (student of St John's College, Cambridge and barrister, born 25 August 1850), Cecil Bridge Norton (born 11 May, died 30 August 1852), Ellen Charlotte (born 25 July 1848, died 3 April 1865), Elizabeth Clare (born 25 July 1853), Louisa Hall (born 1 December 1854) and Henrietta Evelyn (born 7 July 1856).

23. January 1872. There were over 100 institutional and individual members.

24. Publicity Material for Council.

25. First Annual Report, 1873.

26. Ibid.

27. Ibid.

28. Ibid.

29. See: Scratchley, 1875, p.12.

30. The First Annual Report of the Corporation of Foreign Bondholders, 1873.

31. See: Scratchley, 1875. In the table of investment trust trustees, Philip Rose features in more (four) than any other multiple trustee.

32. See: Samuel Laing, *Dictionary of National Biography*.

33. Mackenzie and Laing later quarrelled over Laing's refusal to nominate one of Mackenzie's sons-in-law to a directorship of the London & Brighton. Frederick Rose, *Memoir*.

34. An account of Westbury's life can be found in *The Birth of Foreign & Colonial: The World's First Investment Trust*, Neil McKendrick.

35. J.B. Atlay, *The Victorian Chancellors, Vol 2*, 1908

36. Frederick Rose, *Memoir*.

37. Andrew Mellon, American financier and philanthropist (1855–1937).

38. Rose Family Papers.

39. *The Times*, 20 March 1868.

40. *The Economist*, 28 March 1868.

41. Later the Rt Hon. Sir Francis Jeune, President of the Admiralty and Divorce Division of the High Court.

42. Frederick Rose, *Memoir*.

43. The preceding information compiled from Rose Family Papers, and Frederick Rose, *Memoir*.

44. Frederick Rose, *Memoir*.

45. Rose communicated 'with some of the leading men among the dissidents': Sir Thomas Freemantle (Lord Cottesloe), Sir Charles Jackson, Jonas Levy and Ralph Ludlow Lopes. Frederick Rose, *Memoir*.

46. Rose and Westbury later – 19 March 1868 – founded Foreign & Colonial Investment Trust; Westbury was its first chairman.

47. Rose Family Papers.

48. Ibid. Frederick Rose.

49. Rose knew some of them personally; among them, Sir Frederick Arthur was a personal friend.

50. Rose Family Papers.

51. Agreement between the firm and the London, Brighton and South Coast Railway Company, 21 July 1869.

52. These were Philip Rose's sons, Frederick and George Alfred Ste Croix; the latter became a partner in 1877.

53. *The Directory of Directors*, 1880–94.

54. Ibid.

55. Ibid.

56. Ibid.

57. Share prospectus, 7 April 1864.

58. *Burdett's*, 1873.

59. Share Prospectus, 28 March 1873.

1854–83

Tichborne and After

AT 1 P.M. ON 28 February 1874, a telegram was written from 'Tichbornc, Queen's Bench, Westminster' to 'John Helsby, Lymington, Hants'.[1] It was sent at 1.08 p.m. It read: 'All is lost.'

The Tichborne Case was closed. After a civil action in the Court of Common Pleas which had lasted 102 days, and a criminal trial in the court of Queen's Bench which lasted a further 188 days – the two together making it the longest case ever tried in England – a verdict was reached.

The case had mesmerised the country, fêted the jurors, and divided the firm of Baxter, Rose, Norton & Co. Filling the English and Australian newspapers, from London to Sydney, over eight years, its two-part drama – a civil action of ejectment and a criminal case for perjury – appealed to all levels of English cultural life. The case of *Tichborne v. Lushington* (i.e. the Claimant v. the Trustees of the Estate) opened on 10 May 1871. It achieved instant fame. *The Times* thought it unique:

> The case will in many respects be the most extraordinary on record. Its length must be unexampled, and the issues it raises are such that the wildest romancer could never have ventured to sketch. Such a medley of probabilities and improbabilities, consistencies and inconsistencies was never yet submitted to be summed up by an oppressed judge and disentangled by an unhappy jury.[2]

The *Illustrated London News* included lithographs of the participants arriving at, sitting in and at parting from the court, and called it 'the

The Trial, May 1871.

extraordinary trial which has been going on in the Court of Common Pleas for the last fortnight', adding, 'The facts of this case are indeed remarkable.'[3] The pressure on space in court was great. One aggrieved barrister, turned away at the door during the first week's hearing, was swift to write to *The Times* on 17 May:

> Sir, In your report of the proceedings in the Court of Common Pleas yesterday, the Lord Chief Justice [Bovill] is represented as having stated that "a complete misapprehension existed" as to the necessity for obtaining orders or passes for admission to the Court, and that upon the sitting of the Court both the Bar and the public would be admitted to such seats as were available.

Permit me to say that upon the first day of the Tichborne Trial (Wednesday last), I heard with astonishment that even members of the Bar would not be admitted without orders. I was incredulous and accordingly went to the Chief Justice's clerk, whom I found in his room at Westminster Hall. I asked him if it was true that barristers were not to be admitted without orders. He replied that such were the directions of the Chief Justice. I then said, "I suppose I may give up all hope of hearing any of the case if I do not procure an order of admission?" He replied, "You may."

I enclose my card and beg to subscribe myself, your obedient servant,

A. Barrister.

The case touched legal and popular sentiment, but it also engaged Victorian intellectuals. George Eliot sat in the public gallery – 'an experience of great interest to me', she wrote in her journal. The poet, Robert Browning, who loved knotty legal cases (*The Ring and The Book*, for example), was teased by the great Victorian sage, Thomas Carlyle: 'I bet he'll do the Tichborne case bye and bye, and call it *Gammon and Spinach*.' Browning was a great friend of Sir John Coleridge, the Solicitor-General, who acted for the Tichborne Trustees in the civil hearing.

The after-history of the case is voluminous,[4] but there are extensive records of the firm's role which have never been published. They reveal the inner workings of the firm in crisis: extraordinary meetings, letters to and from the counsel in the case, vital memos and personal records. The firm's involvement continued until the end of the civil action in 1873, although without one of its senior partners.

The case looks simple. In 1854 Roger Charles Tichborne, heir to the Tichborne and Doughty estates and then aged twenty-five, was lost at sea, 'missing, presumed dead'. His brother, Alfred, inherited. But, twelve years later, a man claiming to be the missing Tichborne appeared from Australia and claimed his estates. The Dowager Lady Tichborne recognised him and identified him as her son. The man, who became known as the Claimant, swore on oath in 1867 that he was Roger Charles Doughty Tichborne, but, in 1871, he had to take his claim to court. Here was a case involving money, romance, intrigue, adventure, travel, forgery and high finance spread across three continents.

The great passion aroused by the case was fuelled by the popular Press; it became im-

The Claimant.

possible for the Queen's Judges to enforce rules against contempt of court and the discussion of matters *sub judice*. The case shows Victorian legal process at its most typical. Douglas Woodruff remarks in 1957:

> Today opposing solicitors do not hurry to send to the newspapers the latest piece of evidence which they have collected in support of their clients. Prosecutions are conducted by prosecuting counsel with more restraint. Judges today would be more discreet than Sir William Bovill about the size and conduct of the parties of friends they would invite to sit on the Bench beside them. All branches of the profession were evolving new and better codes in the course of the nineteenth century, but the Victorian public was still a long lifetime away from the greater legal and social decorum of the twentieth century.[5]

The Tichborne family, from Alresford, near Winchester in Hampshire, predated the Norman Conquest. It was one of the oldest and richest

Catholic families in England, but it lay under the spell of the Tichborne Curse. During Henry II's reign, the Lady Mabella Tichborne, lying on her deathbed, implored her husband to help the poor on the estate. He offered the yearly produce of as much land as his stricken wife could crawl round while a torch burned. She managed to cover 23 acres, an area afterwards known as 'The Crawls'.

But she laid a curse on the house of Tichborne: if ever the ceremony – the Tichborne Dole on New Year's Day, then 25 March – were to lapse, the house would fall, the succession end, and unspoken evils would befall the family. The Dole survived the reformation,[6] but in 1794 the family stopped the custom on the advice of local magistrates worried at the increasing numbers of the poor at Tichborne Park.

The background to the case, and the firm's involvement, needs careful explanation.[7] The Tichborne title descended down the male line until 1800, when three brothers – Henry, Edward and James – succeeded one after the other. In 1827 James married Harriet, whom Lord Denning calls 'the evil genius of the story';[8] they had two sons, Roger (born 1829) and Alfred (born 1839). As it became clear that James' elder brothers would have no male heirs, it became equally clear that the line would eventually pass from them to James and then to Roger. In 1845 Henry died; Edward inherited (and combined the names Doughty and Tichborne) but produced only a daughter, Katherine (or Kate as she was known throughout the trial).

Roger's parents, James and Harriet, had been living in Paris but returned to England in 1845 on Henry's death. They sent Roger to the Catholic public school, Stonyhurst in Lancashire. There he shed his French accent, and, following a contemporary craze, was tattooed 'RCT' by a school friend called Bellew. As Kate's cousin and the probable heir to the Tichborne estate, Roger was a frequent visitor at Alresford.

On leaving Stonyhurst, Roger joined the 6th Dragoon Guards ('The Carabiniers'). When on leave in 1850 and 1851, he was often at

Tichborne, and gradually fell in love with Kate. He confided in Kate's mother, but two problems stood in his way. First, the Catholic Church frowned on marriage between immediate cousins; and second, Lady Tichborne had been primed with gossip from Ireland about Roger's excessive smoking, heavy drinking and general dissipation on tour of duty.

On 11 January 1852, over breakfast at Tichborne, Sir Edward had words with his nephew about his unsuitability. Roger never finished his breakfast. He left for London immediately. The love affair with Kate had been more innocent than passionate, but the hint of sexual scandal was to open a vein of salaciousness in the trial and the newspaper reports fifteen years later. On 22 June 1852, he embarked for South America with his regiment. He was twenty-three.

Roger eventually decided to leave the army. He sailed round Cape Horn to Valparaiso, and from there he went by mule over the Andes to Buenos Aires. On 5 March 1853 Sir Edward Tichborne died.[9] His brother James inherited the title, and Roger became heir apparent to the Tichborne fortune. He continued his South American travels for another year, and sailed from Buenos Aires to Rio de Janeiro where he booked a passage to Liverpool on the *Bella*. The ship sailed on 20 April 1854. It was never seen again.

A search vessel found the *Bella*'s longboat 400 miles offshore, floating upside down. Some wreckage of the ship was found but there were, it seemed, no survivors; the insurance was paid, and the death – on 23 April 1854 – of Roger Charles Tichborne was presumed and his will proved in July 1855. Roger had left a sealed packet with the Tichborne estate steward, Mr Gosford, who promptly destroyed it. James Tichborne lived until 11 June 1862, when the estate passed to Roger's younger brother, Alfred. He died in 1866, fathering a posthumous son called Henry, who became the twelfth Baronet.

Roger's mother, the Dowager Lady Tichborne, was distraught at the loss of her son. Convinced that he must have survived the sinking of the *Bella*, she kept a light burning at Tichborne for him. She was prepared to resort to any means of receiving news of him. On 19 May 1865, she read an advertisement in *The Times* of an Arthur Cubitt of Sydney, Australia, outlining his service to find missing persons. She promptly wrote to Cubitt. On the basis of her letter, he duly advertised in the Australian press:

A handsome reward will be given to any person who can furnish such information as will discover the fate of Roger Charles Tichborne. He sailed from the port of Rio de Janeiro on the 20th April 1854, in the ship the *Bella*, and has never been heard of since, but a report reached England to the effect that a portion of the crew and passengers of a vessel of that name was picked up by a vessel [the *Osprey*] bound to Australia – Melbourne it is believed – it is not known whether the said Roger Charles Tichborne was amongst the drowned or saved. He would at the present time be about thirty-two years of age; is of a delicate constitution; rather tall; with very light brown hair, and blue eyes. Mr Tichborne is the son of Sir James Tichborne, Bart., now deceased, and is heir to all his estates ... All replies to be addressed to Mr Arthur Cubitt, etc.[10]

Cubitt's notice was read by the Claimant, then living in Wagga Wagga. He contacted a local solicitor called William Gibbes, and told him, 'I have a little property in England if only I could get hold of it. I am heir to a title but I was shipwrecked and have lost touch.' Gibbes noticed he had the initials 'RCT' carved on his clay pipe; he jumped to a conclusion, and the Claimant was on his way. Cubitt wrote to the Dowager Lady Tichborne; she was overjoyed. The Claimant went to Sydney and booked into the Metropolitan. From that moment on, he referred to himself as Sir Roger Tichborne, Baronet. The Australian papers were full of the news.

While in Sydney he happened to meet a former Tichborne family servant called Bogle, who had known Roger well and who had knowledge of the estate. Supporters of the Claimant at this point rely on fortuity; detractors maintain that Bogle coached the Claimant in Tichborne lore. At any rate, Bogle and his family booked in at the Metropolitan and entered the Claimant's service. Money to pay for the hotel, other expenses and the passage to England was supplied by the Claimant's 'supporters', eager for a share in the estate. The Claimant left Sydney on 22 September 1866 and arrived in England on 24 December, making straight for the family's customary London hotel, Ford's in Manchester Square.

On 29 December, the Claimant made his first visit to Tichborne, staying at The Swan in Alresford. He telegraphed for Bogle to meet him. Four hundred well wishers greeted them at Alresford railway station.

The Dowager Lady Tichborne was, however, in Paris. The Claimant travelled to France and set out to meet her at her hotel in the Place de la Madeleine, but was unsuccessful. After another botched attempt to meet, she went to his hotel, the Hotel de Lille et d'Albion in the nearby Rue St Honoré. Her servant, an Irishman called Coyne, reported:

> I showed her up to the room where the Claimant was. I went in myself, and saw the Claimant. Lady Tichborne walked in first, and I and Mr Holmes [a solicitor advising the Claimant] walked in afterwards. He was lying on the bed with his clothes on. He was lying with his face towards the wall. She stood over him and kissed him, and he stopped so, with his face to the wall. She said, "He looks like his father, and his ears look like his uncle's." As soon as she said that she turned round and asked me to take his clothes off, as he was nearly stifled. I managed to turn him over and took his coat off. He told me to put some coals on the fire. Mr Holmes said, "You witness that; you hear how she has identified him?" and I said, "So do you." … He said nothing but remained lying on the bed.[11]

But for this recognition, the case, according to Lord Maugham, 'would never have occupied the Courts at all, at any rate not for many hours'.[12] On returning from Paris, the Claimant ensconced himself at Essex Lodge, Croydon, where he kept a wild, riotous household, sumptuous and unrestrained in style. By now, he weighed over 350 lb. Roger Tichborne, however, had been:

> about 5 feet 8½ inches in height, but exceedingly thin and spare
> in form, a man of considerable physical energy, delighting in riding,
> fishing and hunting; ... he smoked a great deal and drank more than
> was good for him; ... but not more than an ordinary fox-hunting
> squire of the fifties.... He uniformly behaved with the tact, good
> manners, and discretion of a Victorian gentleman.[13]

Besides being overweight, the Claimant had no 'RCT' tattooed on his arm.[14]

The Dowager Lady Tichborne wanted to believe the Claimant was her son. The retired family solicitor, Mr Hopkins, allowed himself to be convinced; a discontented man, he eagerly offered his services. But the Tichborne Trustees were not so easily swayed. So, in order to displace the child heir, Henry, the Claimant needed to take legal proceedings. On 27 June 1867 the Claimant filed two Bills in Chancery against the trustees of the Tichborne Estates, in effect asking for leave to recover the estates by an action of ejectment. A preliminary hearing took place, during which the Claimant swore that he had seduced his cousin Kate, and that he had left a sealed packet – destroyed by Gosford in 1854 – containing directions for her care should she be pregnant. These personal details were telling in the manoeuvrings before the civil action.

Leave was granted for the Claimant to begin his action of ejectment. But on 12 March 1868 the Claimant lost a chief witness when the Dowager Lady Tichborne died at Howlett's Hotel, Manchester. Then came the death in October of Hopkins, the other pillar of the Claimant's case. But the defence had troubles of its own. The Solicitor-General lodged an appeal to the court in January 1871. *The Times* reported:

> A special application was made on Wednesday to Lord Chief Justice Bovill to postpone the trial of the Tichborne succession Case. The application was made by the Solicitor-General on behalf of the defendant, on the ground that several witnesses whose evidence would be material to the issue were shut up in Paris. Mr Serjeant Ballantine, who is retained for the claimant, said since the time that he had first made his claim as many as ten of his witnesses had died. The Solicitor-General said, "seventeen of ours are dead already, so that the statement tells both ways."[15]

This was a problem that would not disappear; it persisted throughout the case, especially on the eve of the first summer adjournment. *The Times* commented:

> ... among the most important witnesses for the defence are several ladies who are of an advanced age. When persons have reached 70 or 80, four months, including one autumn month, form a very considerable period of their lives, and, should the case be adjourned to November, the chance of all these ladies being able to appear in the witness box is materially diminished.[16]

On 10 May 1871 the case – *Tichborne v. Lushington* – came before the Session Court of Westminster under the Chief Justice of Common Pleas, Sir William Bovill. Leading counsel for the Claimant were the eminent QCs, Serjeant Ballantine and Hardinge Giffard (later Lord Halsbury, three times Lord Chancellor); the Tichborne Trustees were represented by Sir John Duke Coleridge, the Solicitor-General (later Lord Chief Justice), and Mr Henry Hawkins, QC (later Lord Brampton). The Claimant's solicitors were Baxter, Rose & Norton; but it appears that not one of the firm's senior partners was in court with the Claimant, since *The Times* reported on the trial's opening day, 'The plaintiff sat near his attorney, Mr Spofforth, of the firm Baxter, Rose, and Norton.'[17]

How had the firm become involved? Sir Charles Norton's book, *A Man of Many Parts*, suggests that the Dowager Lady Tichborne 'wished her son to be represented by the best firm of Solicitors, in her opinion, and accordingly asked the firm, then Baxter, Rose & Norton, to act for the Claimant, which they proceeded to do, the case being handled, so I have always understood, by the Baxters, father and sons'.[18] The prime mover was the newest of the firm's partners, Markham Spofforth. After losing the Conservative Party agency in 1868, he had contemplated the post of solicitor to the London and North Western Railway. Eventually, he decided to stay with the firm, but by the spring of 1870 he had time on his hands. According to Frederick Rose, this explains why he took up the Tichborne Case on behalf of the Claimant:

> It was truly a case of "Satan finding mischief for idle hands" for there can be no question, I think, that but for Mr Spofforth having lost the Agency of the Conservative Party, and with it the principal part, if, indeed, it did not constitute the whole of his work, Baxter, Rose and Norton would never have touched the Tichborne Case.[19]

In the spring of 1870, a meeting took place in the library of the firm's office at 6 Victoria Street. Spofforth had invited the Claimant, together with Guildford Onslow, MP, one of the Claimant's stoutest supporters; he was an adventurous and flamboyant man, fond of loud checks and brown bowler hats. Woodruff comments wryly: 'Little as he suspected it, Onslow was to devote the remaining fourteen years of his life to the championship of this cause.'[20] The firm was represented by Robert Baxter, Philip Rose and Spofforth. Baxter and Spofforth wanted to represent the Claimant. The climate of opinion – judging from newspaper reports between 1868 and 1871 – favoured the Claimant.

Rayners, Philip Rose's house in Buckinghamshire.

But Philip Rose could not bear to hear the case mentioned. No decision was reached at the first meeting.

Frederick Rose was less intimately involved with the decisions of the firm's partners, and although his account of the case differs from the official transcripts in small particulars, his story of the impact of Tichborne on the firm is supported by letters from Philip Rose published in *The Times* during February 1872.

Philip Rose was not convinced by the Claimant. He left London for his Whitsuntide holiday at Rayners, his house at Penn in Buckinghamshire, assuming that neither Baxter nor Spofforth would agree to represent the Claimant before contacting him there. While at Rayners, Philip Rose suffered what must have been a mild stroke, or 'paralytic seizure'. He had to rest and recuperate. He did so by supervising the development of the farm on the estate, and by overseeing the building of a gamekeeper's cottage, which allowed him to enjoy an outdoor life. His doctors asked the other partners to avoid discussion of business matters.[21]

Rose was therefore surprised to hear, later in the summer, that Baxter and Spofforth had decided to represent the Claimant in the action of ejectment. Spofforth explained to Frederick Rose that while the initial meeting with Onslow and the Claimant had not encouraged the firm to take him on as a client, new evidence had now strengthened the Claimant's case against the Tichborne Trustees:

> ... and that he [Spofforth] fully expected that there would be no necessity to fight the ejectment Action that had been commenced, as he believed the Trustees would never let the case come into court, but would surrender at discretion.[22]

This 'new evidence' in 1870 was probably the Claimant's revelation of the contents of the packet left with the estate steward, Gosford, and which he had destroyed in 1854. Nothing in the firm's records or in the Rose Family Papers is specific on this point.

Spofforth anticipated lucrative work from the Tichborne Estate itself, as well as 'the large business that would accrue' from the publicity.[23] Frederick Rose duly told his convalescing father of the partners' decision to represent the Claimant:

> I told my Father of what had been done with some pride and pleasure that the Firm had been entrusted with such a "Cause Célèbre".
>
> I am sure, from the manner in which my Father received the news, that he was not best pleased at his partners having taken up the case when he was away ill, and when it had been distinctly decided before he left London that we were not to touch it, but what could he say?[24]

The firm relied on the relationship between the senior partners, Philip Rose and Robert Baxter, who both created new business and ensured the proper maintenance of existing railway and commercial clients. Dudley Baxter, Frederick Rose and Markham Spofforth were junior partners. So the decision to represent the Claimant effectively asked the firm who ran it and how.

Philip Rose had been dubious about the Claimant from the first meeting at the firm's office in the spring of 1870, but since Spofforth had already agreed to act for the Claimant, he attempted to make the best of it. He wrote to Spofforth suggesting that the junior counsel to Serjeant Ballantine and Hardinge Giffard should be his own son, William B. Rose, and Francis Jeune. This was a mistake because, although nineteenth-century legal circles were unconcerned by nepotism, this letter made Philip Rose appear an active and enthusiastic player in the case. Frederick Rose defends his father:

> The fact that he had recommended these two to Mr Spofforth for
> Junior Briefs in the Action was afterwards thrown in his teeth, as
> evidence that he had entered as heartily into the Case as any of his
> partners; but, as I have shewn, this allegation had no foundation, and,
> at the time when he committed the indiscretion – as he himself called it
> – of putting forward their names, he knew nothing of what had
> transpired at Victoria Street to cause his partners to alter their original
> determination not to touch the case; and was simply relying upon the
> information that overwhelming testimony in favour of the Claimant
> had been obtained. In fact he made the mistake of relying upon his
> partners – a very natural thing to do.[25]

Philip Rose returned to London in December 1870 after a five-month absence from the firm. But he fell ill again in January 1871 and stayed away from work until the middle of the month. On his return, he immediately met with Spofforth, who arranged for him to see Francis Baigent,[26] a Tichborne family friend from Winchester who identified the Claimant as Roger Tichborne. This changed his mind: as the trial commenced, he defended the Claimant in meetings at the firm's luncheon room in London Bridge Station where the firm's close ally, Ralph Lopes, QC, brought news of the defence tactics and strategy.

But when the Claimant took the stand, Philip Rose again became convinced that the man was an impostor. The firm needed more evidence, and Francis Jeune was despatched to Australia during the long vacation during which the Court had adjourned. Jeune was to check on the background of the Claimant in Wagga Wagga, to discover whether he was who the defence maintained him to be, Arthur Orton (alias Thomas Castro), a butcher from Wapping. Jeune returned in the autumn of 1871. He reported to the partners that the Claimant was not Roger Tichborne but was indeed Arthur Orton, alias Thomas Castro.

On 2 December 1871, Philip Rose wrote to Baxter. He pointed out the serious position of the firm, and urged Baxter to drop the case as soon as possible. Norton and Spofforth received copies. The letter reads:

> I do not know what your decision may be, but, as this is a matter in which everyone must act upon his own lights, I feel that personally I cannot consent to be any longer identified with the Tichborne case; and if it should be my misfortune that you and Norton take a different view, I must, with every feeling of strong and long standing affection to you both, submit, if necessary, to the sacrifice which such a divergence between us may entail.[27]

Baxter and Spofforth called in the barristers to decide whether to drop the case. Philip Rose resisted the pressure of professional rank. He maintained that the decision ought not to rest with Counsel: 'He was never one to take his line from Counsel, however eminent, nor would he admit … any superiority in what is sometimes termed the "higher branch" of the legal profession over the able men who belong to the Profession of Solicitors.'[28] The Counsel, Ballantine and Giffard, duly reported with this self-serving opinion. It is worth quoting at length:

We are Counsel for the Claimant in this case. Our authority to act is derived from him, through the Agency, no doubt, of Messrs Baxter & Co; but still derived from him alone. We are, therefore, called to a Consultation in which the hypothesis must be that we are acting in aid of his rights and in furtherance of his Claim. If the meeting is held upon any other hypothesis ... as the Claimant's Counsel we neither advise the continuance or the abandonment of the Plaintiff's Claims – By his authority we have not been asked to advise on any such question, and our position as Counsel would prevent our acting as advisor to anyone raising such a question adversely to him.

There are cases, no doubt, where counsel may feel absolute certainty that they have been deceived in giving their assistance to a fraudulent Claim, and in such a case we are of the opinion that they are entitled, and indeed bound, to repudiate the connection of Counsel and Client, which has thus fraudulently been put upon them. In this case it is enough for us to say that we are wholly unable to come to any conclusion, at present, which would justify us in taking any such course – Nothing has been proved adverse to the Plaintiff's case which we did not know when the Briefs were originally delivered, and there is most important corroboration of the Plaintiff's narrative which we did not know when we first undertook to be his Counsel. If the Plaintiff were indeed an Impostor we can conceive of no more adroit method of escaping exposure and punishment as the withdrawal of the case, apparently, by his desire, but as it were, against his will. He might then safely attribute his defeat to the defection of his legal advisers, and claim, certainly the legal expenses, possibly the whole of the value of the Estates against them ... We have felt some hesitation even in discussing so far, a question which obviously points to an accusation of the Plaintiff, but we think, should circumstances render it necessary, we ought by placing a copy of this paper in his hands to make him sufficiently acquainted with what has passed ... We have thus explained that the continuance or abandonment of this Cause must be on the responsibility of Messrs Baxter & Co. We positively decline to take it on ourselves, or to share it with them – They did not consult us upon undertaking it. As the Plaintiff's Counsel we are not compelled to advise them as to its abandonment.[29]

The barristers also pointed out that Kate Doughty Tichborne – now Mrs Radcliffe – should have the opportunity of affirming or denying the contents of the sealed packet which Roger Tichborne had left with Mr Gosford. The Claimant maintained that knowledge of its contents would prove his affair with Kate. Victorian proprieties demanded that she be allowed to clear her name.

Philip Rose felt he could not continue as a partner with the firm if he believed the Claimant's suit was fraudulent; but resigning from the firm might damage the Claimant's case and expose the firm to a round of litigation from the Claimant. He again asked advice from his friend, Ralph Lopes, QC, the barrister. He suggested Rose should wait for Mrs Radcliffe's testimony. On 9 December 1871 Rose made a statement to the partners of Baxter, Rose & Norton. Here are the most important extracts:

My partners, Mr Baxter and Mr Norton, though they may entertain grave suspicions, have not perhaps the same settled conviction that I have that the Claim is a fraud, and do not see in the strong light that I do the incumbent duty of retiring from any further support of it – For them the Opinion of Counsel may be a sufficient justification for still representing the Claimant – I wish I could feel it so in my case – It appears to me that if three or four persons are engaged in an object which one of them becomes convinced is unlawful, he is bound in honour and conscience to disconnect himself from it, no matter at what sacrifice, and independent of its surrounding consequences.

Now I am convinced, as strongly as I am of my own existence, that we are involved in the prosecution of a fraud, having for its object to deprive an infant of his rights, and, in furtherance of that object, we are made parties to an attack on the private character of a lady of rank, with grown up Sons and Daughters, who had hitherto borne an irreproachable character; and my earnest and most anxious desire is, if it can be done honourably, and with a due regard to my partners' interests, to have my name disconnected from a proceeding in which I have hitherto been mixed up as an involuntary participator, and sorely against my will.[30]

After a Christmas of ill health, he tackled his partners again through a memorandum[31] to Norton in which he said he was prepared to delay his decision about the case until the Attorney General's opening and the testimony of Mrs Radcliffe ('a duty we owe her'); if, after that, the firm continued to represent the Claimant, further action was threatened:

> … if they [the partners] should still think it right to continue their connection with it [the case], being thoroughly convinced as I am that the Claim from first to last is a conspiracy and a fraud, and that the claimant is all that the Attorney General has described him to be, I shall hold myself free from that moment, to take decisive steps for repudiating my own personal connection with it, and for publishing this to the world. The moral and mental delusion in which those whom I have been accustomed to respect are now wrapped, leaves me no alternative but, either to belie my convictions and appear before the world as supporting what I believe to be an Infamy, or, at all hazards, and regardless of all consequences, to separate myself, and not allow myself to be dragged any further along such a course.[32]

An extraordinary partnership meeting was called on 22 January 1872. Present were the firm's seven partners: Philip Rose, Robert Baxter, Henry Elland Norton, Robert Dudley Baxter, Markham Spofforth, Francis Baxter and Frederick Rose; and with them were the Tichborne Counsel, Serjeant Ballantine, Hardinge Giffard, and the junior counsel,

Jeune and Pollard (a replacement for William Rose, who had died during the case). Philip Rose read the statement he had prepared with Lopes. He concluded:

> I am prepared to bear my share of the necessary expense of carrying on the Case until the close of the Attorney General's opening and until sufficient time has been afforded him to call Mrs Radcliffe. From that moment I will not permit, and, if necessary, I will take measures to prevent, the application of one shilling of the partnership Funds to the further conduct of the Case. If my Partners will now agree to throw up the Case at that time, and state they have allowed our names to be connected with it so far, in order to give Mrs Radcliffe the opportunity we are bound to do, of answering the Claimant's charges, and that we have resolved at our own expense to carry on the Case up to that point, and for that purpose, I should wish to concur with them. But, if they decide upon going on with the Case after that time, then, I shall in the most public manner, at once, repudiate all connection with it so far as I am personally concerned, and denounce it as an imposture and a fraud. I am well aware of the responsibility I shall incur in taking this step, but I am prepared to abide the consequences – So far as concerns the instructions to Counsel which emanate from this Office. I wish it to be distinctly understood that I repudiate all instructions from any quarter which do not assert this much – That we are in possession of evidence and information sufficient to satisfy the mind of every man possessed of ordinary intelligence and common sense, that the Claimant is *not* Sir Roger Tichborne, but *is* Arthur Orton; and that the Claim he has set up is a falsehood and a fraud.[33]

Silence fell: 'The Counsel were evidently dumbfounded at the audacity of the Solicitor who dared to have an opinion of his own.'[34] Counsel asked for an adjournment of the meeting. They made no decision about their role in the case on that day, but three days later, on 25 January, sent a letter to the firm seeking clarification:

> It appears to us that upon the whole we may be justified in
> continuing to act as Counsel for the Plaintiff, but as it is plain that Mr
> Rose seeks to throw upon us the difficulty of deciding between the
> alternatives of abandoning our Client at a time when our doing so will
> be equivalent to a declaration that he ought to be criminally
> prosecuted, or continuing to act in aid of a cause which Mr Rose will
> hereafter be able to say he warned us was fraudulent, we require as
> conditions of our continuing our services:- First: a request from the
> other members of the Firm that we should continue to advocate the
> Plaintiff's Claim and an assurance that they do not share Mr Rose's
> conviction – Secondly – Some effectual guarantee that Mr Rose shall
> have no control whatever over the conduct and management of the
> cause: Thirdly – the supply of shorthand writer's notes, and other
> necessary accessories to the due prosecution of the Trial.[35]

Philip Rose had gambled and won. He had kept the benefits of
partnership by not resigning; he had distanced himself from a case that
would not only be lost, but that would result in the criminal conviction
of the Claimant. In practice, however, the Tichborne case broke up the
firm. Early in February 1872, the Attorney-General said in court that a
rumour – a rumour which he was inclined to believe – had reached him
that Philip Rose had retired from the firm over a disagreement with his
partners over the prosecution of the Tichborne case.

Philip Rose could not have asked for a better or more timely
opportunity, and immediately wrote to the Attorney-General, at the
same time making sure that copies of the letter went to the London
papers and journals. This letter is a witness of his ability to play both
sides of a situation – in effect, to resign from the firm without
resigning. It was cited in the Court of Common Pleas on 7 February
1872 and reported in *The Times* the next day as part of the Attorney-
General's statement.

It is quoted in full, partly because it shows Philip Rose at his best and most subtle (managing to close his letter with an ironic reference that damns, while seeming to praise his partners), and partly because it seems extraordinary that the role of the solicitors in a trial should become the subject of such a statement:

> ... the learned gentleman [the Attorney-General] then said that before proceeding with the case he wished to refer to a matter which had arisen on the previous day, when he mentioned that Mr. Rose was no longer connected with the firm of Baxter, Rose, Norton, and Co. He had received a letter from Mr. Rose that morning, saying that he had not withdrawn from the firm, but he had withdrawn from the case, and in the letter Mr. Rose said:

> Dear Mr Attorney General.
>
> My attention has been called to a statement in your speech this day [6 February 1872] on the Tichborne Case, variously reported in the Evening papers, but to the same effect in all, that I have retired from the Firm of Baxter, Rose and Norton. I trust to your candour and kindness to contradict this statement in your speech tomorrow. It is true that at the commencement of last December difference of opinion arose between me and my Partners as to this Case, which led me to offer at once to withdraw from the Firm, leaving it to Mr Lopes Q.C., by whose advice I have been guided, to settle the time and the mode; but this step not being thought advisable, or even practicable, and as it was subsequently found impossible for us to concur in united instructions to Counsel, the case has since the 22nd January been carried on under new retainers from the other individual Members of my Firm, exclusive of myself and my Son, from which date we have been wholly disconnected with it. I am sure you will be the first to admit that it would be premature to enter publicly [sic] into any further explanation – I trust, however, I

may be permitted emphatically to repeat what, in the midst of this painful divergence, I have desired to impress upon Mr Baxter and Mr Norton, that I am firmly convinced they are acting in the highest sense of what they believe to be their duty, a conviction which will be shared by everyone who knows them.[36]

> The Lord Chief Justice said he should like to know who, then, were the responsible parties having charge of the Plaintiff's case. As matters stood, Messrs. Baxter, Rose, Norton, and Co. [sic] were in the order of the court as the attorneys of the Plaintiff, and Mr. Rose could not withdraw and get rid of his responsibility on simply writing a letter. Mr. Rose's name could be taken out of the order, and the order could be so amended, but this must be done in the proper and usual manner. His Lordship, turning to Mr. Jeune [Junior Counsel], said he did not expect any answer then, but he should espect some notice to be taken of the matter in the course of the day, and the proper course would be that the counsel for the Plaintiff should consult with those who instructed them.[37]

The Times includes an aside from the Attorney-General to the effect that in any other case, the resignation of 'one of the attorneys and his son ... would be thought conclusive as against the plaintiff', but that 'in this case the ordinary rules of action did not seem to apply'.[38] The *Illustrated London News* of 10 February 1872 put the incident more succinctly: 'Sir John Coleridge ... proceeded to correct a statement ... to the effect that Mr. Philip Rose had retired from the firm of Baxter, Rose and Norton [sic], the Claimant's attorneys. Mr. Rose, according to a letter which he had addressed to the learned Counsel, had simply withdrawn from the case.'

It was only a matter of time before the case collapsed. On 5 March 1872, the 102nd day of the trial, the foreman of the jury told the court that the jurors required no more evidence. The Attorney-

General kept the promise he made in November 1871 to deliver a closing speech that 'will be endless'.[39] *The Times* had pleaded in the same month, 'There is a time for all things, and a time has surely come when the public has a right to express an opinion on the indefinite protraction of the Tichborne Case.'[40] On 7 March *The Times* summed up the technicalities of the Civil Action in its concluding article the day after the trial closed:

> It is probable that no private Lawsuit ever excited an interest so widespread and sustained, while it is certain that none was ever reported, day by day, with such minute accuracy. Nor can it be said that public curiosity, idle and capricious as it often is, was in this instance wasted upon an unworthy subject. In all its circumstances – in the magnitude of the property at stake, in the singular antiquity of the family concerned, in the mystery which overhung the early life of the lost heir, in the marvellous coincidences which favoured the cause of the Claimant – this memorable Case well deserved the space which it filled in the popular mind, and may remain for generations to come the most striking example of personation on record.[41]

The Claimant withdrew his claim when his Counsel, Serjeant Ballantine, elected to be non-suited; the claim could be revived at any time, since no judgment had been made against him. But the logic of a failed claim was inexorable. 'Ballantine perhaps thought,' says Maugham, 'that, at the worst, time would elapse before criminal proceedings could be launched against the claimant, who in the meantime would have an opportunity of disappearing.'[42] The Lord Chief Justice acted swiftly. He remanded the Claimant directly to Newgate on bail of £10,000 to await criminal proceedings on fraud and perjury. The Claimant went quietly, and was cheered as he entered the prison. His involvement with the firm ended here; although he reported in later life that he had refused a compromise settlement offered during the case, and had done so for the sake of his own son, Roger.[43]

The Claimant had arrived in England with nothing but his fare and he expected no legal proceedings. The resolute opponents who confronted him taught him that Victorian justice was a costly business. In April 1873, proceedings against him opened in the Central Criminal Court. He was indicted on two counts of perjury, convicted, and sentenced to two terms of penal servitude, each of seven years. The court record reads:

> *Mr Justice Mellor*: The sentence of the Court, which I now pronounce, is that for the perjury alleged in the first count of the indictment upon which you have been convicted, you be kept in penal servitude FOR THE TERM OF SEVEN YEARS. And that for the perjury alleged in the second count of this indictment, of which you have been convicted, you be kept in penal servitude for a FURTHER TERM OF SEVEN YEARS, to commence immediately upon the expiration of the period of penal servitude assigned to you in respect of your conviction upon the first count of the indictment. And that is the sentence of the Court.
>
> *The Defendant*: May I be allowed to say a few words, my Lord?
>
> *Mr Justice Mellor*: No.[44]

As Woodruff concludes in his book of the case: 'One moral is the great importance of being able to employ good solicitors and good counsel; particularly the solicitors.'[45]

The case had left Baxter, Rose & Norton divided along family loyalties. Frederick Rose blamed Baxter for the firm's embarrassment over the case. Part of Baxter's zeal for representing the Claimant may have been due to his fundamental religious opinions which he had acquired as a young man in the 1830s and 1840s. His judgement was clouded by his willingness to see a Catholic family challenged by the avowedly non-Catholic Claimant: 'Mr Baxter's hatred of Catholics and the Catholic Faith was so great that it would have seemed to him a meritorious action to displace an undoubted Catholic by a man who had thrown over his religion.'[46]

Frederick Rose also blamed Baxter 'for his fatuous folly in accepting anything and everything that Mr Spofforth told him ... and for continuing to leave everything to Mr Spofforth's judgement'.[47] Henry Elland Norton seems less to blame, if only because he was less involved in the running of the partnership than Philip Rose and Baxter: he confined himself to the Bills Department (i.e. Costs), where he filled a role not unlike a modern managing partner. The junior partners, Baxter's sons and Frederick Rose, were not consulted.

The year 1872 was important for the firm. If Robert Baxter was the dominant personality within the firm in dealings, then Philip Rose had been the dominant presence outside the firm, much more at ease in City circles than Baxter was. The predominance of Philip Rose and Robert Baxter in the firm was to change; the structure which had served through the turbulent 1840s, the boom years of the 1850s and 1860s was to alter. By the 1870s the firm had developed a structure with three classes of partner: Principals (Robert Baxter, Philip Rose and Henry Elland Norton), Subsidiaries (Dudley Baxter, Francis Baxter, Frederick Rose and Henry Turton Norton) and Salaried (Spofforth and Brewer). Each Principal had the option of retiring when he pleased and nominating his successor.

The Tichborne Case left Philip Rose drained and demoralised: his son, Willie, whom he had suggested as junior counsel, had died during the case in February 1872. Philip Rose, too, was unwell, and, at the age of fifty-six, decided to retire from the firm in the autumn of 1872 in order to pursue company and financial business and maintain his political business and private work for Disraeli. The Tichborne Case precipitated his departure, but he was unprepared for what faced him. In 1872, his capital in the firm amounted to twenty-two sixtieths of £40,000. Baxter had twenty-seven sixtieths, and Norton eleven sixtieths.[48]

Philip Rose agreed to lend his son, Frederick, enough money to buy a share of the firm's capital, to be repaid in instalments from Frederick's share of the firm's profits. An audit was needed. Since the firm's cashier, Edmund Harvey, was suffering from hip pains and absent at his house in Cornwall, the firm commissioned an audit from an accountant (J.W. Richards Adams) and wrote reassuring Harvey that everything was taken care of, urging him to take sufficient time to recover. But Harvey replied, with a request that he should audit the firm's books himself. Rose grew suspicious, and was heard to say, 'I hope to heaven there is nothing wrong with the accounts.'[49] Although extremely ill, Harvey journeyed from Falmouth to his house in Southall. Frederick Rose visited him, and Harvey begged to be allowed to take the audit.

In 1868, Harvey had told the partners that a rich relative had died and left in trust for his son several thousand a year and a small estate in Falmouth, Cornwall. Harvey consulted Norton (whose own son, Henry Turton, was at Cambridge) about a career for his son, the appropriate level of allowance, and other details. He also said that he would have to spend more time at Falmouth, pointing out that the legacy provided him an allowance from his son's estate. Harvey was lying. There was no will, no legacy. He had bought the Falmouth house with money he had embezzled from the firm, using the legacy story to explain his altered circumstances. Therefore in the autumn of 1872, Harvey was worried that Adams' investigations would show the scope of his fraud. It did.

Adams began the audit, and discovered that Harvey had habitually taken bogus cheques to Norton (the Bills partner) for signing; often, cheques would be made out 'To Bearer' or in a bogus name for plausible business. Most of the firm's cheques from the 1860s have Norton's signature rather than Baxter's or Rose's. This shows firstly how few administrative checks and balances there were in the firm, and secondly how the system relied on absolute trust. Adams' initial trawl through the accounts came up with £7,000 of the final total of £17,000 which it was later established Harvey had embezzled. The firm prosecuted, but bail was granted on the grounds of his ill health; Harvey died before the case went to court.

Further financial irregularities surfaced in August 1872. During the Harvey investigation, the firm was contacted by its bankers, Glyn, Mills, Currie & Co. They drew attention to the firm's overdrawn account and in particular a set of loans that had fallen due for repayment in August 1871. In essence, the firm owed the bank £30,000. As the investigations progressed, Harvey's balance sheets were found to be wrong; but even worse, the accounts ignored bad debts – some arising from Robert Baxter's own railway speculation. At this stage, Baxter alone was fully aware of the seriousness of the situation.

Philip Rose announced his retirement on 1 October 1872 and sent a circular to the other partners, appointing his son, Frederick, as a Principal in his place. To retire, Philip Rose needed to withdraw his share of the £40,000 partnership capital. Both father and son were counting on this money being available. But on 17 October 1872, Baxter finally circulated the bankers' letter, revealing the news of the firm's parlous state. From this, Philip Rose discovered that the firm required at least £30,000 fresh capital. Having considered retirement under the impression that the firm's finances were in good order, he faced the task of finding £11,000 of the firm's total debts of £41,000.

Baxter, however, who owed about £30,000 to the firm, had a piece of good luck in 1873. His shares in the colliery companies of Yorkshire and South Wales (and the railways which served them) received a boost from the rise in coal prices that year, so he was able to cover his debts by selling these shares. The energy and daring which had served him so well in the wild 1840s and 1850s had not changed with the increasingly regulated times. But the trust between Philip Rose and Robert Baxter ceased to exist.

The firm, as it had evolved over the middle years of the century, came to an end. In 1873, Baxter formed the firm of Baxters & Co. with his two sons and Markham Spofforth. The two Nortons, Frederick Rose and John Brewer continued in practice as Norton, Rose, Norton and Brewer, still based at 6 Victoria Street. The new arrangement allowed time for reflection:

> The reckless way in which Mr Robert Baxter had acted in the past in taking up business of a highly speculative character, his extraordinary notions of his duty to his partners in the matter of finance, and his obstinate nature, made me [Frederick Rose] highly apprehensive for the future, and I was glad to feel that I no longer ran the risk of being ruined by some act of folly on his part as my partner.[50]

Philip Rose was remarkably resilient. He continued his informal links with the firm (he advised on partnership appointments) through his son and through his directorships. He turned his energies to outside business interests with his friend, the French financier, Baron Emile d'Erlanger; both men worked from the Baron's London office at 43 Lothbury. Their joint projects included the Public Works Construction Company, the Madeira and Marmoré Railway, and the British and Foreign Credit Bank, although these realised much less than they had promised. But Rose seems to have been happier after leaving the firm. The arrangement with D'Erlanger was less arduous and demanding than legal work, and in essence Philip Rose was free to divide his time and energy between office, home and the bench, having been made a JP for Buckinghamshire.

He gradually spent more time at Rayners, looking after the estate and the projects which he had built: the church and school at Tyler's Green, and the St Margaret's Institute, a club for the people who worked on the estate. He became High Sheriff of Buckingham in 1878; and in spring of that year gave a dinner in Aylesbury for the county's practising solicitors: 'He said that his own success in the world being attributable to his professional life as a Solicitor, he felt that there was no body of men he would more like to honour than his brethren in the profession.'[51]

Philip Rose was made a baronet in 1874. He continued an active life in the City throughout the 1870s and died on 17 April 1883, aged sixty-seven. His former partners, Robert Baxter and Henry Elland Norton, were among the mourners at the lavish funeral in Tyler's Green on Saturday 21 April. One hundred mourners took the London train to add to the two hundred local people at St Margaret's Church. The *cortège* left Rayners at 1.30 p.m. with representatives from Rose's professional, personal, philanthropic and local life.

Notes

1. A supporter of the Plaintiff.

2. *The Times*, 30 June 1871.

3. *Illustrated London News*, 27 May 1871.

4. The best book to date is J.D. Woodruff's *The Claimant* (1957); the transcripts of the criminal trial – together with commentary and peripheral evidence – can be found in Kenealy's eight-volume book; there are other useful versions of the case by Atlay (1899), Maugham (1936), W.F. Gilbert (1957) and Denning (1986).

5. J.D. Woodruff, *The Tichborne Claimant* (1957), p.xiv. See also: Maugham (1936), M.F. Gilbert (1957) and Denning (1986).

6. There is a fine painting of the Dole by Tilburg, the Dutch artist, from 1670.

7. Material for this summary is drawn from: Kenealy (8 vols, 1876), Maugham (1936), Woodruff (1957), Denning (1986) and from contemporary newspapers. Information on the firm's role is drawn from the Rose Family Papers.

8. Denning, p.159.

9. The Dowager Lady Tichborne wrote to Roger in June 1853 at Valparaiso.

10. In Denning, p.165.

11. Coyne's evidence. Trial Transcript.

12. Maugham.

13. Ibid.

14. He spoke Spanish rather than French. The Claimant had a remarkable memory, which allowed him to absorb details about Roger Tichborne's life quickly in order to make them appear to be his own.

15. *The Times*, 27 January 1871.

16. Leader, *The Times*, 30 June 1871.

17. *The Times*, 11 May 1871.

18. *A Man of Many Parts*, p.14.

19. Rose Family Papers.

20. Woodruff, p.92.

21. Rose Family Papers.

22. Ibid.

23. Ibid.

24. Ibid.

25. Ibid.

26. Statement printed in Kenealy, III, pp.188ff.

27. Rose Family Papers.

28. Ibid.

29. Ibid.

30. Ibid.

31. 17 January 1872.

32. Rose Family Papers.

33. Ibid.

34. Frederick Rose, Rose Family Papers.

35. Rose Family Papers.

36. Copies appeared in the London papers on 7 February 1872.

37. *The Times*, 8 February 1872.

38. Ibid.

39. *Illustrated London News*, 18 November 1871.

40. *The Times*, 25 November 1871.

41. Ibid, 7 March 1872.

42. See: Denning, p.173.

43. Woodruff, p.418.

44. *The Trial at Bar of Sir Roger C.D. Tichborne*, ed. Dr Kenealy, MP (8 vols, 1876).

45. Woodruff, p.447.

46. Rose Family papers.

47. Ibid.

48. Partnership Deed, 24 July 1866.

49. Rose Family Papers.

50. Ibid.

51. Ibid.

1861–1944

The Tale of Two Firms

ON 23 SEPTEMBER 1903 this report appeared in *The Times*:

> The body of Wilson Mills Roche, of Sunderland, was discovered on a right of way in Knock Wood, Crieff, late on Monday night. The throat was cut, and by the side of the body was a razor. His wife found in his bedroom a letter stating where his body would be found and giving instructions about his funeral. Mr Roche, who was 51, was an authority on Mercantile Marine Law. He was Solicitor to the British Steam Shipowners' Association, the British Shipping Federation, and the British Shipmasters' Association.

In the same week, in Rocamadour, France, another lawyer from Sunderland died. William Atkinson Oliver was also an authority on mercantile shipping law. Together with the London lawyer, John James Dumville Botterell, Oliver had founded the firm of Oliver & Botterell in Sunderland in 1861; Roche had built it into Botterell & Roche in London in 1873.[1] Just before its own centenary, Botterell & Roche amalgamated its practice in 1960 with that of Norton, Rose & Co. (as the firm was known at that time) to become Norton, Rose, Botterell & Roche. There is a shared history which belongs to Botterell & Roche as part of the unified firm which ran parallel to the history of Norton Rose for a century. Botterell & Roche had its own century of history before the amalgamation of the two firms.

Botterell & Roche 1861–1944

William Atkinson Oliver was the son of Dr William Watson Oliver. He started practice alone with an office at 65 John Street, Sunderland. He married Helen Moule (whose family was connected to Bishop Moule of Durham) and their three sons where born in 1870, 1871 and 1874. The middle son, Anthony Moule Oliver, became Town Clerk of Newcastle-upon-Tyne, and was knighted.

William Oliver, the founder of the firm of Botterell & Roche.

But in the 1860s, Oliver had ambitions beyond the north-east. He wrote on shipping law, producing in 1864 a set of 'instructions' for captains. In 1868 James Imray and Sons and by George Routledge and Sons published his *Practical Manual of Shipping Law*, with 141 pages covering charter-parties, bills of lading, loading, the voyage, collisions, storage, delivery, payments, protests and insurance. The book, Oliver wrote in the Preface,

… was originally published … for the purpose of informing them captains of their legal rights and duties, so as to enable them to keep their employers free from disputes and litigation; or, in case any dispute or accidents should occur, to enable them, as far as possible, to save the shipowner from suffering any loss. Although a captain, when from home, has generally no one to advise him, excepting those whose interests are in direct opposition to the interests of the shipowner, no other book of this kind has hitherto been published (so far as the writer is aware), in which the various practical points relating to shipping law are collected together ... It does not profess to be anything more than a short summary of the law on the subject, and the information given has been put in as concise and practical a form as possible.[2]

The first edition sold out within a month. A second edition,[3] in 1869, was expanded to 200 pages and outlined the Merchant Shipping Acts (1854, 1855, 1862 and 1867). The book ran through six editions and had reached 342 pages when it was finally revised in 1879 by Wilson

A

PRACTICAL MANUAL

OF

SHIPPING LAW

BY

WM A OLIVER

SOLICITOR

LONDON
JAMES IMRAY & SONS
89 MINORIES AND TOWER HILL.
GEORGE ROUTLEDGE & SONS
1868

The title page of Oliver's Manual of Shipping Law.

Mills Roche, who had been taken on as a partner. The title changed to *Oliver's Shipping Law Manual*.

In 1873 Oliver stared a practice in London at 1 Quality Court, Chancery Lane, in partnership with John James Dumville Botterell (J.J.D. Botterell, 1847–1923), a London solicitor, who had qualified five years earlier with Wing & Ducane of Gray's Inn. (The Law Lists indicate that Botterell had had a practice as a sole practitioner in Hornsey and in Wood Green, Middlesex, after qualifying and before joining Oliver.) This created two partnerships: Oliver & Botterell in Sunderland and Oliver & Botterell in London; these firms established a complex structure of regional practices with some but not all partners in common. Oliver & Botterell (London) also attracted agency work from Sunderland law firms.[4]

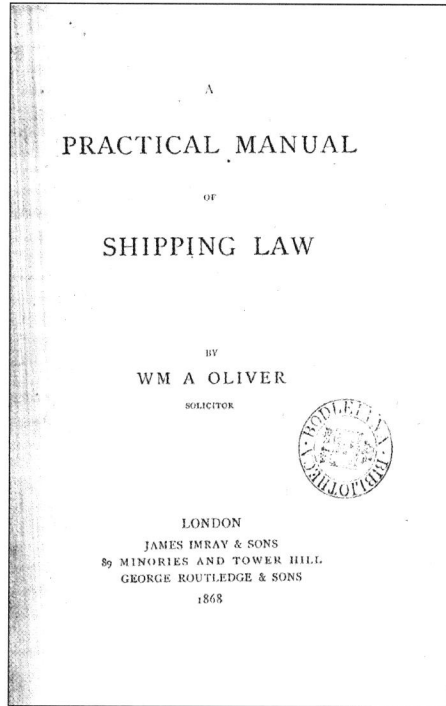

J.J.D. Botterell.

In 1876 Oliver & Botterell opened a practice in Newcastle-upon-Tyne on Quayside. The business in all their three firms was based on shipping, specifically because of Oliver's expertise in the area and because of the succession of Shipping Acts which produced new legislation in the 1860s and 1870s. The firm was especially active in the protection and indemnity business, and was involved with Captain James Henderson of Sunderland, in the British Shipmasters' and Officers' Protection Society (founded in 1873, incorporated in 1878) and in the foundation of the British Shipmasters' and Officers' Insurance Association Limited (established in 1877 and administered by the firm in Sunderland and Newcastle).

In 1876, Wilson Mills Roche (1852–1903) joined the north-east firms as a partner, and for two years the Sunderland and Newcastle firms were known as Oliver, Botterell & Roche; in London, Oliver & Botterell retained the offices at Quality Court and opened a new office, as Botterell & Roche, at 53 Chancery Lane. Roche came from Liverpool, where his father, Dr John Roche, originally from Dublin, was a physician. It is significant that Roche, together with Philip Rose and Oliver, was the son of a doctor. Although the relative status of medicine and the law has changed throughout the nineteenth and twentieth centuries, the firms' founders believed in the kind of education germane to success in the law. In other words, success in a legal career had not begun to depend on a university degree, and was not to do so until the early 1960s.

Wilson Mills Roche, who was educated at Bishops Stortford and Neuweid, Germany, had planned a career in the Indian Civil Service Woods and Forests Department. But instead he took articles in Norwich with the Town Clerk, Henry Blake Miller, later joining the firm of Sharp, Parkers, Pritchard & Sharp. Well-known specialists in local government, corporation and municipal law, the firm had as one of its clients the Association of Municipal Corporations. In the early 1870s, Roche worked extensively in Birmingham, engaged on Joseph Chamberlain's civic projects, and was offered the post of Assistant Town Clerk of Birmingham. He was therefore in possession of a range of skills and knowledge in demand at that time: the Victorians introduced massive changes in local government over the fifty years between the Municipal Corporations Act (1835) and the Local Government Act (1888).

The social and political changes that followed were far-reaching and required leger expertise to implement them.[5] The task tended to fall to the newer members of the legal profession; in fact, solicitors were much more active than barristers in local government administration.[6] Roche moved to Newcastle in 1876 on joining the firm, and to Sunderland in 1877, where he lived in South Sunderland. Both towns at that time were prosperous and growing.

In 1879, Oliver chose to practise alone in Newcastle-upon-Tyne and left the firms – then Oliver & Botterell (which became Botterell & Roche in London), Oliver, Botterell & Roche (Newcastle) and Oliver, Botterell & Roche (Sunderland). Botterell also maintained a sporadic practice in Wood Green. The related firms concentrated themselves in three offices – in London, Sunderland and Newcastle-upon-Tyne – by 1881;[7] and continued to pursue shipping litigation and insurance as their main business. (Total tonnage produced in the Tyne and Wear area in the 1870s had increased fourfold since 1850, despite sharp depressions in the mid-1880s; shipbuilding was not to reach a peak until 1903.[8])

The firms were well placed for work with the new protection and indemnity (P & I) associations[9] which were formed to insure shipowners' liabilities on a mutual and non-profit basis. There was and is a distinction between protection and indemnity. A protection association covered four major risks: personal injury; crew liabilities; collision liability, not covered by hull and machinery insurance; and damage to piers and other objects. An indemnity association covered the shipowner's liability to cargo for short-delivery, damage or overcarriage, and other matters such as immigration, customs and fines which the shipowner may be exposed to through the negligence of officers and crew. The associations were run by managers and solicitors, and gradually expanded their scope of operations as changes in Maritime Law, resulting from the Merchant Shipping Acts of 1894 and 1906, together with the 1897 Workmen's Compensation Act, and the 1901 Factories Act, made shipowning more complex and litigious.

Botterell & Roche in all three locations acted as managers and solicitors for the Mutual Association of Steamship Owners (subsequently the British Steamship Owners Association, BSOA), a legal defence club which J.J.D. Botterell and Wilson Roche founded together in stages during the 1880s, the core of the firms' business for many years. The BSOA was primarily concerned with the legal costs incurred during actions involving deep sea vessels, while the related organisation, the British Steamship Short Trades Association coped with inshore vessels and the coasters which ran up and down the east coast between London and the ports in the North, in particular the ships which carried coal and steel from the North. Over the next twenty years, the BSOA evolved local Associations in the North East, London, and Cardiff–Bristol Channel. The regional nature of the work helped shape the regional strengths of the firms in Newcastle, Sunderland, London, and later, Cardiff.[10]

Roche was the public face of the firms. He was a civic-minded man, and became a Councillor (for St Michael's Ward) of Sunderland Borough Council in 1888. He advised the Council's many standing committees, including Finance and Health. In 1894, as chairman of the Technical Education Committee, he used the 'Whisky Money' raised by the 1890 Local Taxation (Customs & Excise) Act to finance the Sunderland School of Art and to build a new Technical College.[11]

Roche estimated on evidence from similar projects in Leeds, Cardiff and Newcastle that 'to build and equip a Technical School or College sufficient to meet the present requirements of the Borough ... [would] cost somewhere about £15,000'.[12] He promptly held an architectural competition for the design of the new facility in Green Terrace, and began to look for engineers and builders to tender for construction.[13] At 12 noon on 27 September 1897 he laid the first stone and four years later donated the clock to top the building. When it opened, the local paper devoted an unprecedented four-page spread, with engravings, speeches and tributes.[14] In 1903 the *Sunderland Echo* wrote:

> The Technical College is a monument of his [Roche's] municipal work, and not only was it largely owing to his enterprise that the idea was so admirably carried out, but much of the success which has since attended the work of the college has been due to his assiduous efforts. Especially ... in getting together funds for the equipment, in interesting shipbuilders and manufacturers in the institution, and in drawing up schemes for making the college one of immense value to the youth of the town, and particularly to those engaged in its leading industries.

The college later became Sunderland Polytechnic and then, in 1992, the University of Sunderland.

Roche would be remembered by his local community for this achievement, the equivalent of Philip Rose's efforts for the Brompton

Hospital in London fifty years earlier.[15] But in strictly legal circles, he would be remembered for his expertise in shipping law. Through his revisions of *Oliver's Manual*, and through the formation of the British Steamship Owners Association, Roche gained knowledge of shipping law, making him well known in shipping circles. He was a frequent presence at the Board of Trade, advising or giving evidence at enquiries. His greatest achievement – and one of value to Botterell & Roche in London, Newcastle and Sunderland – was the creation of the British Shipping Federation in 1890. A result of the 1889 seamen's strike,[16] which had begun in London and worsened to require police protection for shipowners' property, the Federation was formed to withstand what its historian, writing in 1950, called 'the gravest crisis which the industry had ever had to face'.[17]

Roche helped to devise its form and function, and to arrange its structure and constitution. Throughout 1890, he travelled all over the country to lobby and gain support for a national association of shipowners. In August he addressed the Conference of Shipowners' Associations at Whittington House, Leadenhall Street:

> I think, Mr Chairman, there is very great difficulty in compelling members of the Association to subscribe to what is undoubtedly a Trades' Union, but they have an enormous power in their hands in this way. They can say to a member who is mean and individual enough in the worst sense of the term to say he won't subscribe to that which the great bulk of his trade say he ought to subscribe: "Very well then, sir, we won't insure your ship." ... You will soon find out that those who say they won't subscribe to such a generally desired fund as this, if they were turned out of the Indemnity Associations, would soon reconsider their position.[18]

The extensive minutes of the Shipping Federation show Roche to have been quick in debate and thorough in delivery, swift to intervene and slow to give way. On 19 September 1890 Roche spoke at length about the Articles of Association which he had drawn up for the Federation:

> ... in my opinion it would be impossible to let this be other than a Limited Company, limited by Guarantee, because otherwise you would be having limited companies becoming members of an association without any limit, and the effect would be that they would only contribute to the extent of their limit whilst some shipping companies that might join would be liable to contribute to the full extent, without a limit.[19]

Roche had conducted his research by looking at similar industries. He had spoken at length to the members of the Durham Colliery Owners' Association through their solicitors Phillipson & Cooper of Newcastle: '... and I found them only requesting the vaguest of vague objects, but sufficient for the purpose of covering the terms of working which afterwards you must agree amongst yourselves.' He concluded in his simple, robust and plain style:

> After all, gentlemen, this will be a question of mutual confidence. When you have got to the end of it you do not have to trust one another and if you are not prepared to work together, the whole thing will fall in a fortnight. Therefore I do not care what legal question or legal quibble you raise, you will come to pieces if you do not continue to trust one another ... I know there are heaps of legal points, and I know there are gentlemen who can refine legal straws to any extent, but I advise you not to listen to that kind of advice or you will never do anything in this way.[20]

Roche's speech was well received, particularly when he said he felt able to explain 'the machinery of the thing concerned' in half an hour, that the committee need not adjourn for a fortnight and that 'there is no reason at all why registration should be delayed', rounding off with 'a week, I should say, would be ample for us to complete our labours and meet this day week'.[21]

A week was a long time in the life of Wilson Roche. He reportedly worked in Newcastle on Monday and on Tuesday morning and in Sunderland during the afternoon; travelling overnight to London, he worked there on Wednesday and Thursday, and then on Friday went to Cardiff, leaving on Saturday morning to reach his Northumberland home on Saturday evening.[22] He ably combined his commitments to the firm with his municipal duties in Sunderland, since the Council minutes record regular attendance and few long periods of absence.

By 1891 Botterell & Roche maintained offices at 101 Leadenhall Street, London, at Sandhill, Newcastle-upon-Tyne and at 26 St Thomas Street, Sunderland. But gradually, as business grew, the firms became more distinct, with, in practice, greater demarcation of work. Through the firms' work as founders of and solicitors to the Shipping Federation, new business followed quickly. On 7 April 1893 the Federation set up the Shipowners' Parliamentary Committee, a lobby group which sought to influence the drafting of the Merchant Shipping Bill.[23]

The Committee's twenty-seven founding members amounted to a *Who's Who* of shipping organisations from all round the country, including the Chamber of Shipping, the British Steamship Owners Association, the Shipping Federation, the Owners' Associations from London, Manchester, Newcastle, Sunderland, Cardiff, Swansea, Belfast, Glasgow and Liverpool, and Protection and Indemnity Associations from the West and North of England. Roche was not only the solicitor who drew up the Memorandum and Articles of Association; he was also a representative on the Parliamentary Committee for the North-East Coast. His colleagues and successors on the Federation's committees included representatives from established shipping families and firms such as Currie, Milburn, Miller, Raeburn and Runciman.

Throughout the 1890s the firms' growth matched the growth of the shipping industry as Roche aggressively pursued new members for

Milburn House, Newcastle, 1908.

the Shipping Federation. The firms received a retainer and handled litigation for Federation members. During the decade the firm appears in the Court of Appeal judgements *S.S. Nord Kap v. Sandhill* (1894), *The Owners of Steamship Edenbridge v. Green* (1897) and *The Carleton Steamship Company Ltd. v. The Castle Mail Packets Company Ltd.* (1898). The London firm acted in concert with its regional offices, as in the 1899 case of the *Ruabon Steamship Company* (Botterell & Roche for the associated firm, Vaughan & Roche, Cardiff) *v. The London*

Assurance Co. The staple work of the 1900s, with thirty-seven Court of Appeal cases between 1900 and 1920, was admiralty, marine insurance and commercial shipping work.

The most significant partnership arrangement at Botterell & Roche was its agreement of 1900. It is interesting and worth looking at in detail for two reasons: first, it shows exactly the complex relative status of the firms in 1900, and second, it traces the paths of energy which Roche in particular inscribed across the shipping industry. In 1900 the firms' co-partnership was based in London (Botterell & Roche), Sunderland (Botterell & Roche) and Newcastle-upon-Tyne (Botterell, Roche & Temperley). Henry Temperley had joined the Newcastle firm in 1893 as managing partner; he worked with Roche and in the early 1900s he took over much of Roche's work with the Shipping Federation and it various committees. He and Roche were partners in all three firms, as was Botterell, but he was centred on London. There was a fourth related practice, Vaughan & Roche, in Cardiff, which Roche had established in 1899 with Frederick Vaughan of Vaughan & Hornby who had been using Botterell & Roche as its London agent for a year.

In this complex new agreement between Botterell, Roche, Temperley and two new partners, Arthur Powell Simon (joining in London in 1900) and James Wallace (joining in Newcastle in 1895), the co-partners divided up their firms' areas of interest. This move effectively divided the practice into separate firms and marked a step in the parting of the ways of the London, Sunderland and Newcastle practices. It amounts to a demarcation agreement, dividing up the country in terms, as the document puts it, of 'spheres of influence'. The process accelerated through the appointment of new partners to one firm only. In essence, the group of firms was now held together by the character and energy of Roche, who was the appointed arbitrator for all disputes between the firms. On his death the cohesion between them disappeared.

The work which the firms carried out was, by its nature, liable to involve one or more offices at either end of the country. In the 1890s there had been arrangements, 'partly in writing and partly verbal', concerning the division of work between the offices, as well as 'appointments and remuneration therefor' between the practices. The 1900 agreement describes the practices as 'firms'; and business had formerly been conducted so far as possible so that clients could instruct any one of the firms or offices, depending on which was the most convenient. The agreement evolves the idea of 'spheres of influence', under which each firm maintained its present clients 'so that dispute, misunderstanding and confusion may be avoided in the transaction of business'. The active management of the BSOA remained in Sunderland, which received all the agency fees and then paid out to the other practices a fee for administering their respective local associations. If any firm crossed the demarcation lines, a share of the profits was due to the firm which would otherwise have been entitled to the business. There were provisions to cover work that was distinct from the activities of the BSOA. For example, where conflicts of interest arose in Admiralty actions, the firm which had a general retainer from the client took precedence over the firm merely hired for the work; where more than one firm was retained, the first firm instructed took precedence.

The staple of the firms' business was long-term retained work with the BSOA and the Shipping Federation. Relations between client and firm were informal, perhaps necessarily so. Just as Baxter, Rose and Norton had developed and maintained its railway business by, in a sense, developing the railway industry and growing with it, so too had the Botterell & Roche firms helped alter the shipping industry and allowed itself to grow with it. The Shipping Federation, which Roche had formed, paid an annual retaining fee to the London firm. By 1901, however, the Federation was beginning to balk at the level of the retaining fee in addition to the fees charged over and above. That year, the combined figure was £650; the Chairman at the Annual General Meeting of 26 April 1901 put it like this:

> You know how valuable our solicitors are to us and have been. I think though they have kept us out of a great deal of trouble they have never got us into any trouble … The bills have amounted to something like £300 besides, so that it has cost us about £650 a year. That has been going on for some years now but the firm finds that so much of its time is taken up that they are inadequately paid and therefore they think their retaining fee should be raised [to £600 per year]… I thought it was a little excessive and we discussed it in the Emergency Committee and talked it over thoroughly and we have come to the conclusion that if you will authorise the payment to them of a retaining fee of £500 a year, which they will be pleased to accept, we shall be doing fairly by these gentlemen.[24]

At the same meeting, the General Manager declared:

> … of course we receive every assistance from Messrs. Botterell and Roche. They practically keep open house for us and we are in and out all day long at all hours of the day asking their opinion on little points which we perhaps should not ask about if they were to be included in the bills. We get every attention and I think the Council should pay the increased fee proposed.[25]

And another member, giving a useful sense of the firm's standing at the turn of the century, endorsed this view:

> I do not think there is a firm in London or in the north which could do our special work, our peculiar work, better and very few so well. They have been with us so long that they are family words amongst us and I hope we shall never lose them.[26]

On 21 September 1903 Roche took his own life at Knock Wood, Crieff. He was fifty-one. *The Times* reported the death as suicide; but it was reported in his home town as 'heart failure' by the *Sunderland Daily Post*:

He had apparently been troubled with insomnia, for a letter received from him at the offices in West Sunnyside yesterday morning stated that he had had his first night's sleep, and was feeling much better. The officials at the office, when a representative of the "Daily Post" made enquiries this morning, were unable to state what time death took place yesterday, but it is believed to have occurred in the evening, for some business letters from Mr. Roche were received at the offices this morning, and these had only been posted last night. At the offices no word of the tragic event had been received direct from Strathearn House [Roche's home], the intimation having come through the deceased's Sunderland residence. The news created a sensation amongst the staff, who regarded the news as almost incredible. But unfortunately too true. As soon as the news was received flags at the Town Hall, Conservative and Liberal Clubs, and other public buildings, were hoisted at half-mast. Death is believed to be due to heart

DEATH OF COUN. ROCHE.

SUDDEN COLLAPSE AT CRIEFF.

It is with deep regret that we announce the death of Councillor Wilson Mills Roche, which has taken place at the Hydro. at Crieff, in Scotland. This sad news reached Sunderland this morning by a telegram sent to Mr Roche's office, stating that he had died suddenly last night. At the time this was received there was a letter in the office written by Councillor Roche yesterday at Crieff, in which he said he would be home in two or three days. He had been in Crieff about a week, having gone there for a rest, which he had doubtless well earned, as he was a busy man and did a great deal of travelling, particularly between London and Sunderland, in order to transact his business. For some time he had been undergoing a system for reducing his weight, and this proved effective. Indeed, his friends thought he was in excellent health, and the news of his death caused great consternation among them this morning.

Coun. Roche was born in 1852 in Liverpool. He was the son of John Roche, M.D., of Dublin, who practiced in Liverpool, and was one of the professors of the old school of medicine at Cork. Mr Roche's mother was a daughter of Colonel Gillmer, of Moira, in the North of Ireland, and the colonel was originally in the old East India Company, and went through the Indian Mutiny. Leaving the service of the company, he married and settled at Moira, in the North of Ireland, and was ultimately killed in an explosion on one of the first steam road cars that ever plied when on a journey between Paisley and Glasgow. Mr Roche was, it will be seen, of Irish nationality, though his mother was of Scotch extraction. He was educated at Woodbridge Grammar School and at Neuweid, in Germany, where by a curious coincidence he was a school-fellow of Capt. Arthur Ritson, who is now a member of the Town Council for the Thornhill Ward. After Neuweid he was at Bishop Stortford Grammar School. His intention then was to go into the Indian Civil Service Woods and Forests Department, and he passed the qualifying examinations, but the appointments were so few that he relinquished the idea and went in for law. He was articled with Mr Henry Blake Miller, the Town Clerk of Norwich. After completing his articles he was for several years with the well-known firm of Messrs Sharp, Parkers, Pritchard, and Sharp. Mr Pritchard was solicitor for the Association of Municipal Corpora-

THE LATE COUNCILLOR ROCHE.

Newspaper Report of Roche's death.

> failure. A few years ago Mr. Roche consulted London specialists, and
> he was ordered to make stringent changes in his diet.[27]

The Roche name lived on in various developments of Botterell &
Roche. Roche's son left the country and worked in shipping law in
Buenos Aires, where he became a representative for the British
Protection and Indemnity Clubs in South America.

From 1903, the London firm developed its City shipping business
while the Sunderland and Newcastle firms specialised in protection and
indemnity work in the North East. The firm maintained its prestige and
status in shipping circles by admitting Robert Temperley in 1904. He
was Henry Temperley's brothers, a Scholar of Queen's College,
Cambridge, a barrister of the Inner Temple and a member of the North-
Eastern Circuit. In 1895 he had published *The Merchant Shipping Act,
1894* with notes, cases, and a comparative survey of the current and
previous Acts. (This comprehensive book was expanded by Temperley
in 1907 and again in 1922 and 1932, reaching a seventh edition, *The
Merchant Shipping Acts* in 1976. It remains the standard reference work
in the field.) Robert Temperley was to be instrumental in establishing
during the late 1920s the Baltic & White Sea Conference based in
Copenhagen and dealing with charter-parties, the legal representation of
shipowners and an information service for shipowners. The Botterell &
Roche firms were legal advisers to the Conference.

J.J.D. Botterell became more prominent as a lawyer after Roche's
death. He saw the advantage of highly specialised professional activity
and devoted his energies to the London firm, which grew steadily over
the next thirty years. As shipping work declined in the North East
between the wars and international work concentrated in London,
Botterell's practice flourished. In 1903 he moved with his partners,
Henry Temperley and Arthur Simon, from Leadenhall Street to The
Baltic Exchange Chambers, 24 St Mary Axe, where Botterell & Roche
(London) remained until 1960.

This was a focus for shipping business in London, and through the City, for overseas business. Botterell became more active in the Shipping Federation, joining its Parliamentary Committee as a London representative in 1904 where – as Roche had before him – he sat alongside influential shipping men like Thomas Miller and William Milburn from London, W.H. Raeburn from Scotland, and John and William Corry from Ireland.

J.J.D. Botterell kept a house in London, at 24 Palace Court. In 1896 he bought Colne Park, built in 1775 in the parish of Colne Engaine, Essex, where he lived with his wife, Louise Amelia Webb. He was a stout supporter of the local church and school, just like the Rose family in Penn. In 1902 he found a fragment of statuary in the grounds which is now part of the Elgin Marbles;[28] it had arrived there through the miscarried cargo of a sea captain and friend of a local man, and thence into the possession of Thomas Astle, a palaeographer and antiquarian, and original owner of Colne Park.[29]

During this period, the firm benefited as J.J.D. Botterell's legal career flourished with the Admiralty work of the 1900s and the 'Prize Cases' that resulted from ships taken in action during the First World War. Four new partners joined the London firm between 1907 and 1913, raising the partnership to six. J.J.D. Botterell's elder son, Percy Dumville Botterell (1880–1952) became a partner in 1907 and succeeded his father as senior partner in 1923. He was educated at Harrow and Cambridge, and was originally a barrister. He served as Commercial Attaché at The Hague during the First World War. He was awarded the OBE in 1918 and the CBE in 1920. He had houses in both Hampstead and Hampshire, and was a member of the Garrick Club. His wife, May, led a bohemian life as the model of the Irish post-Impressionist artist, William Leech, whom she married in 1953 after Percy Botterell's death. 'The Sunshade', one of many of Leech's portraits of her, now hangs in the Dublin National Gallery.[30]

J.J.D. Botterell's younger son, John, joined the firm in 1912. He

Percy Dumville Botterell.

became senior partner in 1945 when his brother retired. The year 1913 brought into the firm James Ellis Hammond Sinclair and Henry Millican Cleminson (who took on most of the Shipping Federation work and who was Secretary to the Shipowners' Parliamentary Committee of the Federation from 1918 to 1941). The firm acted in a number of cases at the Prize Court, dealing with seizure and requisitioning of ships and cargo, particularly for Scandinavian shipowners. New business in charter-party, construction, demurrage, freight and marine insurance followed. The firm also prospered from the 1917 Finance Act provisions concerning Excess Profits Duty (a tax on war time profits), which caused many traders to seek legal advice over what could be considered wartime or peacetime profits. After the First World War and its aftermath had expanded the firm's practice, the great depression of the 1920s had the reverse effect. Cutbacks in shipbuilding and shipping activity on the Tyne made the London office of the firm relatively more prominent. The *Law Journal* noted in 1923: 'The firm is engaged mostly in Admiralty, marine insurance, and commercial work, and during the War had an extensive practice in the Prize Court.'[31]

At the age of 76, J.J.D. Botterell, the last of the firm's founders, died at his desk on 11 May 1923.[32] He had seen the shift of power in the firm from Sunderland, where business was steady, to London where business was expanding. He had been a member of the Council of the

Law Society since 1909, and was President of the Law Society in 1921–2. He was also High Sheriff of Essex and a JP. The *Law Society's Gazette* recalls:

John Dumville Botterell.

> Mr. Botterell had reached what even in these days is a ripe old age, having been born early in 1847, and although he was exceptionally young and vigorous in mind, his life's work had practically been accomplished before he was called away, and his mark indelibly left on the pages of good and faithful service to his profession …
>
> Those who came into contact with him in professional life will readily testify to his desire on all occasions to arrive at a fair result, if possible, by the path of conciliation and compromise, rather than by the stony and it must be confessed very uncertain road of litigation.[33]

In the same year, Cleminson left the firm, and Clifford James Temperley (the son of Henry Temperley) became a partner in the London firm, leaving at the end of the partnership agreement in 1928. Work appears to have been steady but not spectacular, and the remaining partners stayed together throughout the 1920s. When the second five-year agreement (1928) between the two Botterells (Percy and John) and Sinclair expired in 1933, Sinclair decided to set up on his own.

The London firm retained the name of Botterell & Roche, which it kept until it merged with Norton, Rose & Co. to form Norton, Rose, Botterell & Roche in 1960. Sinclair took with him the firms' Scandinavian shipping work, Nordisk, and its regional network in the UK for the BSOA.[34] He kept Roche's name in the firm. On 1 January 1934 he established Sinclair, Roche & Temperley with Clifford James Temperley. Shipping work continued steadily during the Second World War, with the Newcastle firm representing, through Robert Temperley and the Treasury Solicitor, the armed services in cases involving civilian loss or injury. Meanwhile, Botterell & Roche in Sunderland and Newcastle continued to act for the BSOA and the British Steamship Short Trades Association. At this point, the history of Botterell & Roche in Newcastle-upon-Tyne and in Sunderland ceases to be germane to the history of the London firm which was to amalgamate with Norton, Rose & Co.

In 1935, Giles Dumville Botterell, the last of the family partners, was articled to his father, John Botterell, in London. He had toured Australia and New Zealand, California and British Columbia in the mid-1930s, but decided to settle in London and join the firm. He was enrolled as a solicitor on 2 October 1939. During the war he served in the East Surrey Regiment in North Africa, Sicily, Italy and Austria, where he was taught to ski in order to patrol the Yugoslavian border. He was mentioned in despatches and awarded an MBE (Military).[35] In 1945 he rejoined the firm as a specialist in Admiralty Law, becoming a partner in 1948.

As Botterell & Roche (London) emerged from the Second World War, it could reflect on its long and honourable involvement with British – and increasingly, international – shipping. It had helped to create a central pillar of the shipping industry in the BSOA; it had formed the British Shipping Federation, and had acted for numerous protection and indemnity clubs, as well as for individual shipping clients.

Norton, Rose & Co. 1894–1944

Norton Rose's second century started well. The City practice was growing rapidly with loans and flotations across a range of commerce and industry. In common with other professional practices, the office was open six days each week and the partners' day started at 10 a.m. Subsidiary partners were able to take five weeks' holiday a year, while principal partners could arrange whatever they felt appropriate. Partners were able to retire at 57.

There were regular monthly partnership meetings, and from the minute books which survive in the firm's archives for the first half of this century, it seems the partnership ran smoothly and the staff numbers remained constant at between forty and fifty, the same as in the 1890s.[36]

The firm's capital in 1894[37] amounted to £7,200 (divided between the partners);[38] subsidiary partners received £350 a year as well as a share in the profits specified by the principals. The amount taken out of

Frederick Rose.

profits was £4,800, divided between the partners according to their respective shares. An articled clerk would have to pay the firm £300 to be taken on.[39]

In 1894 Frederick Rose (now a baronet) retired to concentrate on the London and Brighton railway as its solicitor, a post he passed on to his son, Philip Vivian Rose, in 1908. A new partner was sought. There was a clutch of partnership deeds of note, detailing provisions of enormous length and complexity with the aim of perpetuating the

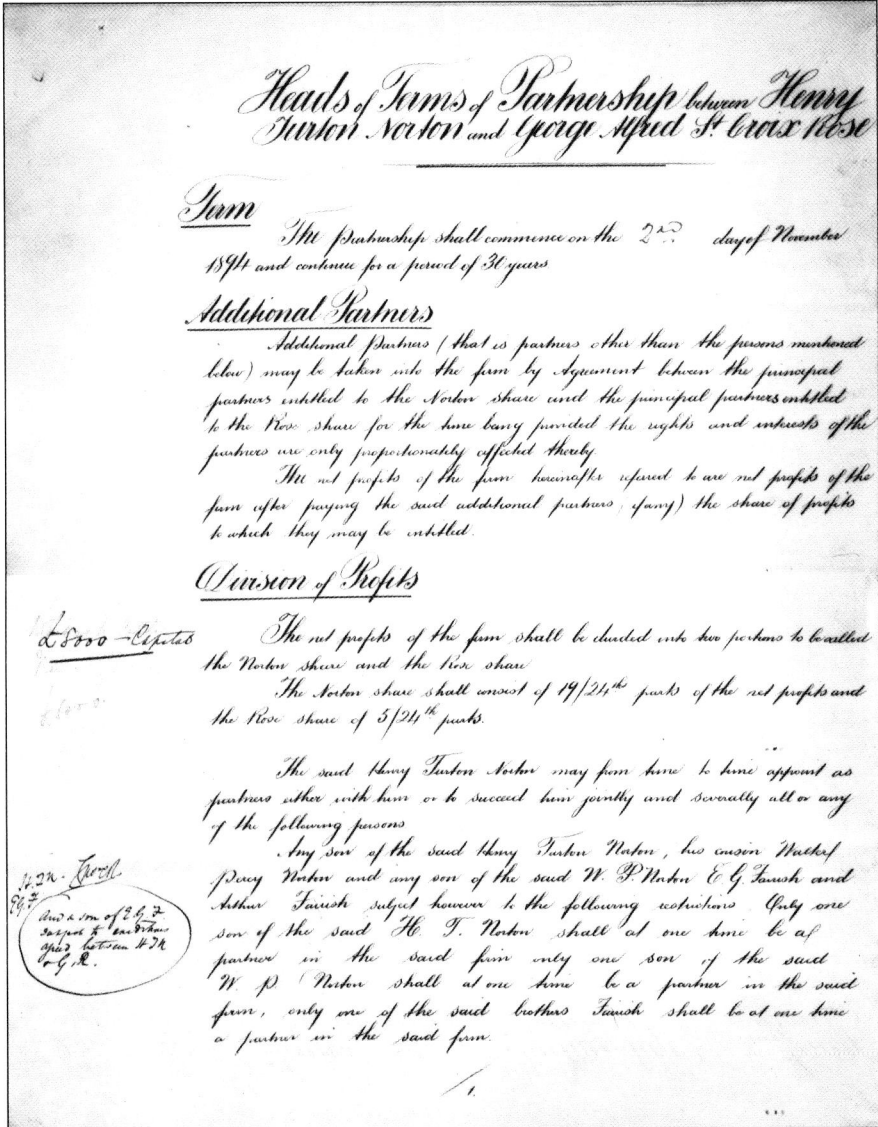

*The Division of Profits between the Rose family and the Norton family
in 1894.*

family interests of the Nortons and the Roses.[40] In effect, the firm was
divided into two parts, named in the agreements as 'the Rose share'
and 'the Norton share'.

The deeds show how far the culture of originally family-based firms changed over the next fifty years. The various deeds assume the partners' right to have their children admitted as articled clerks. The deeds provide for the possibility of non-familial 'additional' partners, but their interests would have to be carved out of the existing family shares, and they would never become principal partners with a voice in the appointment of new partners.

The firm divided again, ironically as a result of City business won by Philip Rose. He had been approached by an old friend, Henry Parkinson Sharp, who ran the firm of W. & H.P. Sharp, and who wished to retire. Sharp simply asked Philip Rose to take over his clients – at least, those who were willing. Asking nothing for the connection or business, he duly passed on the work to the firm. On the strength of Sharp's business, the firm opened a new office at 24 Coleman Street (which runs parallel to Moorgate off Gresham Street).

At the time, Frederick Rose was in America on business, so Henry Turton Norton oversaw the new office. As a result, Frederick Rose had the time and scope to follow John Brewer (who had died in 1881) as adviser to the important London, Brighton and South Coast Railway. This left Norton a monopoly of the profitable business; he was able to dictate terms to Philip Rose's sons, Frederick and George 'Ste Croix', in the draft partnership agreement of 2 November 1894. It reads:

> *Division of Profits*
>
> The net profits of the firm shall be divided into two portions to be called the Norton share and the Rose share.
>
> The Norton share shall consist of 19/24th parts of the net profits and the Rose share of 5/24th parts.

George 'Ste Croix', a junior partner of seventeen years, must have had particularly pressing reasons to agree to Norton's terms which disadvantaged him so actively. His elder brother thought them unacceptable. He recalls:

Victoria Street in 1854.

[Norton] offered such terms of partnership as meant the retention to himself of the whole of the profits resulting from the City Office:[41] but I venture to think that equity and fair dealing should have led him to look at the subject from a very different standpoint ... I feel sure that if my father had lived until 1894 he would have been deeply pained at what took place, and would have bitterly regretted having advised, when the City office was opened in 1874, that Mr H.T. Norton should be selected to take charge of it.[42]

The shape of the firm in 1894 differed considerably from its beginning in 1794. It had expanded through its involvement in some of the century's most exciting developments: railways, investment trusts, new company laws, limited liability, the Tichborne Case. Now called Norton, Rose, Norton & Co., it was an established City practice with four partners and a balance of business between commercial and private clients.

Henry Turton Norton was particularly shrewd in establishing for himself and for his executors the right to buy out partners not only in the Norton share of the firm but in the Rose share too. In essence, these agreements were designed in the families' interest; but they must have had the effect of deterring lawyers who were not members of the two families. Nor could it have been attractive to the incumbent partners that the partnership agreements of 1894 had instituted a system whereby

Henry Turton Norton.

retired partners could maintain a share of the profits. This meant that anything up to half the Norton share continued to go to Henry Elland Norton and, in due course, his son, Henry Turton Norton, even after they had retired; on their deaths, it went to their estates. The situation was partially eased in 1906 on the death of Henry Turton Norton. It is clear that since the death of Sir Philip Rose, the Nortons had strengthened their hold on the firm at the expense of the Rose share.

While the firm organised itself internally, it was gathering its City and commercial business steadily in the 1890s. New business came through railways, investment trusts, foreign bonds and private client work. By 1895, *Leading Men of London* commented on Henry Elland Norton:

> Messrs. Norton, Rose, Norton & Co have, as is well known, one of the largest professional practices in London, and the City office under Mr Norton's conduct has become, since the year 1873, one of the first rank.

The Liberty flotation.

Work of high quality, such as the flotation of the twenty-year-old Liberty & Co. Ltd in December 1894 kept the firm's City business thriving: for the Liberty flotation, the bankers were the Bank of England and the auditors Deloitte, Dever, Griffiths & Co. of 4 Lothbury.

In the late 1880s and 1890s, the work which brought the firm to the public's notice was its involvement in the complex and complicated matter that became known as the first Baring Crisis. This involved the Buenos Aires trading house, S.B. Hale & Co. (Hales), the Buenos Aires Water Supply and Drainage Co. Ltd, and the English merchant bank, Barings. It is already well documented.[43] Barings tended to specialise in American, Canadian and Argentinian securities, both government and private works. After a dozen or so successful issues for railway companies in the United States and Canada, Barings had turned its attention to Argentina which, in the 1880s, was recovering from recession and attracting new foreign investment. By 1888 Barings had granted extensive credit to Hales and had become inextricably tangled with Hales' affairs.[44]

In 1888, the Argentine government granted Hales the concession to extend and run the Buenos Aires Sanitary Works, then being built. For a consideration of $21m payable by three annual instalments of $7m, Hales obtained a lease of the water works and took responsibility for managing the building contracts which the Government had already entered into. The engineering work had been contracted out to the London firm of Bateman, Parsons and Bateman. On 13 November 1888, Hales formed The Buenos Aires Water Supply and Drainage Co. Ltd (BAWSDC) under English company law, with a nominal share capital of £5m. Hales then sold to BAWSDC the benefit of the lease, but remained responsible for the construction of the works. In effect, Hales would run the works, fulfil the management and construction contracts and make the three payments to the Argentine Government in consideration of the issue and allotment to them by BAWSDC of £5m of debentures and all BAWSDC's share capital.

Barings agreed to buy all the debentures with the intention of selling them in London. The 200,000 £10 ordinary shares were to be offered for sale by Hales and Barings on joint account. But the response was disappointing, and by mid-1891 only 15,400 of the shares were in public hands.[45] Barings was effectively left as the largest equity shareholder in the company. Barings did not dare offer the BAWSDC debentures to an unresponsive public. They took them up to secure the large payments and advances made to Hales to meet the cost of the waterworks and the three $7m instalments to the Argentine Government. These commitments put enormous strain on Barings. (A report of 1894 by Price Waterhouse detailing the claims of creditors against Hales shows over £4m owed to Barings; well over half of this was related to claims in respect of the waterworks.) Barings underestimated the scale and costs of the venture. John Baring wrote to his father in 1890:

> I must confess to be surprised to see what a big thing this waterworks business is; you have no idea, I am sure, of the scale it is on. The Grand Service Reservoir is a huge place, four storeys high.[46]

Water rates proved hard to collect; the pumps and filter beds in the works were inadequate. Between October 1888 and July 1890, Hales made a series of agreements with the engineers; an extension to the works was agreed in April 1890. There were disputes over the syphon system and over the condition of the pumping engines. In October 1891 the engineers threatened to withdraw from the works unless arrears in payment were met.

Barings suffered from other unsuccessful Latin American issues in banks, railways and merchant houses. It had also advanced £500,000 to Hales for the benefit of the Curamalan Land Co. in Argentina. Financial crisis loomed in Argentina during the mid-1890s; and the bank was further pressed by withdrawals of large sums on deposit from the Russian Government. Barings was forced to take loans from Glyn, Mills and Martin & Co. and to sell large batches of securities in order to stay liquid.

In November 1890 another payment fell due on the waterworks account. Barings could not pay. Humiliation and liquidation loomed. The Bank of England was asked to step in. A rescue operation was mounted in the form of a loan from the Bank of England to take care of Barings' immediate liquidity problems. This was supported by a fund raised from other city banks and institutions to:

> guarantee the advances which the Bank of England have agreed to make to Messrs. Baring Brothers & Co. to enable them to discharge at maturity their liabilities on the night of 15th November 1890 ... to make good any loss which might appear on the final liquidation.[47]

The guarantee fund amounted to over £17m. The Bank of England loan at its maximum reached £7,526,600. A new company with limited liability, Baring Brothers & Co. Ltd, was formed with £1m share capital subscribed by family and friends; this company took over the business of the old banking house.

After BAWSDC collapsed in 1890, an Argentine Government representative, Dr Victorino de la Plaza, came to London to negotiate new arrangements, which were finally settled in 1891. The original lease of the waterworks was rescinded on condition that BAWSDC completed the original works and handed over the extension works in consideration of the payment of $25,500,000 to be satisfied by Argentine Government bonds. In turn, Hales agreed to cancel its contracts with the BAWSDC and to fulfil BAWSDC's obligation to complete the original works, in return for which Hales would transfer to it some of the Government bonds, eventually issued in 1893.

When BAWSDC was wound up, Barings received £2,500,000 of the Argentine Government bonds (under an agreed arrangement with the creditors) as satisfaction of £2,500,000 BAWSDC debentures held by them. When they received these bonds, Barings passed most of them on to the Bank of England as security for the money they had advanced. Litigation followed in 1894. Barings (represented by Norton, Rose, Norton & Co. and Markby, Stewart and Co.) and the Bank of England (represented by Freshfield & Williams) defended themselves against a suit from one (and by implication all) of the syndicate which was to have underwritten the public issue of the BAWSDC, Charles Morrison (represented by Ashurst, Morris, Crisp & Co.).

Since the public offer had never been made, the syndicate members instead of making underwriting arrangements, had agreed to make loans to Barings on the security of the debentures. The loans were repayable in 1900, or when the debentures were sold. Mr Justice Kekewich held that this agreement and the security under it had been destroyed; but Morrison and the other syndicate members were entitled under the general law to a charge over the government bonds. Barings considered an appeal, but settled out of court in February 1895. Henry Turton Norton dealt closely with Francis Baring in relation to the complex litigation.[48]

Another company, the Baring Estate Co. Ltd, had been formed in 1894 for the purpose of paying off the debts of the old business; to this company were transferred the assets of the old partnership, including the debts due from Hales and the Curamalan Land Co. There was a £1.5m debenture issue by the Baring Estate Co. Ltd, oversubscribed by £2.5m,[49] the proceeds of which went to the Bank of England in final settlement of the loan.[50]

Norton, Rose, Norton & Co. were in fact involved at all stages as solicitors to S.B. Hale & Co. and to C.H. Sanford (a New York entrepreneur and one of its partners). The legal work involved the complex disputes between Hales and the engineers and suppliers on the waterworks project, the negotiations between BAWSDC and the Argentine Government, and the liquidation of BAWSDC. Norton, Rose, Norton & Co. subsequently acted for Barings in partnership matters and for Baring Brothers & Co. Ltd on a £2m Argentine Government loan (1899), the reconstruction of the Curamalan Land Company (1897) and the Western Railway of Santa Fe (1898), and on a proposed share issue by the South Mahratta Branch Railways Co. (1904).

Barings and Hales maintained a joint account with Norton, Rose, Norton & Co. and paid the firm £857 in 1893 and £875 in 1894. The firm dealt with the creditors of S.B. Hale & Co. and coped with flurries of encoded telegrams from Buenos Aires. Many City banks, accountants and lawyers were involved throughout the 1890s in the protracted negotiations to extricate Barings from the mess of S.B. Hale: C.J. Hambro & Son, Brown Shipley & Co., Price Waterhouse & Co., investment trusts, bondholders' associations and law firms. From the evidence in the correspondence files at Barings' archives, Henry Turton

Norton showed himself to be a lawyer capable of dealing with a variety of demanding situations. The firm's reorganisation of the complex affairs of S.B. Hale went beyond legal advice to include management and strategic advice.

This period of international activity was also one of domestic reflection. Henry Turton Norton lived at 103 Lancaster Gate, London, and at an Elizabethan manor house, Kentwell Hall, Long Melford, Suffolk (rented from the Starkie Bence family).[51] He was a JP, a benefactor of his church in Long Melford – where

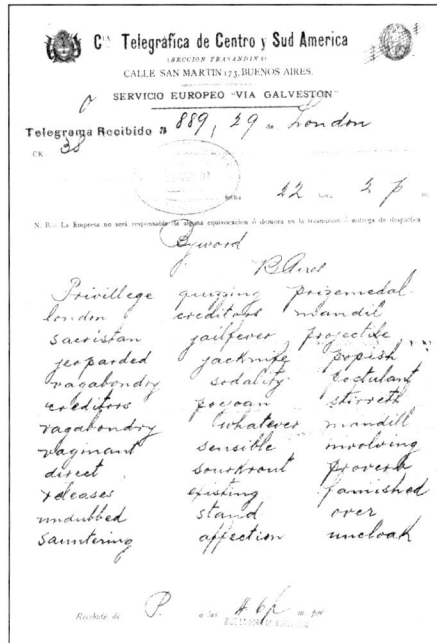

An encoded telegram.

he attended services and often read the lesson – and he made Kentwell Hall the meet for the local pack of hounds. The Norton family exemplified the increasing social acceptability of the legal profession. Henry Turton Norton was a Scholar of St John's College, Cambridge, and his son, Harry was a Scholar and Fellow of Trinity College, Cambridge. Through the university connection, a number of interesting and prominent Edwardians passed through Kentwell. One of them was Harry's friend, John Maynard Keynes, the economist, remembered here by Louisa Norton, Henry Turton's sister:

> … he looked to me so funny – in both senses of the word, both comical and peculiar. To begin with, I thought him … like a poodle, with puffs of black hair on either side of his forehead between very large ears; a large black moustache, and the brightest black eyes imaginable … His clothes seemed peculiar, for whereas the other young men wore coloured blazers and flannel trousers, he always

Kentwell Hall, Long Melford, Suffolk.

appeared, as for formal occasions, in a stiff dark suit ... I now believe that he saw through me and thought me every bit as funny as I thought him.[52]

The Norton family was also on close terms with Lytton Strachey, who lived at 69 Lancaster Gate. Strachey dedicated his book, *Eminent Victorians*, to Harry Norton. Through Strachey, the Nortons came to know Duncan Grant and the Bloomsbury set. The Nortons were doing what Sir Philip Rose had done fifty years earlier: using the firm's success to allow its partners to achieve and maintain a high social profile. Henry Turton Norton and his wife Laura Frances[53] travelled throughout Mediterranean Europe, sometimes with the Cassel family (the great financiers, Sir Ernest Joseph Cassel and Sir Felix Cassel), for whom the firm – and in particular Henry Turton and Walter Percy Norton – acted.[54]

As lawyers, the family had advanced, socially and economically, from its position in the 1840s and 1850s. The solicitor was becoming, in social terms, what the barrister had been five decades earlier.[55] G.W.E. Russell, a keen observer of manners and social trends throughout the century comments on the situation sixty years before, in the 1850s:

> In vain did the solicitor build himself a French chateau a hundred yards off the high road and give tennis parties in the dusty garden. The baronets and their belongings held aloof and the clergy though they attended the parties apologised to their squires for doing so.

The view in the mid-century, expressed here by Anthony Trollope in *Miss Mackenzie*, was still current at the turn:

> Is it not remarkable that the common repute which we all give to attorneys in general is exactly the opposite to that which every man gives to his own attorney in particular? Whom does anybody trust so implicitly as he trust his own attorney? and yet is it not the case that the body of attorneys is supposed to be the most roguish body in existence?[56]

By the 1880s, lawyers of Henry Turton Norton's generation were being drawn from the public schools and the universities. Rose's concern about his baronetcy elevating his son above the profession started to seem outmoded. Why starve at the bar when there was handsome work as a solicitor?[57] The problem and anxiety about the status of the profession and the social status of its practitioners had disappeared by the turn of the century.[58]

In 1899 Henry Elland Norton, the last of the great nineteenth-century partners in the firm, died. Both his sons had followed him into the law: Henry Turton was a solicitor and the other, Frederick Charles, a barrister. He left them each the then considerable sum of £6,000 from an estate worth £134,000.[59] At the turn of the twentieth century, the Norton family members were prime examples of confident and self-confident professionals. In a letter to Francis Baring, Henry Turton Norton found a tone of professional propriety during a litigation involving another well-known London firm. He had written to these solicitors, he reports to Baring:

> ... objecting to the style of their letter and saying that unless they withdrew it we could not carry on any further correspondence with them ... Their reply to this was still more violent abuse which I have not answered or taken notice of.
>
> The abuse annoyed me a good deal and I do not think [these solicitors'] two letters ought to have been written and am from a professional point of view ashamed of them.[60]

Henry Turton Norton was gaining respect in the profession. He had been a member of the City Law Club since 1889, joining or joined by contemporaries like Sir Thomas Paine, Edwin Freshfield and Thomas Bischoff. In June 1902 he addressed the Solicitors' Benevolent Association as Chairman. The report in *The Solicitors' Journal* outlines some of his concerns which bear on his own success as a lawyer:

> He [H.T. Norton] could imagine no system of official remuneration more calculated to create difficulties in the way of any man striving to do his duty than the preposterous system which was the official system of solicitors' remuneration. At every turn the solicitor's interest was eternally opposed to his duty, and that could not be a satisfactory system. Whilst, as everyone knew, there was any amount of personal sympathy between the bench and the solicitors, he thought it would be better for the profession if there was a more practical knowledge on the part of the bench of the troubles and difficulties, and above all the expense, of conducting a solicitor's business.[61]

He became a member of the Carlton Club in 1905. Henry Turton Norton enjoyed the social status which his success brought him. Together with Sir Francis Jeune, an old friend of the firm who had acted for the Claimant in the Tichborne Case, he attended the Queen's levée on 6 March 1899.[62] On 9 June 1906, while still at the height of his powers, he visited his son, Harry, at Cambridge, and fell two floors from the balcony staircase at 17 St John's Street. He fractured his skull but did not die immediately. His wife, Frances, writes in her diary:

> I do not know whether I shall be able to write this, but I shall try ... I found him lying at the foot of the stairs, no wound or bruise visible – paralysed down one side – barely able to speak – hardly conscious – still with the hand he could move he lifted mine to his lips & just murmured my head, my head. He never really spoke again, but for a long time he seemed to know my hand in his & three times in the course of the afternoon he tried to kiss it. No one knew what or how it had happened – the doctors came and went all through that afternoon – he seemed to sink deeper & deeper into unconsciousness.[63]

Norton was placed on a stretcher and moved to the nursing home nearby. He grasped his wife with his right hand – his last conscious action. The doctors decided to operate to remove the pressure on the brain. They were unsuccessful:

> Against all hope I hoped that he might open his eyes on me once more. But this was not to be. He was breathing slowly and noisily but gave no sign of consciousness or moved in the least. Gradually the breathing stopped & he was gone without a struggle or sigh – my arm was under his head – his hand in mine . he seemed just to cease.[64]

The firm felt the loss, and lost momentum after Norton died. He had run the firm without delegation, dealing directly with his City clients; and like Sir Philip Rose before him, he had achieved social and professional status.[65] *The Times* noted three days after his death:

> Mr Henry Turton Norton, whose death, the result of a deplorable accident, took place on Saturday evening, was something more than an eminent City solicitor. Besides being the senior partner

in an important firm, which brought him into contact, more or less intimate, with men and things, he was the trusted adviser in matters of law of several leading men of business, by whom he will be greatly missed. Experience and ability such as Mr. Norton displayed do not come into existence in a day; and the place of a City solicitor who possessed such qualities cannot be easily filled, at any rate as regards his older clients, with whose affairs he had been thoroughly familiar for many years, and with whom he was in relations of friendship.[66]

His death was a second setback to the firm. Edward G. Farish, a partner since 1894, had died in March. In his place, the former managing clerk, Robert Henry Eggar (admitted in 1885) joined the partnership. This left the firm with four partners: Eggar, George 'Ste Croix' Rose, who had become a partner in 1877; Walter Percy Norton, cousin of Henry Turton Norton, who had become a partner in 1892; and the Hon. Walter Bernard Lewis Barrington, who had become a partner in 1905. The firm left its offices at 10 Victoria Street where it had been since 1889, and conducted its business solely from the offices at 57½ Old Broad Street which had been the City branch of the firm since 1888. George 'Ste Croix' Rose became senior partner, and in 1908 his son, Harcourt George 'Ste Croix', joined the partnership. The firm maintained exactly this constitution until 1919.

Few records exist to chart the firm's work during this period,[67] so the status and progress of the firm and its partners are hard to quantify. However, the fact that the two new partners in 1919, Arthur Alexander MacNab (admitted 1892) and Lewis Henry Grundy (admitted 1891), were both former managing clerks showed the limitations placed on the firm by the series of partnership agreements between 1894 and 1906. Talented outsiders may not have been attracted to the firm, and the partnership may have suffered from an over-protectionist and inward-looking approach. Harcourt Ste Croix Rose left the firm after the First World War. Bernard Barrington, a member of the Law Society

Council from 1911 to 1914, left to join the merchant bank Helbert, Wagg at the invitation of Alfred Wagg in December 1919. Barrington cut a colourful figure:

> There was a shortage of money in the Barrington family when Bernie was a child and although living in the stately family home at Shrivenham, he and his brothers and sisters were mainly fed on guinea fowl and moorhens from the lake. The same shortage prevented the tall, elegant Charterhouse cricket captain from going to a university and taking his due place in first class cricket. Instead, he went straight into a lawyer's office. Here he acquired wisdom as well as professional skill, a wisdom which, combined with a gift for conciliation, was invaluable to his partners when he abandoned the law for investment banking … he was an authority on game birds. And like most great English killers of birds he was a merciful man who cherished the victims he slew so cleanly.[68]

Lionel Fraser, one of Barrington's friends and colleagues at Helbert, Wagg, praised Barrington's 'absolute integrity' in everything and noted that he was a 'distinguished solicitor'.[69] Barrington became president of the Legal & General Assurance Society and was a director of both the Gresham Life Assurance Society and the Gresham Fire and Accident Insurance Society Ltd.

In 1924, Walter Percy's son, Charles, became a partner in the firm. He was to be one of the two architects of the firm's expansion over the next fifty years, and he was the last of the Norton family to hold a partnership in the firm. Born in Kensington on 24 May 1896, he was educated at Winchester and then served in the 9th Battalion of the Royal Sussex Regiment. He was as a Lieutenant at the Battle of Loos (September 1915, for which he was awarded the Military Cross), then at Ypres through the hard winter of 1915–16, and finally at the Somme during the terrible battle of July 1916. He fell ill, and was shipped to Oxford (Somerville College) to recuperate from 'trench fever'. He subsequently became an army instructor at Newmarket, where there was bustling social activity around racing, horses and training.

Charles Norton, demobilised in February 1919, joined the firm in March, and was briefly articled to Barrington and subsequently Walter Percy Norton. He qualified as a solicitor in May 1921, and received a salary of £350 initially, rising to £500 as a partner (£750 with his 4 per cent share in the firm's profits). He recalled in his memoirs:

> The offices and equipment were very old fashioned. The General Office was presided over by Mr. Benfield who always wore a tail coat and was at the office from 8.30 a. m. until very often 8 in the evening. Letters were partly written in long hand and partly typewritten and every outgoing letter was "press copied". The press copy machine was similar to a large Company sealing press on a substantial stand. Letters were inserted with a flimsy sheet and damp flannel squares between the top and bottom press. When sufficient were inserted the press was closed and clamped down. A few minutes later the clamp was undone. The letters and flimsy sheets which now bore a reproduction of the letters then had to be dried. If the flannel squares were too damp the letters and flimsies were smeared. In the case of two or more pages to a letter the flimsies were held together by a pink wafer. It can well be imagined the time it took to get the post away each night. All stamps were affixed to envelopes by hand.[70]

The firm remained stable throughout the First World War, the depression, the 1930s and until the end of the Second World War. Until 1929, the offices were at 57½ Old Broad Street (renumbered in 1924 as 111); the firm then moved to Stone House, 128 Bishopsgate, but returned in 1934 to Old Broad Street and remained at No. 116 until these offices were bombed in 1940. The partnership changed little in the 1930s, except for the absorption of Greenwell & Co. in the form of Edward Eyre Greenwell (the father of Charles Norton's first wife) and his partner, Frederick Johnson. They joined the existing partners

(Walter and Charles Norton, Grundy, Eggar and McNab) in 1935. Greenwell, then aged 75, took little active part in the firm; he died in 1938. Johnson became the conveyancing partner as the firm sought to diversify and build on the City business of clients like the stockbrokers of the same family, W. Greenwell & Co., the finance house, Arbuthnot Latham & Co., and the investment trust, Foreign & Colonial. Private work for City families like the Cassels was the staple diet for the firm in those years.

The partnership of the firm in 1932 was five, with one assistant solicitor and twenty-three clerks and secretaries.[71] Records were kept by a lone clerk, a Mr Sage, who lived with the old files in a house in Chelsea. That year, 1932, Maurice Bennett joined the firm as a member of the general office. He was one of the firm's most popular clerks, and subsequently became a partner in 1958. The day-to-day work of the firm was borne by two managing clerks, E.E. Hills in Trust and Probate, and Bernard Gould in Litigation, Company and Commercial business. Gould joined the firm in 1933 from Guedella & Co., and replaced Robert Henry Eggar's son, Humphrey, who had left to become the legal adviser to the Pilkington Glass Company. Gould was also popular in the firm, and became a partner in 1945.

Walter Norton did not retire until 1939, but by then he had delegated the running of the firm to his son, Charles Norton. Realising the need to expand, even in such difficult times, Charles Norton searched for new partners from outside the family. One such was Michael Armitage, who came to the firm in 1934 and was made a partner in 1936. David Matthew, was with the firm briefly from 1937 to 1939 as a salaried partner. In 1937 there were six partners in the firm, now called Norton, Rose, Greenwell & Co. A partnership was offered to Con Surtees in 1939. He was to change the shape of the firm and become senior partner of the firm thirty years later.

Surtees was born in 1907, the fifth child of a solicitor. He took a First in Law at Balliol, Oxford, and left for New York in 1929 for a banking job with Fairfax & Co. The depression made banking both difficult and risky, and so he returned to England as an articled clerk with Slaughter and May. When his own family firm – Surtees & Co. – was in difficulties, he left to help his father. It was from there that he joined Norton, Rose & Co. at the instigation of his old school friend from Rugby, Mike Armitage. In 1939, with the outbreak of war, Surtees joined the Ministry of Aircraft Production under Beaverbrook and then went to Washington to serve in the Civil Affairs department of the Combined Chiefs of Staff, concerned with economic planning in Eastern Europe. He was awarded the US Legion of Merit for his work.

Charles Norton and Fred Johnson were the only partners to remain with the firm during the war. Both were too old for active service. Charles Norton became Chief Air Raid Warden for the City of Westminster, and was on duty throughout the blitz. The offices were severely damaged by the mine that fell on the adjacent Dutch Church in Austin Friars in August 1940. The firm was immediately offered the vacated offices of Arbuthnot Latham in St Helen's Place. By 4 p.m. the following day, the firm was back in business: Charles Norton had prepared circular letters to the firm's clients for this eventuality, and the staff simply filled in the new address and mailed them. He writes of the period:

> There is not much to say of the Firm during the Second World War years. Short hours had to be worked during the Blitz period to enable staff to get home before the air-raid warning went in the evening, especially during the winter of 1940/41. Conditions were difficult and although the temporary loss of 116 Old Broad Street might have been much worse, the experiences of other firms were in many cases dreadful with total loss of offices and contents. It was by no means uncommon to hear from some other Solicitors who had lost all, asking whether we could lend them our papers so that they could carry on with the action or conveyancing transaction.[72]

In 1944, after 150 years, the firm was balanced between the debility of the war and the promise of the future. For the United Kingdom, as for other Western European countries, the end of the Second World War signalled the final passing of empire. After the task of domestic reconstruction, post-war opportunities overseas depended on the hard-won peace. The first century and a half of the firm's existence coincided with the zenith of British Empire; the Victorian achievement in the nineteenth century had kept armies in the field throughout the world, yet had brought about a domestic stability after 1848 during which work and wealth increased steadily. Now, after the ebb and flow of commerce throughout the nineteenth century, after the Great Depression of the twentieth, and after two World Wars, the firm entered the longest period of international peace in its history.

Notes

1. *A note of offices:* The complex record of the different offices of Botterell & Roche from 1861 has been traced through local trades' directories and the Law Lists of the relevant period. In brief, the offices are as follows:

   65 John Street, Sunderland (1861–79)

   1 Quality Court, London (1873–9)

   27 Quayside, Newcastle-upon-Tyne (1876–81)

   53 Chancery Lane, London (1879–82)

   41 West Sunnyside, Sunderland (1881–90)

   Wood Green, Middlesex (1868–73, 1883–5)

   101 Leadenhall Street, London (1882–1903)

   Sandhill, Newcastle-upon-Tyne (1885–94)

   26 St Thomas Street, Sunderland (1891–1902)

   King Street, Newcastle-upon-Tyne (1895–1906)

   Maritime Buildings, St Thomas' Street, Sunderland (1903–)

   24 St Mary Axe, London (1903–60)

   Milburn House, Newcastle-upon-Tyne (1907–)

2. Preface, 1868, pp.iii–iv.

3. Simpkin Marshall co-published the second edition in 1869.

4. 1883 Samuel Alcock; 1883 David Duncan Smith; 1885 Charles Thomas Stockdale.

5. For a brief history of demographic, municipal and industrial change in Sunderland in the nineteenth century, see B.R. Mitchell, *Abstract of British Historical Statistics*, Cambridge, 1962.

6. *Law Journal*, vol. 35 (1901), p.609.

7. 53 Chancery Lane, London; 27 Quayside, Newcastle-upon-Tyne; 41 West Sunnyside, Sunderland.

8. See: *Sunderland· River, Town and People, A History from the 1780s*, ed. Geoffrey Milburn and Stuart Miller, Sunderland, 1988; *The Great Age of Industry in the North East*, ed. W. Sturgess, Durham, 1981; *Lloyd's Register* for the period *100 Years of Shipbuilding – J.L. Thompson Ltd*, 1946; and *Industrial Resources of the Tyne, Wear and Tees*, ed. W. Armstrong et al., 1864.

9. The first, the Shipowners Mutual Protection Society, was formed in 1855. See: N.F. Ledwith "An Address Delivered to the Marine Discussion Group of the Insurance Institute of London" (19 October 1954) and *The History and Development of Protecting and Indemnity Clubs* (Insurance Institute of London Advanced Study Group 109, 8 January 1957).

10. The firms were linked by Roche to the practice of Vaughan & Hornby as Vaughan & Roche, Cardiff in 1899. Noel Davies, a partner in Botterell & Roche, 1945–60, was articled to Fred Vaughan of Vaughan & Roche in 1908 and after military service in the First World War became a partner of Vaughan & Roche in 1920. His son, Michael Davies, also served his articles with Vaughan & Roche.

11. See: W.G. Hall (M.Ed. Thesis, 1964; Sunderland Archives), *The Provision of Technical Education in Sunderland Before 1908*.

12. Sunderland Borough Council Minutes.

13. Messrs. Potts, Son, and Hennings was the firm which won the First Prize Design for the Municipal Technical College. John William White was the chosen builder.

14. *Sunderland Daily Echo*, 13 September 1901.

15. See: Minutes of the Meeting of the Council of the County Borough of Sunderland, 3 p.m., 14 October 1903 which record Roche's contribution to council and community.

16. See: J. Stanley Todd, *Memories*, private, 1947.

17. L.H. Powell, *The Shipping Federation, A History of the First Sixty Years, 1890–1950*, London, 1950, p.4.

18. Minutes, of the Conference of Shipowners' Associations, 19 August 1890. British Chamber of Shipping Archives.

19. Minutes, 19 September 1890. British Chamber of Shipping Archives.

20. Ibid.

21. Ibid.

22. Historical note by Mr Smart, Managing Clerk of Sinclair, Roche & Temperley (formerly of Botterell & Roche).

23. This was a consolidating measure enacted as the Merchant Shipping Act 1894. It remains the principal Merchant Shipping Act at the time of writing.

24. Minutes of Annual General Meeting of the Shipping Federation. Chamber of Shipping Archives.

25. Ibid.

26. Ibid.

27. *Sunderland Daily Post*, 22 September 1903.

28. Top left-hand corner, slab xxxvi, British Museum.

29. Local archives, Colne Engaine.

30. Leech's biography is by Denise Ferran, not published at time of writing. See also: the *Daily Telegraph*, 15 March 1988.

31. *The Law Journal*, 19 May 1923.

32. Memorial Service, St Andrew Undershaft, St Mary Axe, on 22 May 1923.

33. *The Law Society's Gazette*, June 1923.

34. Interview, Michael Davies, 1993.

35. His Colonel insisted Giles Botterell write the Citation himself.

36. Four partnership minute books cover the period from 1874 to 1938.

37. A valuation of office moveables, furniture and books was made in 1894 by the accountants, Vernon & Sons, of 29 Cockspur Street, Charing Cross, London: the valuation came to £576. Norton Rose archives.

38. George 'Ste Croix' Rose, £1,500; Henry Elland Norton, £5,700. Norton later received from Walter Norton and Edward Farish £750 and £1,050 for their shares.

39. It was not until the 1950s that the practice of charging articled clerks for their articles ceased, and City firms began to pay the clerks.

40. Deeds dated: 1 November 1894 between Henry Turton Norton and George 'Ste Croix' Rose (with additions on 6 May 1894 and signed by Norton, Rose and Edward Garthwaite Farish); an amended version of 1 November 1894 dated 10 May 1894 between Norton, Rose, Farish and Walter Percy Norton; three copies of the partnership deed of 1 November 1894.

41. In 1888 the firm's City office moved from 24 Coleman Street to 57½ Old Broad Street. The main office had been at 6 Victoria Street since 1857, but in 1889 it moved to 10 Victoria Street. After 1906 the firm based itself solely in Old Broad Street until 1929.

42. Rose Family Papers. Frederick Rose.

43. See: Philip Ziegler, *The Sixth Great Power: Barings, 1762–1929*, London, 1988, and John Orbell, *Baring Brothers & Co., Limited. A History to 1939*, London, 1985. I am grateful to James Leaver of Norton Rose for his help in unravelling the intricacies of the Baring crisis.

44. Argentinian and Latin American business came to Barings through Nicholas Bouwer, a Buenos Aires agent who joined the staff of the London house of S.B. Hale: firstly, by marrying a senior partner's daughter, secondly, by joining the house in 1884 and, thirdly, by becoming a partner in 1887.

45. 40,000 were with a finance house; the remaining 144,600 were left with Hales but in the name of Barings.

46. In Orbell, pp.57–8.

47. Ibid, p.59.

48. Barings Archives.

49. H.T. Norton applied for shares in the company.

50. The Estate Company's debentures were redeemed in 1897 and 1898 and the company wound up in 1899.

51. From 1650 to 1676 the house was owned by Sir Thomas D'Arcy (a lawyer), and from 1676 to 1683 by Sir Thomas Robinson (another lawyer); its present owner is also a lawyer.

52. Lucy Norton, 'Kentwell' in *Folio*, Spring 1985.

53. In 1884 Norton married Laura Frances, the eldest daughter of Nathaniel Lawrence, lawyer (of New Square, Lincoln's Inn), and granddaughter of the Right Hon. Sir James Bacon, Vice-Chancellor.

54. There are extensive records of Frances Norton's travels in the Eastern Mediterranean in the Norton Family Archives. The reference to Cassel is in Sir Charles Norton's book, *A Man of Many Parts*.

55. See: Thomson, *The Choice of a Profession*, London, 1857, pp.93ff.

56. In Kirk, *Portrait of a Profession*, p.211.

57. Harding, *Social History of English Law*, London, 1969, p.289.

58. Periodic slumps in status and self-confidence still occur. This from 1959, *Law Society Gazette*: 'The fall in the standing of our profession expressed in terms of social esteem and remuneration caused much heart-searching.' p.689.

59. Norton Family Papers.

60. Barings Archives. Henry Turton Norton to the Hon. Francis Baring, 11 October 1893.

61. 7 June 1902.

62. *Morning Post*, 7 March 1899, and the King's on 30 May 1904 (see *The Times*, 31 May 1904).

63. Norton Family Papers.

64. Ibid.

65. Norton left estate worth £161,000 gross.

66. City page, *The Times*, 12 June 1906.

67. Charles Norton writes in *A Man of Many Parts*: 'If reference is made to the time of the introduction of Joint Stock companies – say from 1870 to 1914, it will be found that in practically all Company issues the firm acted either for the Company or the Trustees for the Debenture Holders, Ashurst Morris & Co. being the other Solicitors concerned.' p.17.

68. *The Times*, 16 May 1959.

69. *The Times*, 28 May 1959, lists those who attended Barrington's memorial service, representing a range of city firms and institutions.

70. *A Man of Many Parts*, 1976, p.18.

71. Maurice Bennett, *Memoir*.

72. *A Man of Many Parts*, p.23.

1944–94

The Amalgamation and Beyond

IN THE TWENTIETH century, lawyers – like many professionals in the City, in universities, in medicine or in government – developed as managers. Just as changes in law and commerce affected the content of lawyers' work, so changes in their firms' structure affected the style in which it was conducted. These cultural and economic changes shaped the two firms which became Norton, Rose, Botterell & Roche in 1960. The single most important event in the history of Norton, Rose & Co.[1] and of Botterell & Roche was their establishment as an amalgamated practice.

The amalgamation was a benchmark union of two middle-sized firms, creating a larger, more powerful organisation. The union reflected the new ways in which lawyers were organising their working lives. For the profession in general, which doubled its membership of the Law Society in the ten years after the Second World War, practice was becoming more streamlined, more regulated and more specialised. The post-war years yielded new ideas, initiatives and economic development. And lawyers gained from the explosion of legislation.

For the two firms in particular, successful practice beyond post-war recovery meant larger and more specialised partnership; logic pointed to the amalgamation. Norton, Rose & Co. and Botterell & Roche had both arrived at this point by developing their business through the late 1940s and 1950s. It is easy to see the union of the two firms as in some senses inevitable, but each had distinct successes and requirements in the 1940s and 1950s. It is worth looking closely at the way the partnership of each firm evolved into the two groups of partners who formed the amalgamated firm on 1 May 1960.

Botterell & Roche

The London office of Botterell & Roche, based in St Mary Axe, had been independent of the regional offices since the turn of the century. Percy Dumville Botterell retired from the firm in 1945 through ill health and was replaced by 'Jimmy' Freeland. Freeland had verve and ambition. Having qualified as a Scottish lawyer in Glasgow, he moved to London in 1926.[2] He had gone to 24 St Mary Axe as an articled clerk in Constant & Constant, and was a partner there from 1934 to 1945. He tempered wild unpunctuality with accurate draftsmanship. He had a gift for inspiring confidence in clients regardless of the nature of their business; and he possessed great commercial acumen. This quality in particular attracted clients. His drive and connections helped to build the practice, and many leaders in shipping joined a clientele which also included industrial companies, investment trusts and banks. It was his departure in 1959 to pursue a career in shipping with the Naess Group that precipitated the fusion of the two firms in 1960.

'Jimmy' Freeland, John Botterell and Edward Pryce were joined by Noel Davies, who also became a partner of the firm in 1945. Davies, a marine lawyer, specialised in personal injury, charter-parties and bills of lading disputes. He was a gentle and gentlemanly figure. After serving in Palestine during the First World War, he had qualified as a solicitor in June 1920, and had been the senior partner in the firm of Vaughan & Roche,[3] Cardiff. During the Second World War he worked as a part-time consultant to the London firm, making the difficult journey from Cardiff for two days each week.

His son, Michael, was to play an important part in the amalgamation of the firm with Norton, Rose & Co. and in the shipping business of the combined practice. He was a fine lawyer: modest, immensely hard-working, gentle and courteous. His contemporaries later acknowledged him to be one of the City's leading commercial shipping lawyers. He qualified in 1946 after war service in North-West Europe and joined Botterell & Roche in 1947. The senior partner, John Botterell (brother of Percy Dumville Botterell), had spoken to him in 1946, emphasising the family nature of the firm, but suggesting that a partnership would be available in due course. Michael Davies became a partner in 1949. He worked as assistant to the ebullient Freeland, who concentrated on shipping company work, ship finance and purchase, mortgages and shipbuilding.

In 1948 John Botterell's son, Giles, who had been admitted before the war, joined the firm as a partner. He was the last of the Botterells and was to become senior partner of the amalgamated firm in 1976. He was, in the late 1940s, developing into a fierce Admiralty litigator (he became an Examiner in Admiralty in 1971) and a decisive lawyer. In 1959 Douglas Hamilton was the last partner to join Botterell & Roche before the amalgamation. He had joined the firm in 1955, and worked as Michael Davies's assistant solicitor in the firm's ship finance department, dealing with building contracts for new ships, sale and purchase agreements for existing ships and the raising of finance generally. Hamilton was to emerge as one of the most powerful lawyers in the amalgamated firm, as executive partner and then senior partner during a period of rapid change and swift growth.

The partners' work was supported by the managing clerks. The Botterell & Roche ledgers for the 1950s list cases of assault, indiscipline and stowing away which had to be prepared for court, as well as matters of personal injury claims which had to be filed with insurers. Much of the work on these cases was dealt with by the managing clerks. They were important figures, highly experienced but unadmitted; with the increasing prominence of assistant solicitors, however, their numbers declined.

Prominent among the managing clerks at Botterell & Roche was Geoff Lewsey, active in Admiralty work. Two of the other most industrious and effective managing clerks during this period and into the 1970s were Gerry Driscoll and John Mackie, specialising in personal injury work. Before them, men like Harry Spreckley, the senior managing clerk who dealt with the affairs of the British Shipping Federation, served the firm well for many years, becoming widely known in professional circles.

In the 1940s and 1950s, Botterell & Roche's business was mainly shipping work. One of the longest standing clients was the British Shipping Federation; work from this source provided a flow of varied cases which involved breaches of the Merchant Shipping Acts. It was through the Shipping Federation that the firm acted for shipowners. The firm had wide experience of marine work, from ship finance to high-volume, low-cost personal injury work involving individual seamen. Botterell & Roche also gathered, through Jimmy Freeland, a solid City clientele, including the Baltic Mercantile Shipping Exchange, for which the firm drew up new rules of membership; other continuing work from the Exchange members followed.

Norton, Rose & Co.

Meanwhile, at 116 Old Broad Street, Norton, Rose, Greenwell & Co.[4] was entering a period of change. It moved from a family-based enterprise to a more open meritocracy. Charles Norton, Fred Johnson, Mike Armitage, Con Surtees and Bernard Gould took the firm and its thirty-six staff into the post-war era.[5] As senior partner, Charles Norton ran the firm as a benevolent autocrat. Johnson specialised in property and retired in 1950. Armitage, a partner for over thirty years before he became a consultant in 1970, was a family practice lawyer; he accumulated a private clientele through giving clear simple advice, which the clients liked. Gould was the general litigation partner and a master of every subject. He had been the first

Charles Norton.

to join the post-war partnership, in 1945; he too became a consultant to the firm in 1970.

Con Surtees earned a reputation as an outstanding company and banking lawyer in the City. It was largely he who built up the firm's corporate finance practice in the 1960s. He became senior partner in 1970, one of the architects of the amalgamated firm's structure. His distinguished bearing and austere appearance at first intimidated those who did not know him; in reality, he was kind and generous, particularly to younger partners and assistants.

In 1946, Charles 'Chips' Jewell joined Norton, Rose, Greenwell & Co. as an articled clerk. He had served in North West Europe and in

Egypt during the Second World War. When he arrived at the firm, which had acted for his father, he was articled to Mike Armitage. There was little formal instruction for articled clerks. Jewell gained his practical training through listening to conversations or reading the 'white carbons' – a form of tuition not unusual in the profession at that time.[6] He qualified in 1949 and became a partner in 1951.

In the 1940s and 1950s, the firm had concentrated on building its commercial, company and litigation practice. The company work grew largely through Con Surtees' association with Hambros Bank. The energy of Bernard Gould was invaluable: he made an effective litigator, since he recognised the value of reaching a strong position to achieve a good settlement; this was a vision less obvious in the 1950s than in the 1970s and 1980s when high litigation costs became more prominent.[7]

While taking new initiatives, the firm kept its established strengths. It acted for twelve Argentine railway companies, the largest of which was the Central Argentine Railway; and together with Linklaters & Paines, Ashurst Morris Crisp, Bischoff & Co. and Barnett Tuson, handled a complex restructuring of the Argentine railways throughout 1947 as a prelude to the sale of the railways to the Argentine government.[8] Railway work followed in Brazil and Cuba with the nationalisation of the Leopoldina Railway Company and the United Railways of the Havana and Regla Warehouses (URHRW).

Maurice Bennett had joined the firm in the 1930s as an office boy. He had served in the Second World War in Scapa Flow, Malta, and – as commander of a landing craft – in Normandy. His war service brought out qualities of leadership and pragmatism. He became a managing clerk and then a full partner in 1960. He made an excellent, all-round company lawyer, knowledgeable and dependable, and one from whom seniors and juniors sought advice on abstruse points of law and practice. He rose to become senior partner of the amalgamated firm's Company Department. He was a man of general good humour, incisive wit and retiring modesty; and he was held in great affection by those who knew him.

The tangled matters of Cuba's railways had fallen to Bennett and Con Surtees. The URHRW was sold to the Cuban government in 1953, but action concerning the company's liquidation persisted for a further seven years. The House of Lords made a ruling over some outstanding loan notes called Equipment Trust Certificates which had become the responsibility of the new owners of the railway, the Government of Cuba. But when Fidel Castro took over from General Batista, the new Cuban government decided it was not responsible for liabilities incurred under the outgoing regime. The negotiations were described by Bennett as 'a very interesting but at times traumatic experience'.[9]

Outside the firm, Charles Norton followed his interests at the Law Society, where he had been on the Council since 1934; he was its President in 1955–6 (knighted in 1957). This marked a stage in a public career which brought him personal recognition. He had been elected to Westminster City Council in 1948, and was elected Mayor of Westminster in May 1957. As Mayor, Sir Charles performed the usual range of duties across the administrative, social and ceremonial spectrum. He still went to the firm's office most mornings, but with two or three official engagements during the day and into the evening, his mayoral duties occupied most of his time that year.[10] His managing clerk, George Dunn, shouldered the burden of Sir Charles' work during the necessary absences; this effectively enabled Sir Charles to pursue a public career without detriment to the firm's clients.

Sir Charles Norton was the public face of Norton, Rose & Co.; his work in local government and the Law Society brought the firm recognition and prestige in wider public circles. In the 1950s, the firm's City practice helped to balance its private property and trust work. By 1960, immediately prior to the amalgamation, Norton, Rose & Co. had eight partners (Sir Charles Norton, Mike Armitage, Con Surtees, Bernard Gould, Chips Jewell, John Norton, Maurice Bennett and

Christopher Dixon – the last partner from the constituent firms to hold a partnership in the amalgamated firm).[11] The firm specialised in personal finance, banking and general company work and in litigation. Norton, Rose & Co.'s clients were principally members of the peerage and landed gentry, banks and institutions. The firm's weakness lay in the composition of its commercial client base: it relied too much on too few clients.

The Amalgamation

In 1959, Botterell & Roche approached Norton, Rose & Co. So began the negotiations which led to the formation of the amalgamated firm. The amalgamation made sense for both firms. It was triggered by Botterell & Roche's need for a merger or other means of strengthening the partnership after the announcement of Freeland's imminent departure,[12] both unexpected and unwelcome for the Botterell & Roche partners. They thought their commercial shipping practice would be at risk unless the partnership expanded. The attractions to Norton, Rose & Co. of Botterell & Roche were the spread of its client base and the complementary nature of its work.[13]

Freeland's departure meant that Botterell & Roche required more partners to handle the commercial shipping business. Michael Davies in particular needed others to share the burden. Over a period before 1959 he had worked on transactions with partners from Norton, Rose & Co., namely Con Surtees and John Norton. Davies worked for shipowners raising loans from the Ship Mortgage Finance Company for which Norton, Rose & Co. acted. Botterell & Roche was faced with either advertising for experienced solicitors or amalgamating with another firm. The practices of the two firms were sufficiently dissimilar for it to be unlikely for there to be any loss of clients through conflicts of interest. Norton, Rose & Co. had strengths in corporate finance (under Con Surtees) and private client work (under Sir Charles Norton). In turn, Botterell & Roche brought an extensive shipping finance business which in due course evolved into aviation and asset financing on a wider scale.

The negotiations between the two firms were tough and protracted, but from 1 May 1960 when the two firms effected the union, they worked harmoniously under Sir Charles Norton. He was an experienced chairman, who ensured that the firm was managed in an ordered and systematic way. Weekly Tuesday partner lunches were introduced not only for social reasons but also as a forum at which partnership matters could be aired. The partnership remained hierarchical, and discussion muted. At the outset there were nine profit-sharing partners[14] and three salaried partners.[15]

The new firm was called Norton, Rose, Botterell & Roche and kept this name until 1987. The partners then decided to change it to Norton Rose in keeping with the more streamlined and shorter names of City firms of lawyers, accountants and bankers. This meant the loss of two famous names, Botterell & Roche, which had been part of the legal environment since 1879.

The partners and staff of the amalgamated practice united under one roof on Monday 3 May 1960. Their offices had been moved during the weekend from their respective premises at Old Broad Street and St Mary Axe to the newly completed Kempson House in Camomile Street, a late example of post-war austerity design. To those who had previously worked in semi-dark offices, the unobstructed views of London from the twelfth floor of what was, at that time, the highest office block in London, were extensive.

The firm took a long lease at competitive terms of the top three floors. There had been hesitation about the third of these; two floors were thought to provide too little room and three too much. The partners thought that they could sub-let unused space. The surplus space was used, initially, to provide recreational facilities for staff but soon the table-tennis tables had to be replaced by office furniture. The firm quickly outgrew all three floors and was searching for further accommodation. As the firm expanded at an ever-increasing pace from the mid-1960s through the 1970s and into the 1980s, accommodation – or the shortage of it – was its most pressing problem. Floor by floor the firm took over Kempson House.

In 1976, Norton, Rose, Botterell & Roche committed itself to a long lease of Bishops House in Bishopsgate, adjacent to Kempson House. Some partners were against the firm taking on Bishops House, thinking it reckless and likely to lead to bankruptcy. The optimists prevailed. The firm outgrew this space too. This time the firm expanded into two buildings (Stone House and Staple Hall) opposite Bishops House and Kempson House in Houndsditch. Those additions gave the firm the flexibility of a 'legal village' of four buildings closely situated.

Increases in partners and staff followed the amalgamation, slowly at first but accelerating during the late 1960s and the 1970s. The culture of the firm began to change as it became less the familial organisation of the early twentieth century and more a meritocratic institution. Commercial work became more prominent. The partners responded to and anticipated clients' commercial needs in being more outgoing and entrepreneurial than they had been before 1960. They worked longer hours to meet the demands of international work, and brought commercial judgment to augment the legal aspects of clients' business.

Increasing commercial activity in the 1960s was to be found in the creation and rapid development of the London markets in Eurodollars and Eurodollar Bonds. These markets were led by Hambros Bank, S.G. Warburg and N.M. Rothschild from 1963 onwards. Eurodollar Bond loans and facilities financed governments, utilities, capital projects and commercial working capital on an international scale. Hambros, one of the firm's major clients, was an innovator in this area. As the market grew, the firm benefited in turn. John Norton and then Christopher Dixon were particularly active in this area.

The firm also gained from the growth of the international shipping market in the same period, especially after the 1964 Shipbuilding Credit Act and the 1967 Shipbuilding Credit Scheme resulting from the 1967 Shipbuilding Industry Act. The firm acted for clients of the Ship Mortgage Finance Company as agents for the Department of Trade and Industry. Other important work in the mid-1960s included the nationalisation of British Steel and the after-arrangement of its subsidiary companies; general insolvency work; export credits; investment trusts; rights issues; company flotations and mergers and acquisitions.

The firm grew organically. The one exception occurred in 1961 when the firm absorbed a personal finance practice, Langlois Harding,[16] following the retirement of one of its two partners. As a result the remaining partner, Nicholas Rowntree, joined the firm as an equity partner. In 1961, two additional salaried partners, Peter Purton and Michael Brown, were appointed. Purton had arrived at the firm in 1953 through his father, a senior manager of Hambros Bank. He played an active part in the Law Society, where he was a Council Member for seventeen years (1969–86). In the 1970s, he developed the firm's planning practice which led to the environmental practice of the 1980s. Brown joined as an assistant to Noel Davies and worked for the Protection and Indemnity Clubs and for the Shipping Federation, specialising in disciplinary cases and personal injury cases.

Sir Charles Norton resumed his public career in 1965 when he began his second Mayoralty of Westminster. During this term, the office of Mayor of Westminster became the office of Lord Mayor of Westminster by Royal Charter. He became the first Lord Mayor of Westminster, newly created from the union of Paddington and St Marylebone into the Borough of Westminster.[17] He gave time to charities through the Westminster Housing Trust, Westminster Hospital, the Westminster Amalgamated Charity and Old People's Welfare (which became Age Concern).

Sir Charles held directorships in electronic, insurance and transport companies.[18] As chairman of the Hurlingham Club which he had joined in 1925, he helped to reconstruct it after the Second World War. Lord Denning saw much of Charles Norton in the 1960s, recognising him to be an important and influential member of legal and City circles as a member of the Law Society Council and the architect of the status of the City of Westminster as its first Lord Mayor.[19]

Sir Charles instituted a series of mechanisms for change which allowed Norton, Rose, Botterell & Roche to capitalise on the commercial opportunities of the 1960s and 1970s. On 1 May 1960 there were twelve partners (equity and salaried). Seven years later, in 1967, legislation which removed the twenty-partner limit helped to speed the numbers of new partners joining the firm; by 1 May 1970 there were twenty-five partners.

In October 1963, Norton, Rose, Botterell & Roche convened for its first weekend Triennial Conference, a professional and social occasion involving partners and their wives. It was held at the Queen's Hotel, Hastings. Debate covered inter-departmental work, office organisation and lay-out, and the future of the Marine and Admiralty Department after the retirement of Noel Davies, which was to be in April 1964.

The principal outcome of the 1963 conference was the decision to promote the five salaried partners (Bennett, Hamilton, Dixon, Purton and Brown) to equity partnership. In the early 1960s, the salaried partners[20] were given no assurance that equity partnership would necessarily follow their salaried partnership. Equity partners in many City law firms – as well as in banks, accountants or brokers – were often connected through blood or long-established friendship to the families which ran them. Others were seldom appointed unless they could enhance an established client base or bring capital to a firm. By 1963, Sir Charles Norton and the other partners recognised that if the firm was to be a force in the developing City legal scene, young talent had to have the incentive of a share in the equity.

Once the conferences had established a triennial pattern for regular and profound reflection, the partners were able to turn their expertise towards their own organisation and to improve the running and management of the firm's affairs. In essence, the management of the firm changed from the autocracy of Sir Charles Norton in the early 1960s to a form of government by consensus in the late 1960s. The 1968 conference, at Bournemouth, marked the birth of government by committee system.[21] The partners also responded to the lifting of restrictions in partner numbers, discussing the economics of scale, and the benefits of concentrating talent and expertise.

The management problem of a growing staff (already 168) had been exacerbated in 1966 by Sir Charles Norton's mayoral duties. A partnership manager was needed to take the firm to a higher stage of organisation. That year the partners appointed Dick Clifford, a former colonial administrator who had been secretary to the Governor of Tanganyika (now Tanzania). In 1968, he reflected on two years' service: 'My position is not unlike that of the District Officer with his relationship to government and the people of his district – save that sadly I lack the private powers of fining and imprisonment.'[22] The role of partnership manager evolved and developed with Clifford's successors into that of the Director of Administration.[23]

Partners were beginning to exert an influence through committees and reports, to share their expertise,[24] and to look for new ways of managing the growing firm.[25] These cultural changes coincided with the retirement of Sir Charles Norton in 1970. He had joined Norton, Rose & Co. fifty-one years before, spending forty-six years as a partner and thirty as senior partner.[26] Con Surtees took over as senior partner, maintaining some of the autocracy of Sir Charles Norton, but allowing this to be mollified by the new and growing committee system.

That committee process continued through the next four years and emerged fully formed at the 1972 Brighton Conference. The firm was run through an Executive Committee which received recommendations from standing committees.[27] The partners also reported to each other through departmental notes and summaries. This was the age of collective management. The 1972 Report featured for the first time a structural diagram of the firm, with extensive notes on management structure.[28]

The firm's business had begun to alter, too. With the change in domestic business during the secondary banking crisis of the early 1970s, new issue work tended to be less prominent and had been replaced by work connected with corporate crises and their aftermath in liquidation or litigation. The firm also sought business elsewhere, and found it overseas.

In the early 1970s, the firm increased its shipping finance practice. This was also the time of the firm's entry into aviation work: asset finance and aircraft leasing.[29] The partners developed their expertise in Euro-currency finance, North Sea oil operating agreements, export credits and project finance, unit trusts, foreign investment trusts[30] and banking.[31] Litigation kept constant: the departmental report for the period flatly characterised its work as 'not usually adversely affected by political and economic changes'.[32]

Con Surtees remained powerful until the mid-1970s. He retired as senior partner in 1976, to be replaced by Giles Botterell. He in turn held this position until 1982 while continuing full-time practice. Accordingly in 1976, Douglas Hamilton became 'executive partner' with responsibility, as Chairman of the Executive Committee, for the day-to-day co-ordination of the firm's administration.[33] He remained in management until he retired in 1994.

The firm was beginning to conduct itself more like a large corporation. Aside from a plethora of short committee and departmental reports,[34] the partners addressed themselves to tighter billing procedures, recruitment policy, new partner procedure, promotions to salaried partnerships, pay scales and retirement ages. The finance report included schedules of capital ratios, assets and liabilities, profit-shares, turnover and profits figures for 1973, 1974 and 1975. At the 1978 conference, the partners heard reports from ten standing committees.[35] But even by consolidating the firm's committees, there was an increasing tendency towards bureaucracy and red tape in partnership matters and decision-making.[36] The firm also reviewed the issue of appointments in the firm for children of partners. A conference resolution tackled this and made the partners' views plain.[37]

On 1 May 1980 there were sixty-one partners. The partnership meetings were no longer the formal weekly occasions they had been in the 1960s. The partners kept in touch with each other through the informal lunches held every Tuesday. The only formal requirement became an annual meeting; but full partnership meetings could be called at other times. By the early 1980s, the government-by-committee system had reached the extent of its usefulness: the partners needed a new form of government. It arrived in 1981 as the result of a working party under Christopher Dixon which reported to the partners' triennial conference.

Dixon's report advocated a move from self-government by committees to a more corporate management structure involving fewer partners, making the rest freer to deal with clients. It promised a flatter and less hierarchical structure. The partners adopted the working party's proposals. The role of senior partner was akin to a non-executive chairman of a commercial company. The executive partner (later 'managing partner') was akin to a managing director. The small partner management group oversaw a team of dedicated administrators who brought technical and non-legal management expertise to the firm.

The first managing partner, in 1982, was David Mullock; he was succeeded by Tony Kay in 1987 and Roger Birkby in 1994. Between 1982 and 1994 the firm's managing partners evolved a streamlined and more efficient system of management. This system recognised the firm's complexity and presence in various legal markets; and it met the need for consistent service and the efficient use of resources, in the UK and overseas. The management of Norton Rose became a science. The system also allowed for a period of expansion: the partnership increased from sixty-one in 1980 to one hundred in 1994.

The senior partner from 1982 to 1994 was Douglas Hamilton. In the 1960s he had been active in the new business of Eurodollar ship finance, producing a great deal of business for the firm. He became one of the finest commercial shipping lawyers in the City. That much of the firm's practice in the 1980s and 1990s stemmed from the Botterell & Roche practice was due in part to him.[38] Tony Kay succeeded him as senior partner on his retirement.

The great boom in commerce during the 1980s benefited the firm, since over half of its work was in corporate finance (including mergers and acquisitions, equity issues and flotations), banking, project and asset finance and corporate services. In 1982, the shipping finance section of the firm suffered a setback when three partners left to form their own practice.[39] However, the section re-established its position in the field, and then expanded the firm's aviation finance practice. The firm made strides in other areas, with progress which matched the boom in commercial litigation. The property department grew in the 1980s to handle all aspects of commercial property work, including the new disciplines of planning and environmental law.

The firm developed specialisms in competition and European Community law as the European Commission applied more scrutiny to takeovers and mergers of all levels in the European Community. Such developments in the legal world embraced all forms of legal expertise within the practice; they typified the impact of new legislation. In essence, the firm's departments were already cutting across disciplines: taxation and litigation, for example, called on a variety of legal and commercial expertise. One feature of the 1980s was the firm's increased involvement with policy-forming and regulatory bodies like the Monopolies and Mergers Commission, the Takeover Panel, the

Stock Exchange, the European Commission, and the range of self-regulating bodies formed under the Financial Services Act. The firm retained its private client practice dealing with trusts, wills, estates and investments.

Changes within Norton, Rose, Botterell & Roche reflected not only the changing identity of the firm but the new interdisciplinary demands on partners working across departments. The first truly inter-disciplinary department was the Taxation Department, developed in the 1970s by the partner, L.E.T. Jones, whose career had already spanned the Inland Revenue and Cooper Brothers. It was a model of how a department could provide expertise and information to the firm's other departments.

Throughout the 1970s and 1980s, the firm had been developing specialist groups of partners concerned with precedents and library and information systems. Both were energetically advocated by Michael Sayers, who took over the leadership of the Corporate Finance section on Con Surtees's retirement in 1976. Norton, Rose, Botterell & Roche was one of the first firms to institute and develop a comprehensive working library. Having established this, the firm instituted a system of precedents which developed into a central and departmental source of legal know-how and models for transactions and contracts. The emphasis on precedents increased in the late 1980s. In parallel with these, the firm pursued an innovative training policy in the early 1970s and 1980s, even though the concept of Continuing Professional Education was not introduced by the Law Society until the mid-1980s. In 1993 precedents, information services and training were drawn together in a Professional Resources Group.[40]

The firm's internal changes matched the commercial environment of the 1980s. In the UK, successive governments throughout the decade brought ideas of competition from commerce and industry and applied them to the professions.[41] The spirit of the age frowned on regulation, restriction and monopoly across all forms of commerce and the UK governments in the 1980s applied that spirit to professions already exposed to purely economic pressures. An ethos of competition grew among and between the professions; buyers of commercial services became more sophisticated and informed; and the economies of the developed countries suffered a recession at the end of the 1980s longer and more profound than any since the 1930s.

The 1980s were a time of greater internationalisation of commercial and legal services. While law firms in New York balanced their international practice with a large domestic practice, law firms in London prospered overseas from the international standing of the City of London as a financial services centre. UK law firms benefited from the popularity of English as a commercial language and the use of English law as a commercial medium.

Norton Rose responded to these changes at home and abroad with a policy of internationalisation from a domestic base. In the UK the firm strengthened its domestic position in 1990 by linking with six leading law firms outside London. These firms had for some time been members of a group intriguingly named the M5 Group.[42] The new grouping became known as the Norton Rose M5 Group, recognising the unique association between a City and international firm and leading UK regional firms. The seven firms operated as independent practices but shared training and other professional development and resource costs. Norton Rose and the other members of the group offered a network of offices in the UK and abroad to domestic and international clients.

On the international scene, the firm responded to the new commercial environment of the 1980s by resuming the overseas expansion begun in Hong Kong in the 1970s. In 1975 the firm was approached by the prominent Hong Kong firm of Johnson Stokes & Master, and the two firms established a joint practice. The first managing partner of the firm's section was David Shaw, who became Norton Rose's senior partner in South-East Asia and a force in

Hong Kong law circles. The association between Norton Rose and Johnson Stokes & Master proved successful for both. Within five years, the firm opened offices in Singapore in association with the leading Singaporean firm of Lee & Lee and in Bahrain. Those first overseas offices were the start of a strong international network.

The 1980s brought more opportunity. During the late 1980s, demand for UK domestic legal services levelled off, but multinational businesses were seeking legal advice from leading City of London law firms concerning jurisdictions outside the UK, particularly those of South-East Asia and Central and Eastern Europe. The preparation for and impact of the 1992 Single European Act had a profound effect on all UK law firms as European and Community law became fundamental to UK legislation.

After 1987, Norton Rose added five European offices to its international network: three within the European Community in Brussels, Paris and Piraeus (Athens); the others in Prague and Moscow. The European Community offices dealt with the increasing volume of European and Community Law as well as with general corporate, commercial and competition work. The Moscow office opened in 1990, followed by the Prague office in 1994, to deal with new commercial opportunities in the former Soviet Union and Eastern Europe. At the same time, the firm strengthened its offices in Hong Kong, in Singapore and – after the 1992 Gulf War ended – in Bahrain.

The 1990s brought the challenge of wider markets. These became more integrated, competition more global and operations at once more centralised and more devolved. Each small alteration in the 1990s' global markets had the potential to affect commercial decisions worldwide. Approaching half of the firm's business in 1994 was international.

The City of London suffered two bomb attacks in the early 1990s. On the evening of Friday 11 April 1992 a bomb exploded in St Mary Axe, near the firm's offices, injuring several staff. The four buildings occupied by the firm were damaged, and serious disruption to regular work persisted into the following week. A year later, on Saturday 24 April 1993, another bomb exploded in Bishopsgate and wrecked the area of the City where the firm's offices were situated. The City of London Corporation police cordoned off the area. The management partners with Patrick Stone, the Administration Director, were able to survey the scene. They recognised that the offices were too badly damaged to be occupied and that the firm would have to obtain temporary accommodation while the damage was repaired. In this regard they implemented the contingency plans which had been drawn up after the 1992 bomb.

Partners and staff reacted with the spirit of August 1940, when Sir Charles Norton had moved the firm after the offices had been destroyed. Colin Graves, the Administration Partner, with Patrick Stone concentrated on moving 800 partners and staff to various City locations. The management team under Tony Kay ensured that the firm met its commitments by enabling staff to work either from home or from the offices of clients and other law firms. The business survived intact because of the stamina and ingenuity of partners and staff, and because of the generous response of the firm's friends and competitors in the City who gave accommodation to all or part of the firm's departments; for example: Freshfields hosted the management team; Linklaters & Paines the taxation department; Clifford Chance and Slaughter and May the corporate and finance departments; Herbert Smith the commercial property department; and D.J. Freeman the marine department.

By June 1993, the firm was able to make full use of two buildings recently vacated by other law firms, 25 Cannon Street and Blackfriars House on New Bridge Street. From these two temporary locations, partners and staff were able to provide the full range of the firm's services to its UK and international clients. The partnership also continued planning and strengthening its overseas capacity and

Bishopsgate after the April 1993 bomb.

financial services. The Triennial Review Group under Roger Birkby (Managing Partner 1994) continued with preparation and planning for the firm's future. The firm extensively refurbished the damaged Bishopsgate offices and returned to them in December 1994.

In 1794, Robert Charsley could not have predicted that the firm he founded would become a major international law firm in the City of London with offices in a number of other countries. Nor could he have known that the partnership would broaden into an international body with partners from the European Community, South Africa, Australia and New Zealand. For Charsley in Uxbridge, London itself seemed distant; it certainly was for William Oliver in Sunderland. Norton Rose initially built itself on City business anchored in the City of London.

Bi-Centenary banquet, Guildhall, London, 1994.

But both firms reached beyond the UK with railways, shipping, foreign investment and foreign government loans. Since the time of Sir Philip Rose, Henry Turton Norton and Wilson Roche, the English language itself became a medium and means of export, carrying legal, commercial and financial expertise with it. Technology made the spread easier and more rapid.

The firm's great nineteenth-century partners, Robert Baxter and Sir Philip Rose, were at the heart of transport infrastructure and project finance in their day. The railways represented the best and latest in technology, engineering, organisation and investment. By 1994, those aspects of national enterprise and ingenuity had become international project finance and corporate finance for companies and capital works in aviation, shipping, railways and road transportation; the technology of railways had been replaced by the information technologies of the 1990s. The international investment of the 1890s had evolved into the firm's broad international finance practice of the 1980s and 1990s.

Since 1794 the firm's partners have, individually and collectively, matched and led developments in commerce and the law. The two firms which amalgamated in 1960, each of which began with one practitioner and flourished under family cultures, evolved into a unified social and commercial institution. The partners had chosen a management style consistent with the individualist culture of the firm's pioneering partners, and which recognised the needs of partners and clients to spend time on business rather than administration. And the firm over the years saw the results of consistent investment of the kind Baxter, Rose and Norton had made in the 1840s when they took on 300 clerks to run the railway bills.

For some, history is circular or cyclical, for others direct and linear. The history of Norton Rose is both: the firm developed from the rational ideals of the eighteenth century and the commercial spirit of the nineteenth into the international environment of the twentieth. Over the two hundred years to 1994, as the law grew, so did the firm; as commerce and industry grew, so did the firm's commercial and corporate departments; and as law became more international in the latter part of the twentieth century, so too did the firm's practice. It makes the best kind of history, and holds the best promise for the future.

Notes

1. This was the firm's last name change before amalgamating with Botterell & Roche.
   Its names since 1794 are as follows:

   1794 Charsley

   1805 Charsley & Bond

   1808 Charsley

   1821 Charsley & Barker

   1831 Charsley, Barker & Bridge

   1833 Barker & Bridge

   1838 Barker & Rose

   1844 Barker, Rose & Norton

   1845 Baxter, Rose & Norton

   1860 Baxter, Rose, Norton & Spofforth

   1861 Baxter, Rose, Norton, Spofforth & Rose

   1865 Baxter, Rose, Norton & Co.

   1873 Baxter, Rose, Norton & Brewer

   1881 Norton, Rose, Norton & Co.

   1904 Norton, Rose, Norton, Farish & Co.

   1906 Norton, Rose, Barrington & Co.

   1919 Norton, Rose & Co.

   1935 Norton, Rose, Greenwell & Co.

   1955 Norton, Rose & Co.

2. He was Managing Assistant in the Company Department of Stephenson, Harwood & Tatham.

3. The other partners in the 1920s were Frederick Vaughan and Harold Venables with a staff of twenty.

4. This was the firm's last address before amalgamating with Botterell & Roche. Its premises from 1794 are as follows:

   1794 London Road, Uxbridge

   1805 23 Billiter Lane, Leadenhall Street, London

   1806 18 Mark Lane, London

   1814 66 Mark Lane, London

> 1820 25 Mark Lane, London
>
> 1821 21 Mark Lane, London
>
> 1829 50 Mark Lane, London
>
> 1845 50 Mark Lane, London and
>
>   3 Park Street, Westminster, London
>
> 1850 3 Park Street, Westminster, London
>
> 1857 6 Victoria Street, London
>
> 1874 6 Victoria Street, London and
>
>   24 Coleman Street, London
>
> 1888 6 Victoria Street, London and
>
>   57½ Old Broad Street, London
>
> 1889 10 Victoria Street, London and
>
>   57½ Old Broad Street, London
>
> 1906 57½ Old Broad Street, London
>
> 1924 111 Old Broad Street, London
>
> 1929 Stone House, 128 Bishopsgate, London
>
> 1934 116 Old Broad Street, London
>
> 1940 St Helen's Place, London
>
> 1942 116 Old Broad Street, London
>
> 1960 Kempson House, Camomile Street, London

5. Like Botterell & Roche, Norton, Rose & Co. had a number of managing clerks. They included an 'outdoor clerk' called Hancock. He had an immaculate copperplate hand. One of his file notes recorded under the client's name reads: 'Attending you at your offices. Engaged waiting 20 mins but finding that you were absent.'

6. C.F.P. Jewell, Interview, 1993.

7. Anthony Surtees (partner), Interview, 1994.

8. The firm acted in railway matters in South America and Canada during the 1950s.

9. Bennett, *Memoir Notes*.

10. *A Man of Many Parts*, p.41.

11. See: Appendix A.

12. He became managing director and then chairman of Naess Denholm & Company Ltd. He retired in 1969.

13. 'In the field of ship finance, every shipping finance document that is currently used in the City can be traced back to an original draft of Michael Davies.' (Michael Brown, partner. Interview, 1993.)

14. Sir Charles Norton, Noel Davies, Mike Armitage, Con Surtees, Bernard Gould, Giles Botterell, Michael Davies, Chips Jewell and John Norton.

15. Maurice Bennett, Douglas Hamilton and Christopher Dixon.

16. The firm was founded by John Walter Langlois and Lewis Marks Biden in 1885 with offices at 11 Leadenhall Street. In 1911 it moved to 170 Bishopsgate as Langlois, Harding, Warren & Tate, and by 1935 it had become Langlois, Harding, Tate & Johnson.

17. Local Government Act, 1963.

18. At this time, the firm permitted partners to hold directorships outside their family interest. This ceased in the mid 1970s.

19. 'I never talked over a legal subject with him, or matter of legal concerns... He was a good solicitor ... in the sense of seeing the clients, discussing policy with them and things of that kind – from that point of view he was a good administrator. In other words, he was a good senior partner.' Interview, 1993.

20. Maurice Bennett, Douglas Hamilton, Christopher Dixon, Michael Brown and Peter Purton.

21. Thirty-nine-page Administration and Committee Report. Michael Brown, Peter Purton, Dick Clifford.

22. Dick Clifford, 1968 Conference Papers.

23. Clifford's successors were Robert Staveley and Patrick Stone, both recruited from the Ministry of Defence with the rank of Major-General.

24. E.g.: Michael Brown's memo on Protection and Indemnity Clubs. 1968 Conference Papers.

25. E.g.: N. Rowntree, 1968 Finance Committee Report: 'I believe in basic principles, simplicity and streamlining.'

26. He remained a consultant until his death in 1974.

27. Finance, New Partners, Planning, Accommodation, Articled Clerks Selection and the Library.

28. 1972 Conference Papers, pp.11–14, 18.

29. 1975 Conference Papers.

30. The firm founded the first Brazilian investment trust in the UK.

31. 1975 Conference Report.

32. Ibid.

33. Ibid.

34. The departments were: Company, Litigation, Marine, Property, Taxation, Trust and Administration.

35. Executive, Finance, New Partner, Accommodation, Recruitment, Overseas Offices, Technical, Insurances, Library and Charities.

36. 1978 Conference Papers.

37. 'Children of partners or consultants then appearing on the firm's paper should not be employed by, or be eligible for partnership in, the firm.'

38. Christopher Dixon, a partner at time of writing, remains the last partner from the pre-1960 firm of Norton, Rose Co.

39. Watson, Farley & Williams.

40. The group is headed by David Lewis, a prominent corporate finance partner.

41. Government initiatives for the legal profession evolved through 'Green' and 'White' papers from the Lord Chancellor's Department.

42. It was founded in 1977 and now comprises: Addleshaw, Sons & Latham (Manchester), Bond Pearce (Plymouth and Exeter), Booth & Co. (Leeds), Burges Salmon (Bristol), Mills & Reeve (Norwich and Cambridge), and Wragge & Co. (Birmingham).

Appendix A

THE TWO FIRMS merged in 1960 to form the new firm **Norton, Rose, Botterell & Roche** which changed its name to **Norton Rose** on 1 May 1988.

This appendix lists the partners and their dates of joining and leaving.

Norton, Rose & Co. *(1794–1960)*

Robert Charsley (1794–1833)

Albany Carrington Bond (1805–8)

William Barker (1821–45)

Thomas Mann Bridge (1831–8)

Philip Rose (1838–73)

Henry Elland Norton (1843–92)

Robert Baxter (1845–73)

Markham Spofforth (1860–73)

Henry Rose (1861–6)

Robert Dudley Baxter (1865–73)

Francis Eldon Baxter (1865–73)

Philip Frederick Rose (1866–94)

Henry Turton Norton (1872–1906)

John Brewer (1873–81)

George Alfred Ste Croix Rose
  (1877–1926)

Walter Percy Norton (1892–1939)

Edward Garthwaite Farish (1894–1906)

Walter Bernard Lewis Barrington
  (1905–19)

Robert Henry Eggar (1906–34)

Harcourt George Ste Croix Rose
  (1908–19)

Arthur Alexander MacNab (1919–34)

Lewis Henry Grundy (1919–39)

Walter Charles Norton (1924–)

Edward Eyre Greenwell (1935–8)

Frederick Johnson (1935–50)

Philip Michael Armitage (1936–)

David Matthew (1937–9)

Conyers Alfred Surtees (1939–)

Bernard William Gould (1945–)

Charles Francis Patrick Jewell (1951–)

John Eyre Norton (1955–)

Maurice Bennett (1958–)

Christopher Dixon (1959–)

Botterell & Roche *(1861–1960)*

William Atkinson Oliver (1861–79)

John James Dumville Botterell
    (1873–1923)

Wilson Mills Roche (1879–1903)

Henry Temperley (1893–1923)

James Wallace (1895–1903)

Arthur Powell Simon (1900–09)

John Charles Peace Thomson (1904)

Percy Dumville Botterell (1907–45)

Robert Temperley (1909)

John Dumville Botterell (1912–57)

Henry Millican Cleminson (1913–23)

James Ellis Hammond Sinclair
    (1913–33)

Clifford James Temperley (1923–8)

Edward Calcott Pryce (1936–60)

James Gourlay Freeland (1945–59)

Noel Hier Davies (1945–)

Giles Dumville Botterell (1948–)

Michael Baddeley Davies (1949–)

Douglas Owens Hamilton (1959–)

Norton, Rose, Botterell & Roche *(1960–1988)*

Sir Charles Norton (–1970)

N.H. Davies (–1964)

P.M. Armitage (–1970)

C.A. Surtees (–1982)

G.D. Botterell (–1982)

B.W. Gould (–1970)

M.B. Davies (–1973)

C.F.P. Jewell (–1982)

J.E. Norton (–1965)

M. Bennett (–1982)

D.O. Hamilton (–1994)

C.J.A. Dixon (–)

N. Rowntree (1961–82)

M.A. Brown (1961–89)

P.J. Purton (1961–92)

A.C. Surtees (1965–91)

M.B. Sayers (1965–94)

J.M. Woodrow (1965–91)

W.A.J. Leaver (1966–92)

D.J. Freeland (1968–93)

G.F. Chronnell (1968–)

J.N.L. Chalton (1968–94)

H.M. Crush (1968–91)

J.P. Lansdell (1969–94)

D. Mullock (1969–94)

D.S. Burnand (1970–)

M.R. Macfadyen (1970–)

R.J.B. Heasman (1970–88)

G.C. Sutton (1970–)

D.J.G. Hurst (1970–84)

W.N. Rouston (1971–80)

D.D. Alexander (1971–88)

A.C. Ayres (1971–94)

J.M. Maskell (1971–93)

L.E.T. Jones (1971–87)

C.P. Robinson (1972–)

J.R. Lingard (1973–93)

I.M.S. Swabey (1973–)

D.J. Shaw (1973–)

M.J.A. Lee (1973–)

F.I. Sumner (1973–)

J.W. Ody (1973–)

P. Fergusson (1974–)

G.C. Williams (1974–82)

R.A. Powell (1974–)

A.H. Farley (1974–82)

M.V. Fowke (1974–)

N.D.F. Bohm (1975–94)

M.A. Watson (1975–82)

T.A. Kay (1976–)

A.C. Graves (1976–)

N.J.C. Richardson (1976–83)

R. Birkby (1976–)

J.G.R. Harding (1976–)

D.A. Ashworth (1977–)

P.G. Thorne (1977–)

P.L. Graham (1977–)

H.R. Jackson (1977–)

D.L. Jones (1977–91)

D.T.R. Lewis (1977–)

D.J. Colliver (1978–)

C.J.L. Ryan (1978–)

J. Clark (1978–94)

T.C.M. Howard (1978–)

J.V.C.L. Barratt (1979–)

E.C.D. Norfolk (1979–)

M.P.G. Taylor (1979–)

P.M. Skelsey (1979–89)

P.A.J. Woods (1980–94)

D.F. Potter (1981–)

A. Pouteaux (1981–83)

Sarah C. Holt (1982–90)

O.R. Jonathan (1983–94)

S.L. Sackman (1983–)

E. Lee-Smith (1984–94)

S.W. Parish (1984–)

Isla M. Smith (1985–)

D.R. Crane (1985–)

P.M. Martyr (1985–)

N.W. d'A Mason (1986–91)

N.P. Edgell (1986–)

Valerie E.M. Davies (1986–)

Margaret A. Coltman (1986–)

R.H. Mitchell (1986–)

R.J. Calnan (1987–)

Patricia Watson (1987–91)

P.J. Rees (1987–)

J.H. Shelton (1987–)

D.P.R. Stannard (1987–)

Norton Rose *(from 1988)*

B.J. Greenwood (1988–)

J. Challoner (1988–)

S.R.G. Pratt (1988–)

S.F.T. Cox (1988–)

C.L. Proctor (1988–)

G.C.C. Hall (1988–)

Susan A. Wright (1988–)

A.M. Crookes (1988–)

R.G. Brooks (1988–)

H.R. Heward (1989–)

P.M.G. Burrows (1989–)

P. Haslam (1989–)

Lindsay B. Morgan (1989–)

Barbara Stephenson (1989–)

P. Farrell (1989–)

C.J. Cook (1990–)

T.J.T. Walker (1990–)

W.N.T. Ward (1990–)

P.L. Williams (1990–)

M. Mattiuzzo (1990–)

Lynn West (1990–)

T.F.A. Emmerson (1990–91)

R.P. Falkner (1990–)

M.A. Coleman (1991–)

Louise Higginbottom (1991–)

M.D.K. Scott (1991–)

P. Shadarevian (1991–)

A.W.J. Bamber (1991–)

P.J. Whale (1992–)

P.J.G. Williams (1992–94)

Cynthia J. Witcombe (1992–)

A.G. Phillips (1992–)

C.C. Pearson (1992–)

J.J. Logie (1992–)

J.H. Ellis (1992–)

R.W. Butler (1992–)

T.P. Theochari (1992–)

J.R. James (1993–)

A.J.S. Bagge (1993–)

P.T. Vallance (1993–)

S.R. Lippiatt (1993–)

Melanie Tether (1993–)

T.J. Marsden (1993–)

K.J.G. Gray (1993–)

M.J. Lloyd-Williams (1993–)

F.O. Mackie (1993–)

P.A. Hardy (1994–)

T.I. Soames (1994–)

R.W. Barratt (1994–)

M.D. Ings (1994–)

C.L. Swift (1994–)

T. Polglase (1994–)

M.A.L. Bankes (1994–)

P.M. Hall (1994–)

Appendix B

A SELECTION FROM the records of the Legal & Parliamentary Committee of the London, Brighton and South Coast Railway showing its relationship with Baxter, Rose, Norton & Co. (Source: PRO Railways). The first entry here is an example of the form and function of a meeting of the Legal & Parliamentary Committee, and is given in full. Other minutes are excerpted.

**At a Meeting of the Legal & Parliamentary Committee
London, Tuesday, 8th June 1869**

Present:	Jonas Levy, Esq. (in the chair)
	F.F. [Fremantle], Esq.
	A.J. Lopes, Esq.
In attendance:	P. Rose, Esq.
	Mr. Brewer

Mr. Farmer's
defalcations

1. Resolved,

That the Secretary and Accountant do furnish the Solicitors with the detailed cases of Mr. Farmer's defalcations and embezzlements, especially of those in which the total amount of charges from any station have been unaccounted for by Mr. Farmer, and to have them put in a shape for the Solicitors to submit to Mr. Lewis who is advising the Company on the whole of the case.

Jennings' claim

2. A letter from Messrs. Drummond, Robinson and Till appealing on behalf of Jennings with reference to a loss of £15 which he had enclosed between the leaves of a book sent as a parcel from Croydon to London having been read, it was Resolved

That Mr. Rose be authorised to give £5 to Jennings as matter of charity.

Button's claim

3. Mr. Rose reported an action brought by Button for £29 for the loss of a portmanteau, said to have been entrusted to the charge of the Company's servants in the cloakroom at Lewes Station, but which did not appear to have been booked.

Mr. Rose was instructed to continue to resist the claim.

4. With reference to an action brought by Messrs. Gray Beavis & Co. in respect of a claim for Naphtha destroyed by force at the Three Bridges accident, Mr. Rose was authorised to inform those gentlemen that the three Directors on this Committee will undertake the arbitration of the claim, as proposed by them.

5. A claim by Payne for the loss of two packages by Goods train between Brighton and Norwood Junction having been discussed, Mr. Rose was authorised to settle the matter on the best terms he can obtain and take such steps in following up the lobby as he may think desirable.

6. Resolved,

That the particulars of all Passengers or Goods claims to compensation for losses, damages, injuries or otherwise be in future entered in a book, with a short history of the case, and the terms of settlement, with due reference to the papers and memoranda appertaining to each claim, and that in all important cases the Traffic Committee be consulted by the Traffic Manager before any settlement be made unless in cases of emergency, and that such book with the papers and memoranda be submitted to each meeting of the Traffic Committee.

7. With reference to an action brought by Cramer and Company for damage to a harp said to have been repaired for £20 which they state they are prepared to settle on receiving payment of that sum with the costs of action to the present time. Mr. Rose was authorised to compromise the same by payment of £30 inclusive of costs.

Further entries follow the same pattern of minuted decisions, advice and resolutions.

9 November 1870 — The Solicitors were requested to use every effort to complete without loss of time the agreement with Messrs. Will Smith & Sons for their rental of the Company's bookstalls and advertising spaces at Stations, their [hearing] of which commenced on the 1st January 1868.

17 May 1871 — The Solicitors having reported upon a claim for £100 preferred by Mademoiselle Vidal for the detention in transit of a box, part of her luggage, containing testimonials, the non-production of which she alleged had lost her a valuable situation as governess, they were instructed to decline liability as the damages appeared too remote.

21 June 1871 — Mr. Rose reported that the Isle of Wight, Cowes and Newport

Railway ... had just passed the Committee of the House of Lords and had been sent down to the House of Commons. Mr. Rose reminded the Committee that the proposed line, being an offshoot from the Isle of Wight Railway would be a direct communication with this Company's system at Portsmouth, and being well calculated to develop this Company's Isle of Wight traffic should be supported by this Company so far as is consistent with their relation with the London and South Western Railways.

22 August 1873   Mr. Brewer having reported upon a claim preferred by Kierman for broken chemicals improperly placed in a perambulator as passenger luggage, the Committee decided that nothing should be paid or given either as a matter of charity or obligation, the conduct of the party being unjustifiable.

25 March 1874   The Solicitors reported that a County Court Summons having been issued against the Company for damage done to a Hay Stack and other property of a Mr. Flint, in consequence of a fire caused by sparks from a passing engine, the same had been settled by payment of £49.15s. 0d. for damage and costs, as the Company's liability could not have been successfully contested.

1 March 1882   Read report from the Solicitors upon the following action which had been commenced. *Frederick Brandon*, Pianoforte Tuner, claims £100 for having had his finger pinched in a carriage door at London Bridge Station last Christmas day while seeing a friend off by train. Papers are before Counsel for an opinion as to the liability.

5 April 1882   The Solicitors reported that an action had been commenced and others threatened by Consignees of Gorgonzola Cheeses and

perishable articles shipped at Dieppe by the S.S. *Dieppe* last December which had been sold under the direction of Experts appointed by the Tribunal of Commerce in consequence of damage caused by tempestuous weather. The Solicitors were authorised to consult Counsel and defend the proceedings if so advised.

9 August 1882   The Solicitors verbally reported that out of the £66.13s. 4d. awarded to Mrs. Barnes by the Board … they had advanced £5 to enable her to purchase a mangle, and upon their recommendation they were authorised to advance a further sum of £5 to enable her to visit the seaside for the benefit of her health.

31 January 1883   The Solicitors reported that as notices had been served upon the Company by several Electric Lighting Companies, of their intention to apply for Provisional Orders to supply different towns and places in the Company's system, and the consequent crossing of the railway etc. by their men, they had draft clauses prepared by the Company's Parliamentary Agents to be delivered to the Promoters and the Board of Trade, in accordance with the Electric Lighting Act, 1882, which were submitted and approved.

9 April 1884   The following prosecutions were reported … Robert Fuger (a boy) for stealing some coal from a barge which was being unloaded at the Pumping Engine House at Rotherhithe … ordered to be sent to a Reformatory ship until he is 16 years of age.

Thomas Knight, for stealing a small piece of beef from Willow Walk Station … sentenced to two months' hard labour.

3 April 1885   Upon the Solicitors' report they were authorised to prepare and present a Petition against the United Telephone Company's Bill

of this Session, in which power is sought to lay, suspend and maintain wires over, under and along any railway within 100 miles of London.

10 November 1885   The Solicitors having verbally reported upon the case of W.J. Pritchett who had been discovered travelling last September between Tulse Hill and London Bridge without payment of fare, which he said he had intended to do for two months in pursuance of a bet that he could do so without discovery, they were authorised to settle the matter on such terms as they may think fit.

8 December 1885   Read report of the Solicitors upon the following Notices which had been given of intended application to Parliament which appear to affect this Company:

(i)   London, Chatham and Dover and London, Brighton and South Coast Railway Companies Bill.

(ii)   London, Chatham and Dover Railway Further Powers Bill.

(iii)   London and South Western Railway Various Powers Bill.

(iv)   Wimbledon and West Metropolitan Railway Bill.

(v)   South Eastern Railway Various Powers Bill.

(vi)   Southward and Vauxhall Water Company's Bill.

(vii)   Bexhill District Railway Bill.

(viii) Brighton, Rottingdean and Newhaven Railway Bill.

(ix)   Brighton, Rottingdean and Newhaven Direct Railway Bill.

(x)   Eastbourne, Seaford and Newhaven Railway Bill.

(xi)   Portsmouth and Hayling Railway Bill.

Resolved.

That it be a recommendation to the Board not to oppose any of the Bills or standing orders, but that Mr. Knight and Mr. Bannister do communicate with the authorities of the Southwark and Vauxhall Water Company and endeavour to come to some arrangements as regards the land at Battersea let by the Company to Mr. Corington for the storage of dust which the Water Company seek to acquire compulsorily.

16 February 1886

The Solicitors submitted a print of the clauses which they had settled with the Solicitors of the East London Company and East London Joint Committee upon which their oppositions to the powers sought in this Company's Various Powers Bill as regards the railways at New Cross will be obviated.

16 February 1886

The Solicitors having requested instructions as to the course to be pursued for the acquisition of property required for the Oxted and Groombridge Line having regard to the altered time in the Company's Bill of this Session for the completion of the railway, they were authorised to obtain all the property required for the line as soon as possible by private arrangement where they can do so, otherwise to take possession under the compulsory powers of the Lands Clauses Act.

11 May 1886

James Sullivan, for card sharping in a train between Victoria and Pulborough on 30th January last sentenced to two months' imprisonment with hard labour.

24 May 1886

The Solicitors having submitted a draft of the agreement with Mr. Clark for the proposed supply of omnibuses at the London termini, a long discussion arose on the provisions with regard to the term of the privilege, the option to the Company of purchasing the vehicles during the term, and the minimum rate of line which it was suggested should be reduced from 4s/- to 3s/- for distances under 2 miles, when it was ultimately decided to leave the final settlement to Mr. Lopes and the Solicitors.

8 June 1886	The Solicitors reported that the Company's Various Powers Bill had received the Royal Asset on the 4th instant.

6 July 1886 The following prosecutions were reported:

Lewis and Fiddy, two boys, absconders from the Philanthropic Farm School, Red Hill, for stealing a platelayers clothing from Earlswood – 21 days' imprisonment with hard labour.

Signalman W. Gray for stealing vegetables from a hamper at Cheam Station – fined £2 and dismissed from the service.

Porter C.F. Day for stealing an empty sack at Willow Walk Station – fined £1 and dismissed from the service.

7 December 1886 The Solicitors having reported upon the notices for the following Bills for next Session:

(i)   Brighton, Rottingdean and Newhaven Direct Railway.

(ii)   West London Extension and Surrey Commercial Docks Company.

They were instructed not to oppose on Standing Orders.

26 April 1887 The Solicitors submitted a draft clause as to the consolidation of the 4% Preferential Stocks which was accidentally omitted by the Parliamentary Agents from the Company's Various Powers Bill of next Session, which they stated could be inserted in the Bill when in Committees.

26 April 1887   The Solicitors verbally reported that Tuesday next had been fixed by the Board of Trade for their enquiry into the cause of the stranding of the S.S. *Victoria* off Cape D'Ailly and that they had retained Sir Walter Phillimore QC to represent the Company.

10 May 1887   … the West of France Railway Company having pressed for the approval of this Company to a settlement of the claim for £1,360 preferred against that Company by Messrs. Fenwick for the loss of diamonds by the robbery on board the S.S. *Bordeaux* – after consulting Sir Philip Rose … [the Company] agreed to a settlement of £1,269.5s. 1d.

27 September 1887   Read report from the Solicitors on the progress of the settlement of the claims arising in respect of the wreck of the S.S. *Victoria* for lost and damaged luggage, compensation for persons drowned and for lost and damaged merchandise.

26 October 1887   The Solicitors having reported that the action for the limitation of the Company's liability in respect of the loss of the S.S. *Victoria* had been heard yesterday and the application granted, a cheque was drawn for the amount required to be paid into Court, viz:

513 2/25ths tons @ £15 per ton £7,696.4s. 0d.
Interest @ 4% from 13th April to 25th October   164.9s. 4d.
TOTAL £7,860.13s. 4d.

8 November 1887   The Solicitors having reported that Dr. Eady had on three occasions travelled from Sanderstead or Caterham Junction to London without paying his fare and had intimated his intention to continue to do so until such fare amounted to 8s/- which he had incurred for cab hire owing to delay in the delivery of a

special letter sent down by train from Caterham Junction to Brighton – they were instructed to send him the balance of his claim but to point out the illegality of his proceeding.

20 December 1887   The Solicitors having reported upon points that had been raised in settling the new contract with the postal authorities for the conveyance of mails, with respect to the definition of the term "mails", and the issue of tickets or passes for the officials of the Post Office in connection therewith, the matter was referred to the Solicitors to make the best arrangements they can.

23 May 1888   Upon the recommendation of the Solicitors a cheque was ordered to be drawn in favour of Messrs. Griffith and Eggar for 100 guineas, their fee including out-of-pocket expenses, for obtaining signatures in Brighton and Worthing etc. to a petition against the South Eastern Company's Various Powers Bill of the present session.

17 July 1888   Upon the Solicitors' report they were authorised to draw up a special contract with the Royal Mail Steamship Co. for the conveyance of bullion, diamonds etc. between London and Paris and obtain the approval of the West of France Railway Company thereto.

25 September 1888   Upon the recommendation of the Solicitors it was decided not to prosecute James Morris, a stone mason, for altering the date of a return ticket as he was a poor man, in ill health and was probably not aware that he had acted fraudulently.

6 November 1888   Upon the Solicitors' report an expenditure of £25 was authorised for renewals and additions to the Company's law library.

26 March 1889   The Solicitors reported that they had prepared the necessary clauses for insertion in the Shortlands and Nunhead Railway Bill of this session to protect this Company's interest, which having been accepted by the promoters, it would now be unnecessary to present a petition against the Bill.

7 May 1889   The Solicitors reported that they had applied to the Board of Trade for the revival of the Company's powers under the Regulation of Railways Act, 1842, for the purchase of a piece of land from Mr. Glasier and Cowdene, and had received the necessary certificate. They were instructed to serve the usual "notice to treat" and to resist any action that may be taken to delay the completion of the purchase.

22 April 1890   Upon the Solicitors report a fee of 120 guineas and £20 to cover disbursements was authorised to be paid to Mr. S.G. Edridge for his services in getting up a local case for the Company against the Croydon and Crystal Palace Railway Bill of this session.

17 June 1890   The Solicitors having reported that Mr. A.E. Griffin, a clerk in the Borough Surveyor's Office at Brighton, conveyed a bicycle from Brighton to Victoria without paying the ordinary charge, by producing an old excess luggage receipt which had been altered to suit the circumstances, and gave a false name and address on arrival at Victoria, the matter was referred back to them to take such proceedings as they may think advisable.

Read report by the Solicitors upon a conference they with Mr. Sarle and Mr. Cripps had had with representatives of Messrs. W.H. Smith and Son with regard to the renewal of their advertisement and bookstall licence, recommending "that there should be separate licenses for the advertising and bookstaff and newspaper business to run for three years certain and then continue from year to year until terminated by either party giving six months' previous written notice; that the percentage allowed to the Company for the advertisement licence be 60%, instead of 50% as here before, with a fixed minimum of £10,000 per annum, and with regard to the bookstalls, the percentage be 10% for London Bridge, Victoria, Brighton and Eastbourne and 5% for other stations with a minimum of £7,500 per annum; Messrs. Smith and Son to pay all rates, fares and assessments of every hand ... approved and negotiations to be continued on such recommendations.

20 May 1891

T. Belam, porter, for stealing two cards of Blakey's boot protectors at Willow Walk – sentenced to seven days' hard labour.

Mr. Sarle having read a report he had received from Captain White on the conduct of Major Fowkes, whereby a Mlle. Josephine Roger, a passenger from Dieppe, was pushed off the bridge on to the other sponson of the S.S. *Paris* on its arrival at Newhaven on the 19th instant, necessitating her removal to the hotel and receiving medical assistance, and stating that Major Fowkes had not yet paid the fares for himself and his nurse who accompanied him on the passage, and that he had on a previous occasion caused annoyance to passengers while under the influence of drink, the case was referred to the Solicitors to investigate and report what action may be taken against the Major.

14 July 1891

The Solicitors submitted a letter they had received from Messrs. Lowless and Co. declining on behalf of the owners of the tug *Challenge* to accept £100 in settlement of their claim for salvage in respect of assistance rendered to the S.S. *Normandy* when aground off Beachy Head, and putting forward a claim, without prejudice, for £750. They had therefore retained Sir Walter Phillimore, and upon their recommendation, they were authorised to take the joint opinion of that gentleman and Dr. Raikes with a view to contesting the exorbitant claim.

12 August 1891   Seven boys named Kerchie (2); Simmons; Page; O'Leary; True and Smith for being found without visible means of subsistence at Chichester – each sentenced to 14 days' hard labour.

3 November 1891   The Solicitors reported that at the trial Lucy Clarissa Holloway for stealing passengers' luggage at Paddington, Waterloo and Clapham Junction stations – the jury found her guilty and she was sentenced to four years' penal servitude.

　　　　　　　　The Solicitors reported upon the Company's position in regard to the £100 Bank of England note found by cash-boy B. Bone on board the S.S. *Paris*, recommending the retention as long as possible should it not be claimed after advertising for the owner.

9 February 1892   The Solicitors verbally reported that the draft deed of grant by the Board of Trade of the foreshore and bed of the River Adur required for the columns of the new Shoreham viaduct did not include that portion of the bank above high water mark; they had been in communication with the Board of Trade who informed them that the crown rights did not extend beyond the high watermark, but were vested in Mr. Carr Lloyd, the lord of the manor. The Solicitors to make enquiries as to the existing rights of the Company and report the result.

23 February 1892   The Solicitors having submitted a draft of a petition they proposed to lodge against the National Telephone Company's

Bill of this session, the same was approved and ordered to be submitted to the Board for the seal of the Company to be affixed thereto.

29 November 1892   The Solicitors reported that an action brought by Mr. Wilkinson, a commission agent, claiming £40 damages for the non-delivery of a Gladstone bag, some betting poles and placards deposited by him in the cloakroom at Chichester during the last Goodwood races, which had been handed to a man who claimed them, stating he had lost his ticket, was heard at the Southwark County Court, when a verdict was given for the Company.

Upon the Solicitors' report it was decided to break off the arrangement with the Automatic Fire Check Company for the maintenance of Douse's patent fire checks in the carriage shops at Brighton, the insurance company being paid the amount allowed by them off the premium on account of the installation of the checks.

10 January 1893   The Solicitors reported that having been in communication with the other railway companies on the question of deductions from employees' wages, it had been considered advisable to let the matter slumber.

21 February 1893   Read report by the Solicitors upon the Chipstead Valley Railway Bill of this session, and on their recommendation they were instructed to secure the services of Sir John Fowler and Mr. Scotter to supplement the evidence of the officers of this Company in its opposition to the scheme in Parliament.

16 May 1893   Upon the Solicitors' report that the Select Committee appointed by the House of Commons to consider the London

Improvement Bill would meet formally today to discuss the course of proceedings, they were on their recommendation, instructed to appear by agent and retain Counsel, so as to be in a position to intervene at any time during the progress of the Bill in support of protective clauses on behalf of the Company, which had been proposed to the London County Council.

19 September 1893   T. Hughes for loitering and begging in the station at Victoria – sentenced to one month's hard labour.

31 October 1893   The Solicitors reported that Mr. Bidder Q.C., had accepted a general retainer from the Company in parliamentary matters.

Read report by the Solicitors submitting a draft notice of the Company's Various Powers Bill of next Session ... the Solicitors were instructed to apply for a separate Act extending the Company's powers provided under their Act of 1864 to include Newhaven as one of the English ports from which they may provide a service of steamboats to Caen etc.

Bibliography

I DREW MOST of the material for this book from archives never before published. However, I found numerous secondary sources of use, and I have listed them in the bibliography.

Abel, R., *The Legal Profession in England and Wales*, Oxford, 1988

Ackworth, W.M., *The Railways of England*, London, 1889 et seq.

Anderson, G., *Victorian Clerks*, Manchester, 1976

Anon., *The Right Honourable Benjamin Disraeli, M.P.: A Literary and Political Biography*, London, 1854

Bagehot, W., *Works*, ed. N. St-John Stevas, London, 1965–86

Baxter, M.D., *In Memoriam R. Dudley Baxter, MA*, London, 1878

Baxter, R., *Argument for Judgement to Come*, London, 1823

> *Narrative of facts concerning supernatural manifestations …*, London, 1833

> *Irvingism in its rise, progress and present state*, London, 1836

Birks, M., *Gentlemen of the Law*, London, 1960

Blake, Lord R., *Disraeli*, London, 1966

> *The Conservative Party from Peel to Thatcher*, London, 1985

Boase, F., *Modern English Biography*, London, 1965

Bradshaw's Railway Guide

Bramsen, B. *and* Wain, K., *The Hambros 1779–1979*, London, 1979

Briggs, Lord A., *Victorian People*, London, 1954

Carr-Sanders, A.M. *and* Wilson, P.A., *The Professions*, Oxford, 1933

Carter, A.T., *A History of English Legal Institutions*, London, 1910

Chalmers, M.D., *Bills of Exchequer*, London, 1883

Christian, E.B.V., *A Short History of Solicitors*, London, 1896

 Solicitors: an Outline of their History, London, 1925

Conder, F.R., *Recollections of English Engineers*, London, 1868

Cornish, W.R. *and* Clark, G. de N., *Law and Society in England 1750–1950*, London, 1989

Cottrell, P.L., *Industrial Finance, 1830–1914*, London, 1980

Cowling, M., *1867, Disraeli, Gladstone and Revolution*, Oxford, 1967

Davenport-Hines, R.T.P. (ed.), *Speculators and Patriots*, London, 1986

Davies, M.B., *Belief in the Sea: State Encouragement of British Merchant Shipping and Shipbuilding*, London, 1992

Davis, R.W., *The English Rothschilds*, Chapel Hill, 1983

Davis, W., *Merger Mania*, London, 1970

Dennett, L., *A Century in the City*, Cambridge, 1989

 Slaughter and May, Cambridge, 1989

Denning, Lord A.T., *Leaves From My Library*, London, 1986

The Dictionary of National Biography

Disraeli, B., *Letters* (1815–51, 5 vols), Toronto, 1993

 Works (ed. E. Gosse, 20 vols), London, 1904–5

Drummond, A.L., *Edward Irving*, London, 1937

Evans, D.M., *The Commercial Crisis 1847–8*, London, 1840

 The History of the Commercial Crisis 1857–8 and the Stock Exchange Panic of 1859, London, 1859

Faith, N., *The World the Railways Made*, London, 1992

Feuchtwanger, E.J., *Disraeli, Democracy and the Tory Party*, Oxford, 1968

Findlay, Sir G., *The Working and Management of an English Railway*, London, 1889 et seq.

Foot, M.R.D. *and* Matthew, H.C.G., *The Gladstone Diaries*, Oxford, 1968–94

Francis, J., *History of the English Railway*, London, 1851

Fraser, W.L., *All to the Good*, London, 1963

Froude, J.A., *Lord Beaconsfield*, London, 1890

Fryer, M., *A Newcastle Century: One Hundred Years of the Newcastle P & I Association*, Newcastle, 1987

Gibson-Watt, A., *An Undistinguished Life*, London, 1990

Gilbert, M.F., *The Claimant*, London, 1957

Goodall, F., *A Bibliography of British Business Histories*, London, 1987

Goode, R., *Commercial Law*, London, 1982, 1985

Grayson, T.J., *Investment Trusts*, London, 1928

Grinling, C.H., *The History of the Great Northern Railway*, London, 1966

Hanham, H.J., *Elections and Party Management in the Time of Disraeli and Gladstone*, London, 1959

Hansard's Parliamentary Debates

Harris, L., *London General Shipowners' Society 1811–1961*, private, London, n.d.

Herepath's Railway Magazine

Holdsworth, W.S., *A History of English Law, 1938–1966*, London, 1966

Jeremy, D., *Dictionary of Business Biography*, London, 1984

Jones, Sir L.E., *Georgian Afternoon*, London, 1958

Kellet, R., *The Merchant Banking Arena*, London, 1967

Kellett, J.R., *The Impact of Railways on Victorian Cities*, London, 1969

Kenealy, Dr., *The Trial at Bar of Sir Roger C.D. Tichborne, Bart*, London, 1876

Kirk, H., *Portrait of a Profession*, London, 1976

Kitson Clark, G., *The Making of Victorian England*, Oxford, 1962

Kynaston, D., *Cazenove & Co: A History*, London, 1991
    The City, London, 1994–

Ledwith, N.F., *Ships That Go Bump in the Night*, London, 1974
    The Best of All Possible Worlds, London, 1984

Lewis, J.R., *The Victorian Bar*, London, 1982

Lucas, P., 'Blackstone and the reform of the legal profession', *English Historical Review*, London, 1962

Lytton, Earl of, *The Life of Edward Bulwer, first Lord Lytton*, London, 1913

Moneypenny, W.F. *and* Buckle, G.E., *The Life of Benjamin Disraeli, Earl of Beaconsfield*, London, 1910–20

Morley, J., *The Life of W.E. Gladstone*, London, 1903

Norton, Sir C., *A Man of Many Parts*, private, 1974

Oliphant, M., *The Life of Edward Irving*, London, 1862

Oliver, W.A., *A Practical Manual of Shipping Law*, London, 1868; 1879, ed. W.M. Roche

Orbell, J., *Baring Brothers & Co, Limited. A History to 1939*, London, 1985

Ottley, G., *Bibliography of British Railway History*, London, 1966, 1988

Parris, H., *Government and the Railways in Nineteenth-Century Britain*, London, 1965

Perkins, H., *The Origins of Modern English Society*, London, 1969

Phelps, B., *Power and the Party: A History of The Carlton Club 1832–1982*, London, 1983

Polson, A., *Law and Lawyers: or Sketches and Illustrations of Legal History and Biography*, London, 1840

Powell, L.H., *The Shipping Federation: A History of the First Sixty Years 1890–1950*, London, 1950

Reid, S.J. (ed.), *Memoirs of Sir Edward Blount*, London, 1902

Rudz, D.L., *The Parliamentary Agents*, London, 1979

St George, E.A.W., *JOH: The Biography of Jocelyn Hambro*, Cambridge, 1992
> *The Descent of Manners*, London, 1993

Sayers, R.S., *The Bank of England 1891–1944*, Cambridge, 1976

Scratchley, A., *On Average Investment Trusts*, London, 1875

Shannon, R., *Gladstone, I: 1809–65*, London, 1982
> *The Age of Disraeli (1867–81)*, London, 1992

Simmons, J., *The Victorian Railway*, London, 1991

Slinn, J., *A History of Freshfields*, London, 1984
> *Linklaters & Paines: The First One Hundred and Fifty Years*, Cambridge, 1987
> *Clifford Chance: Its Origins and Development*, Cambridge, 1993

Stewart, R., *The Foundation of the Conservative Party 1830–67*, London, 1978

Temperley, R., *The Merchant Shipping Act, 1894*, London, 1895; *The Merchant Shipping Acts* (ed. M. Thomas and D. Steel), 7th Edition, London, 1976

Thirwell, A., *A Century of Practice*, London, 1985

Thomas, D. St-J. and others (ed.), *A Regional History of the Railways of Great Britain*, London, 1960–89

Thompson, G.C., *Public Opinion and Lord Beaconsfield, 1876–80*, London, 1886

Tillotson, K., *Novels of the Eighteen-Forties*, London, 1854

de Tocqueville, A., *Democracy in America*, New York, 1961

Turner, J.H., *The London, Brighton & South Coast Railway*, London, 1977–9

Weintraub, S., *Disraeli*, London, 1993

Woodruff, D., *The Tichborne Claimant*, London, 1957

Wrottesley, J., *The Great Northern Railway*, London, 1979–81

Zarach, S. (ed.), *British Business History*, London, 1987, 1994

Ziegler, P., *The Sixth Great Power: Barings, 1762–1929*, London, 1988

Law Advertiser

The Law Journal

The Law Lists

Law Magazine

Law Magazine and Review

Law Quarterly Review

The Law Review

Law Society's Gazette

The Law Times

Lawyer's and Magistrate's Magazine

Legal Advertiser

Norton Rose News & Views

Solicitors' Journal

Index

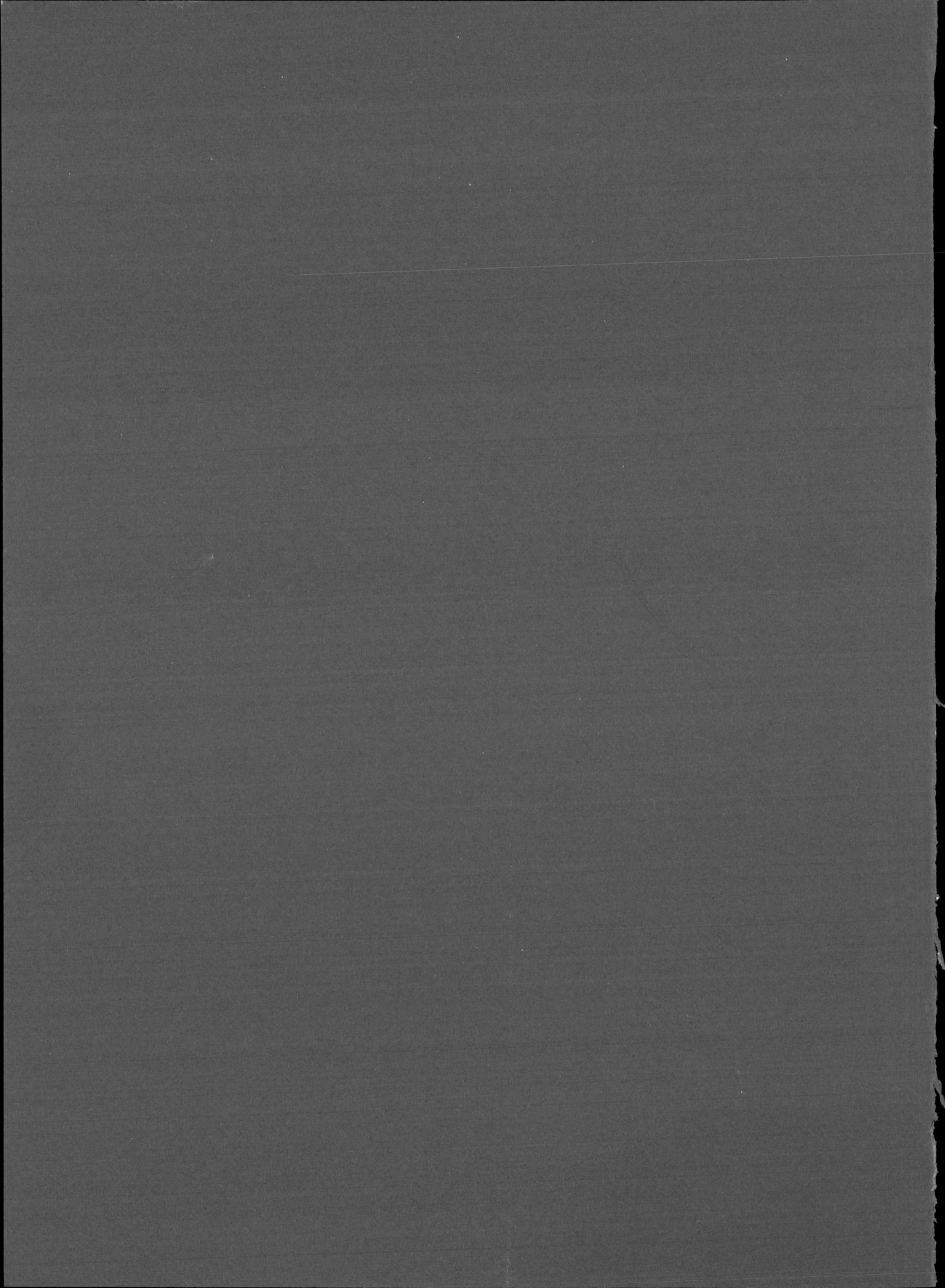